WHAT RECONSTRUCTION MEANT

THE AMERICAN SOUTH SERIES

EDWARD L. AYERS, EDITOR

WHAT RECONSTRUCTION MEANT

HISTORICAL MEMORY IN THE AMERICAN SOUTH

BRUCE E. BAKER

UNIVERSITY OF VIRGINIA PRESS

CHARLOTTESVILLE AND LONDON

University of Virginia Press
© 2007 by the Rector and Visitors of the University of Virginia
All rights reserved
Printed in the United States of America on acid-free paper

First published 2007
First paperback edition published 2010
ISBN 978-0-8139-2877-7 (paper)

1 3 5 7 9 8 6 4 2

The Library of Congress has cataloged the hardcover edition as follows:

Library of Congress Cataloging-in-Publication Data

Baker, Bruce E., 1971–
    What Reconstruction meant : historical memory in the American South /
Bruce E. Baker.
        p. cm. — (The American South series)
    Includes bibliographical references and index.
    ISBN 978-0-8139-2660-5 ((hardcover) : alk. paper)
    1. Reconstruction (U.S. history, 1865–1877)—Public opinion.
    2. Reconstruction (U.S. history, 1865–1877)—Social aspects.
    3. Reconstruction (U.S. history, 1865–1877)—Historiography. 4. Memory—
Social aspects—Southern States—History. 5. Southern States—Social
conditions—1865–1945. 6. Public opinion—Southern States—History—19th
century. 7. Public opinion—Southern States—History—20th century.
8. Southern States—Politics and government—1865–1950. 9. United
States—Politics and government—1865–1933. 10. United States—Politics and
government—1933–1945. I. Title.
    E668.B155 2007
    973.8—dc22

                                                                    2007007346

FOR AMANDA

CONTENTS

ACKNOWLEDGMENTS

I would like to start by thanking someone who has been with me longer than this book, longer than I have been a historian—my wife, Amanda Gillespie Baker. Two historians have been particularly influential in my development and the growth of this project. Fitz Brundage helped me make the transition from folklore to history and introduced me to many of the questions about historical memory in the South with which I have been working ever since. My dissertation adviser, Jacquelyn Dowd Hall, has encouraged me for several years now as I turned this project from a curiosity to a dissertation to a book. Her insight and enthusiasm and many careful readings of draft after draft have helped make this study what it is. I cannot imagine how one could complete a doctorate and a book without a supportive family, especially my mother, Peggy Baker, and my in-laws, Ben and Jeanne Gillespie.

The staff of a number of excellent archives and libraries helped ferret out material I wanted to look at and suggested other things I had not even known about. Three archives in particular—the Southern Historical Collection at the University of North Carolina at Chapel Hill; the Rare Books, Manuscripts, and Special Collections room of Perkins Library at Duke University; and the South Caroliniana Library at the University of South Carolina—were central to my research, and I cannot thank those who work there enough, especially John White, Laura Clark Brown, Elizabeth Dunn, Sam Fore, Henry Fulmer, and Robin Copp. I could almost cite the entire staff of every local library and museum in South Carolina here as well, but I should certainly single out Donna Roper of the Pendleton District Commission and Pelham Lyles of the Fairfield County Museum for their unlimited generosity and deep knowledge. Vernon Burton is an example of the best sort of person South Carolina can produce, and I appreciate his encouragement and hospitality.

Many people read parts of this book at one stage or another, but the person who saw it in its rawest, most incoherent form was Andy Arnold, and for that I am eternally grateful. My interdisciplinary dissertation writing group—Marc David, Liz Fournier, Brian Thomas, Div Thornley, and Thomas Pegelow—gave me great feedback and pushed for clearer arguments and explanations. Other helpful readers were Barb Hahn, Brian Puaca, Paul Quigley, Kerry Taylor, Mark Bradley, Blain Roberts, Cary Miller, Rondall Rice, Scott Nelson, Peter Lau, Scott Poole, Matt Reonas, Bethany Keenan, and Amy Crowe. For assistance with particular bits of information, I need to thank Glenda Gilmore, Gaines Foster, John Chasteen, Jim Farmer, and Bryant Simon. My dissertation committee helped as I was writing the dissertation and gave me great suggestions on how to make it into this book. The signatures on the front page of my dissertation confirm my opinion that Chapel Hill was the best possible place to undertake this study: Jacquelyn Dowd Hall, Joel Williamson, Richard H. Kohn, Joy S. Kasson, George B. Tindall, W. Fitzhugh Brundage.

Writing American history in England has been made easier by excellent colleagues in the department of history at Royal Holloway, University of London, especially John Kirk, Dan Stone, and Justin Champion. In my first year here, I had four occasions to present parts of this work, and I would like to thank Richard Godden, Donald Ratcliffe, Jon Bell, and Tony Badger for facilitating exciting opportunities to talk about historical memory of Reconstruction in places quite far removed from South Carolina.

Finally, working with Dick Holway at the University of Virginia Press has been a delight. We began discussing this book while I was still working on the dissertation, and he has consistently suggested ways small and large to make it a better piece of work. The two readers gave me many important and helpful ideas and will hopefully not be disappointed with the results.

WHAT RECONSTRUCTION MEANT

INTRODUCTION

What does Reconstruction mean? People have answered that question in many ways in the past century and a half. Those answers varied, depending on who was asked, and when, and where. A freedman casting his first vote in 1867 to send a delegate to a state constitutional convention might have one answer, but his notions of what Reconstruction meant would be very different from those of a white member of the United Daughters of the Confederacy at a Confederate Memorial Day celebration in the 1910s. She would be likely to talk about the "horrors of Reconstruction" and might even relate stories from her own childhood of the upsetting, disorienting things she remembered from that time. An African American college student in the mid-1940s attending the Southern Negro Youth Congress convention might have yet another opinion on what Reconstruction meant. She might vehemently disagree with both the UDC woman and the 1867 freedman. Her understanding of the period could be shaped by the stories she might have heard from her grandparents who had lived through the period, but it would also have been influenced by her education in segregated southern public schools and by the works of the Negro history movement and even by the Marxist histories of Reconstruction emerging in the 1930s and 1940s. The ongoing World War against Fascism, and the possibility that, like the Civil War, this war might be followed by an attempt to set things right in America, would also be factors in her thinking. Such a simple question with so many answers.

This book is a history of the meaning of Reconstruction in a particular time and place. Before I explain a bit more about what that entails and how I propose to get at such an amorphous question, I should explain briefly what this book is not. It is not a history of Reconstruction, of the years after the Civil War between the Emancipation Proclamation and the removal of Federal troops from the South in 1877 when Rutherford Hayes became president. There are many excellent studies of this period, and I draw on those for my own understanding of what was happening then. This book is also not a theoretical study of what meaning is or, to borrow a phrase from poet John Ciardi, "how history means." I set out my ideas about history, meaning, and social memory here in this introduction, and I may make a few points in this regard from time to time in the notes, but for the most part I follow the history of the meaning of Reconstruction, attempting to show how many different sorts of people held different views on the subject and how those views changed over time.[1]

When we speak of the "meaning of history," we are combining two separate ideas into one handy phrase. First, the "meaning of history" contains in itself a particular understanding of just what that history is, of what actually happened. That is to say, one of the features of history, in a commonsensical way, is that it is a narrative of events that corresponds accurately to the events that actually happened. In this sense, there is "good" history that corresponds well to the past, and "bad" history that deviates substantially from correspondence with the past. It is easy to see how much room for variation there is here. All the facts of "what happened" might not be known equally to everyone. Assumptions that color how one views "what happened" might be equally diverse and divisive: allowing African American men to vote during Reconstruction was viewed favorably by those who believed they were inherently equal and deserving of full citizenship rights, but for people, especially white elites, brought up to see African Americans as racially inferior and fit only for the lowest position on society's hierarchy, allowing them to vote would seem a disaster, a world turned upside down. As we account for the various strands of social memory, we must pay close attention to exactly what different people thought actually happened, where they got those ideas, and how those ideas developed.

The second idea contained in the "meaning of history" is that what has happened in the past influences the present and the future. Fortunately, we are never completely trapped by history, but at the same time, as Karl Marx observed, "men make their own history, but they do not make it just as they please; they do not make it under circumstances chosen by themselves, but under circumstances directly encountered, given, and transmitted from the past." The meaning of history here is as a reservoir of knowledge that can be applied to contemporary questions and problems. If someone believes that allowing African Americans to vote during Reconstruction had disastrous results, he is likely to use that as an argument for continuing to prevent African Americans from voting in 1930; that is one of the meanings Reconstruction holds for him. On the other hand, if someone thinks that African American political participation during Reconstruction was right and just, then the meaning that history might hold for her could be that it would also be right and just to restore those political rights in 1930. After we have figured out how people came to hold the differing views they had on what happened during Reconstruction and what they thought about it, an important part of this book is following the changes in how people thought those events might be significant for themselves in later times.[2]

What Reconstruction Meant, therefore, falls within the broad category of "social memory studies," a field that originated in the early twentieth century but only came into its own in the late 1980s. The most comprehensive survey of this field's historiography suggests that memory became a topic of interest to scholars as part of a more general "desacralization of traditions" and a growth of interest in understanding not just the ideological reasons for which power was exercised, but the instrumentalities by which it was exercised. More recently, French historian Pierre Nora has suggested that the shock of the oil crisis of the 1970s on industrialized nations, along with "the end of the revolutionary idea" as the Soviet Union's slow collapse began, discrediting the idea that Marxism would bring an end to history, created interest in continuities with the past. Of the many variations of social memory studies that have developed since, the one that I have found of most use for addressing the questions in which I am interested is what Jeffrey K. Olick and Joyce Robbins term "a historical approach to social memory," one that "instead of trying to fix conceptual distinctions theoretically . . . sees such distinctions as emerging in particular times and locations and for particular purposes."[3]

Although no historians have systematically examined social memory of Reconstruction in the twentieth century, quite a number have studied other aspects of social memory in the South in ways that provide a useful foundation for this study. Most recently, W. Fitzhugh Brundage has surveyed historical memory in the South since the Civil War, providing a compelling framework for more specialized studies such as this. There is a rich literature on the southern glorification of the Confederacy in the late nineteenth and early twentieth centuries, known as the "Lost Cause." An earlier watershed in this historiography was the decade of the 1980s, which saw the publication of Charles Reagan Wilson's *Baptized in Blood: The Religion of the Lost Cause, 1865–1920* and Gaines M. Foster's *Ghosts of the Confederacy: Defeat, the Lost Cause, and the Emergence of the New South,*

1865 to 1913. Wilson discussed the Lost Cause as a "civil religion" for the South, while Foster saw the ritual celebration of the Lost Cause as one of the mechanisms for instilling the necessary discipline in the New South's white workforce. Neither of these works, however, succeeded in incorporating African Americans in their analysis in a central way. The study that accomplished this was David W. Blight's *Race and Reunion: The Civil War in American Memory* (2001), which, like the works of Wilson and Foster, looked at the first half-century after the war's end. Blight's argument, to reduce it to its barest bones, is that after the Civil War, three overarching views of the war's significance emerged. One was the war's emancipatory legacy of bringing African Americans into America's democracy, exemplified by Emancipation and the Reconstruction amendments. Another was a white supremacist view that held that while slavery may have ended, and for the best, America could not exist except with a clear racial hierarchy. These two views were incompatible. A third view valued reconciliation of the nation as its highest priority. Over time, the reconciliationist position merged with the white supremacist position, shutting out the emancipatory vision of the Civil War and its memory. Grace Hale, in her study of the cultural history of segregation, did discuss the role memory of Reconstruction played in justifying Jim Crow, but her discussion focused more on major novels and the works of historians and was but part of a much larger project.[4]

Three books relating specifically to South Carolina provide helpful intellectual framework and background for the arguments I present here. Steven Kantrowitz's biography of Ben Tillman also explains how the form of white supremacy of the slave system was transformed in the years up to World War I into the mature form of white supremacy under segregation and disfranchisement. Kantrowitz's key insights are that the process was never smooth or uncontested, that it involved reconfiguring power relationships along the bases of class and gender as well as race, and that the old model of Tillman as an all-powerful demagogue manipulating the masses of his white followers at will was too simple: "White supremacy," writes Kantrowitz, "was hard work." The memory of Reconstruction, as shaped by Tillman and others, made that hard work much easier. W. Scott Poole shows how the South Carolina upcountry's religious heritage turned the Civil War into a crusade and then helped transform defeat into the indispensable foundation for a social and political conservatism that steeled resistance to Reconstruction. Using case studies of four conservative intellectuals, mostly centered in Charleston, Charles J. Holden traces the persistence of the conservatives' belief in white supremacy, aristocracy, and their own right "to remain on top of a hierarchical social order," a set of beliefs that helped keep South Carolina a bastion of conservatism from the Civil War to World War II. Memories of Reconstruction grounded in white supremacy were important components of the conservatism Poole and Holden describe.[5]

Although I am more concerned here with a specific historical question than with developing innovative ideas about the nature of social memory, it is helpful to lay out some of the key concepts I am using, explain where they come from and with what other literatures they intersect, and indicate where I differ from those studying similar topics. The history of social memory sheds light on many other large historical processes, and for the purposes of this study, one important observation about the development of interest in memory and the past is particularly important. In an influential book on "invented traditions," English historian Eric Hobsbawm argued that "one period which saw them spring up with particular assiduity was in the thirty or forty years before the first world war." Changes in the nature and power of the state and rapid social changes "called for new devices to ensure or express social cohesion and identity and to structure social relations," and both official and unofficial "traditions" fulfilled these tasks nicely. In his study of historical memory in the United States, Michael Kammen notes a transformation at the same time, noting that "anyone who probes historical sources for this period will be figuratively assaulted by the nation's arsenal of memory devices and by the astonishing diversity of its stockpile." This is exactly the period of Reconstruction in the United States, and the intensification of interest in the past just as the contest over the fate of Reconstruction was raging made participants on both sides keenly aware of the importance of shaping the legacy of Reconstruction even as they fought over it.[6]

Pierre Nora occupies an important place in social memory studies, in large part for his exhaustive study of memory and the French nation. But as careful observers will soon realize, France is not the American South. Nora's basic paradigm for the relationship of history and memory argues that "memory" is the organic, continuous connection of a people with their past. Following the lead of Walter Benjamin, Nora suggests that modernization disrupts the traditional ways of life that anchor memory, and that as memory disappears, the people's relation to the past takes the form of an official, systematized "history" instead. In France, writes Nora, "we speak so much of memory because there is so little of it left." This model simply collapses if we apply it to the American South, for a variety of reasons I can only point toward here. Because of the sectional conflict in the United States and its lasting effects, the South never had the sort of strong central administrative structure that in France could create a dominant national history. Though both places remained largely agricultural through the period under consideration, the South had no metropolis to compare to Paris as a national center of intellectual activity. As France was urbanizing and industrializing, it suffered through two wars, emphasizing the rupture between past and present. The equivalent transition in the South, while often harsh and sporadically rapid, had nothing like that kind of disruption after the Civil War until, arguably, World War II. Applying Nora's ideas about memory in France to the American South without very careful consideration is likely to lead to false comparisons and confusion.[7]

My approach in this study, to the extent it is systematized, rests on three enthymematic ideas, somewhere between assertions and assumptions. First, oral tradition on the local level provides the basis for social memory. Second, making a careful distinction between social memories operating in public discourse and those operating in private discourse allows us to present a more fine-grained picture of the range of social memories and their interconnections. Third, to the extent that a given social memory becomes dominant in public discourse (in the case of this study, that dominant social memory is what I refer to as a "white supremacist narrative of Reconstruction"), we should look out for the structure and operation of countermemory. Each of these points requires some elaboration. In his studies of African history, Jan Vansina developed a careful system for using oral tradition as historical evidence, though the studies that have influenced me more profoundly on this matter come from folklorists and oral historians interested in how groups view their own history, especially those community members recognized to have authoritative knowledge of the community's history, individuals Henry Glassie calls "historians of the countryside." The best example of this sort of work is Glassie's magisterial study of an Ulster community, *Passing the Time in Ballymenone*. In considering the entire range of a community's folk culture, Glassie was able to explain the Ballymenone residents' conceptions of their history in their own terms. A similar attempt to get a community's inside view on its history propels William Lynwood Montell's study of homicide in a part of the Cumberland Plateau. Other folklorists have studied the development of historical folklore around real events, such as a Texas border hero studied by Américo Paredes. In their book *Social Memory*, James Fentress and Chris Wickham build a theory of how social memory works around just this sort of an oral base, and I shall return to their ideas throughout this book.[8]

Public commemorations provide an opportunity to see the interface between official and vernacular memory, between public and private discourses of memory, as it is shaped. Commemorations contributed to social memory by providing an official platform from which leaders might preach their views of the past to the masses, but also, more importantly, by spurring the formation and reformulation of memory at a variety of levels at once. Social memory at any given moment exists only as an abstract generalization, a way of speaking about a multitude of memories, residing in individual minds, which have some appreciable resemblance to one another. Individual memory remains more or less unmalleable so long as it remains undisturbed; we seldom reinterpret our views of the past of which we have been a part without some stimulus to do so. Public commemorations provide such a stimulus. An orator speaks of the "dark days of Reconstruction"; the listener compares that to his own memory of Reconstruction. Now individual memory may begin to change if the listener is convinced by a version of the past that differs from his own. Yet this view of how official memory reshapes individual memory casts the listener in a purely passive role and gives too much credit to speakers on lecture platforms for molding the memory of their listeners. Individual memory becomes malleable at precisely the point when the individual must articulate that memory to others. The necessity of marshaling abstract recollections, ideas, and values into coherent concepts and narratives that can be transmitted to others gives shape to memory. It is at this point of socialization that new influences might reshape memory. Public commemorations provide many opportunities for individuals to absorb official memory, but just as important, they offer many opportunities for individuals to articulate—to make social and thus to expose to potential revision—their own memories.[9]

Social memory is a body of knowledge about the past that is both a product and medium of social interaction. That is, social memory is constituted in part by one's position in the various social groups of which one is a member. This statement merely acknowledges the influence of one's social position on the kinds of knowledge about the past one would have access to and need for, but does not suggest that such influence is determinative. Social memory is one of the key elements that constitutes social groups; social groups tend to share an understanding of their common past, though not, as we will see, without dissenting voices.

Another important theoretical consideration is the relative importance of oral tradition and literate tradition in the production of social memory. To state it baldly, social memory is primarily an oral product. This is not to say that social memory is only a product of oral tradition or that any print-based aspect of social memory must be derived from the oral foundation. This is, roughly, the position adopted by Pierre Nora when he argues that "memory" is something oral, informal, and constantly being supplanted by history—written, formalized, official, and all-consuming. However, this takes a very limited view of the significance of oral communication, even within highly literate societies. There is no reason to think of oral and literate modes of social memory as mutually exclusive. Rather, social memory in highly literate societies inevitably blends the two modes, just as individuals blend the modes of communication in their daily lives. By keeping oral tradition at the center of my account of social memory, it is easier to get a balanced view of social memory across the breadth of society without giving undue emphasis to the well-educated middle class. This is especially important in a region such as the South in the early twentieth century, where education levels, and even basic literacy levels, were fairly low compared to modern standards.[10]

A conception of social memory as something based primarily on oral communication arises out of the pathbreaking work of Milman Parry and Albert Lord, who studied Homeric epic poetry. They suggested that rather than originating as fixed texts, the Homeric epics took shape as oral performances that used a body of stock phrases and formulas to retell a basic narrative, producing slightly different versions to suit the conditions of each performance. Later scholars have built on this insight to argue that narratives are remembered in terms of sequences of visual images and interlocking chains of concepts. As individuals take information about the past—whether that information came from direct personal experience or from a secondhand source matters little—and assimilate it to their memories, it is remembered in these structures. One effect this has is to tend to simplify complex and subtle information into simpler narratives that are easier to remember. When a person sets out to communicate this memory to others, the memory is articulated in the form of narrative, drawing on the conventions of narrative available within that culture. These conventions will have been shaped by the other aspects of the culture, so narratives will tend to take on somewhat standard forms and use elements that can be found in more than one narrative.[11]

The distinction between public discourses of memory and private discourses of memory is related to the idea of countermemory and derives from several sources. Political scientist James C. Scott introduced the idea of a "hidden transcript," "a critique of power spoken behind the back of the dominant." This concept, along with Scott's interest in "the hegemonic purpose behind displays of domination and consent," is particularly useful for this study, since the white supremacist narrative of Reconstruction that is so central to my study consisted of exactly such a display of domination and consent in the register of history and memory. If the hidden transcript is the record of the resistance to power in the face of hegemony, then the social spaces within which that occurs are what Nancy Fraser terms "subaltern counterpublics . . . parallel discursive arenas where members of subordinated social groups invent and circulate counterdiscourses to formulate oppositional interpretations of their identities, interests, and needs." In the context of social memory in the United States, John Bodnar has employed categories roughly analogous with these when he discusses the nation's "official" memory and the multiplicity of "vernacular" memories. There is a danger, however, that Bodnar's use of "official" suggests a potency to the social memory thus endorsed that is largely illusory until well into the twentieth century, more so in the case of the South than the Midwest, where Bodnar's study centers. Simply put, as we noted in relation to Nora's ideas about France, the South did not have a strong enough state to make the writ of "official" memory run very far: low literacy, little or no compulsory education, strapped state budgets in a region with an unsteady economic foundation.[12]

Finally, the alternative social memory that circulated in the counterpublics described above may be included under the portmanteau term "countermemory." The most useful definition of countermemory comes from Yael Zerubavel, who writes: "The alternative commemorative narrative that directly opposes the master commemorative narrative, operating under and against its hegemony, thus constitutes a *countermemory*. As the term implies, countermemory is essentially oppositional and stands in hostile and subversive relation to collective memory." Countermemory is more than a will-o'-the-wisp that floats around automatically whenever one social memory achieves dominance in the public discourse. A countermemory may have its origins in configurations more or less separate from those that gave rise to the hegemonic memory, or its origins may be entangled with those of the hegemonic memory; we must consider such questions on a case-by-case basis. To understand countermemory's significance, at least as I am using the concept, we must keep in mind its relationship to the distribution and functions of power in the societies in which countermemory circulates, and for that we turn to the leading analyst of knowledge and power, Michel Foucault. In an interview expanding on his book *Discipline and Punish,* Foucault articulated with exceptional clarity his sense of how power operates: "We all know about the great upheavals, the institutional changes which constitute a change of political regime, the way in which the delegation of power right to the top of the state system is modified. But in thinking of the mechanisms of power, I am thinking rather of its capillary form of existence, the point where power reaches into the very grain of individuals, touches their bodies and inserts itself into their actions and attitudes, their discourses, learning processes and everyday lives." Likewise, my concern with countermemory, with memory more generally, is less with how it operates at the broad level of institutions and more with the capillary form of memory, of memory experienced at the individual and community level as it encounters and competes with other memories in the shaping of something that can be said to have a collective or social existence.[13]

Before examining what Reconstruction meant, I would like to justify why I have chosen to focus the book as I have. As mentioned above, it is neither possible nor desirable to account for what Reconstruction meant to each person who might have had an opinion in the last one hundred and forty years. Rather than make sweeping claims about huge regions, I tried to turn my attention to what seemed to be the most significant place and time. I hope this has allowed me to present a picture of how social memory of Reconstruction worked and also to avoid confusing the reader with too many different stories and details. Although many aspects of Reconstruction were shaped at the national level—such as Emancipation, the Reconstruction amendments to the U.S. Constitution, and the various laws passed by Congress—all those national events played out differently in each state, due to differences in demographics and politics. As a result, it makes sense to follow the story of Reconstruction and its memory at the state level.

I chose South Carolina because it was the crucible of Reconstruction, bringing together many of its most powerful features in their most concentrated forms. First, more than in any other state, newly freed and enfranchised African Americans held real political power in South Carolina throughout the Reconstruction period. Second, Reconstruction lasted longer in South Carolina than in any other state except Louisiana and Florida, ending only with the withdrawal of Federal troops in April 1877. Studying the historical memory of Reconstruction in South Carolina, moreover, is particularly fruitful because Reconstruction in the state ended so abruptly and dramatically, with several deadly interracial clashes, the paramilitary mobilization of a substantial proportion of the state's Democratic voters, a residual and ineffective federal military presence, widespread and flagrant voter intimidation and election fraud, and a tense six-month standoff between rival state administrations. The contest over the fate of the Reconstruction government, waged from July 1876 to April 1877, sparked debate and discussion of all aspects of Reconstruction. The intensity of Reconstruction's demise in South Carolina made it eminently memorable and easy to simplify into narratives that could be transmitted to others in the state and beyond. Social memory of Reconstruction has been broader, deeper, and more enduring in South Carolina than in other southern states precisely because so many people across the state were directly involved in the 1876 campaign, either as the terrorists or as the terrorized.

As we will see, this more intense experience of Reconstruction in South Carolina also meant that many of the most influential debates over Reconstruction and depictions of it were about South Carolina specifically. The experience of Reconstruction in South Carolina had a much greater effect on the national understanding of the meaning of Reconstruction than did that of any other state, and far out of proportion to its mere population. This is not to say that there were not influential features of Reconstruction in other states that were incorporated into the national memory of Reconstruction. Louisiana is important in this regard, and in some ways a similar study could have been written on that state. Throughout this book, I try to point out parallels from other states, but my study focuses on South Carolina. At the same time, much of what I consider is how later national changes and influences—World War I, the New Deal, the Cold War, and others—played out in the context of the social memory of Reconstruction in South Carolina. With some modifications, I am confident that much of what I argue here would be applicable to other states and the nation as a whole.

The structure of this book is roughly chronological, starting in chapter 1 with an account of the contemporaneous shaping of the memory of Reconstruction in the 1870s. Chapter 2 shows how southern politicians used the memory of Reconstruction as a tool to build Jim Crow, at the same time that patrician leaders of the fight against Reconstruction, such as Wade Hampton in South Carolina, were elevated to heroic status. The third chapter is set after the turn of the twentieth century, when the mechanisms of disfranchisement were in place in South Carolina and segregation was gathering pace; in such an environment, the white supremacist narrative of Reconstruction employed in the political maneuvering of the previous decade was given free rein and came to dominate public discourse. In chapter 4, I retreat from the public sphere to the private, to examine how white individuals constructed their memories of Reconstruction and how a countermemory persisted among African Americans. Politics is again the topic of chapter 5, which traces the use of memory of Reconstruction as South Carolina's political landscape was reshaped by Franklin D. Roosevelt's years in power. Radicals attempting to change the South and the nation entirely found in Reconstruction a useful model for interracial alliances between black and white workers in the South, and their story, stretching from the 1920s to the beginning of the Cold War, and developing parallel to the liberalization of politics in the Roosevelt years, is told in chapter 6. When the federal government began to take an active part in the civil rights movement, many white southerners saw parallels to Reconstruction once again, but as I argue in chapter 7, some liberal, white southern historians, led by C. Vann Woodward, reclaimed the idea of a "Second Reconstruction" from the segregationists. The conclusion gives a quick glance at the developments in social memory of Reconstruction in South Carolina after 1957, a story that is still developing in interesting ways as I write.

ONE

CREATING MEANING DURING RECONSTRUCTION

In the years following 1870, southern whites were able to combine their practical resistance to Reconstruction, exemplified by the Ku Klux Klan, with a powerful ideological attack on the very foundation of the Reconstruction program. This attack proved to be appealing enough to northern Republicans that the national support necessary to make a success of Reconstruction withered away. Just as South Carolina had been the place where the federal government tried and failed to stop the Ku Klux Klan, South Carolina would be the decisive battleground in this new war of ideas. The depictions of Reconstruction by its opponents would form the basis for what would become the dominant social memory of the period.[1]

Even before the Civil War ended, South Carolina was poised to be the place where free labor ideology would begin transforming the South. Occupied by Union forces since the early months of the war, the Port Royal area had seen the old plantation system crumble, gangs of slaves raising cotton replaced by freedpeople on family farms raising food for themselves. This and other hopeful developments were brought to a halt when President Andrew Johnson imposed easy terms on former Confederate leaders, allowing them to regain their lost lands and political control of the state, all in the interest of stability and a swift recovery for the damaged region. In power, the former Confederates lost little time in passing a "Black Code" to govern the lives of their former slaves, ensuring that they would not share the same legal and political rights as whites and that their productive capacity would be harnessed to white employers' interests in ways that differed from slavery in little more than name. Voters in the North, though, were hardly willing to see the South so little changed, and in the fall 1866 elections they returned a Radical Republican majority to

Congress. The new Congress took control of Reconstruction policy, drafting the Fourteenth Amendment and passing the Reconstruction Acts in March 1867. As a result, former Confederates were out of southern state governments and freedmen were in. A constitutional convention rewrote South Carolina's organic law in January 1868, and elections later that year brought African Americans into a variety of state and local offices. Opposition to black political power, and the economic opportunities it enabled the freedpeople to enjoy, sparked the opposition of the Ku Klux Klan, which interfered in the 1868 election and later instituted a reign of terror in the upstate in the months around the 1870 election.

The Reconstruction Acts of 1867, as well as the Thirteenth, Fourteenth, and Fifteenth Amendments, all grew out of the free labor ideology that drove the Republican Party from the time of its creation in 1854. The Republican free labor ideology began with the Protestant notion that labor was inherently dignified and that through labor individuals might improve their position in a fluid society that had no preexisting hierarchies. This ideology was incompatible with slavery and the values and structures of southern society. As Reconstruction began, Republicans saw the newly freed slaves as ideal workers in a free labor system. Starting with nothing, they would be able to work hard and become substantial citizens in a South transformed by the free labor ideology. At the same time, Republicans worried about white workers in the urban North, who were likely to vote for the Democratic Party and rely on legislative solutions to their problems rather than hard work.[2]

Freedmen might have become the ideal free labor workers Republicans envisioned but for the insistence of southern whites on maintaining the hierarchies that had thwarted the free labor system in the first place. In the face of this opposition from southern whites, freedmen and their advocates called for measures, such as the Enforcement Acts, which would protect their rights so that they might enjoy the fruits of their labor. Many northern Republicans, however, came to see such protective legislation as "class legislation" that would give one group in society an unfair advantage over another and nullify the principle of unencumbered competition between individuals that was the underpinning of the free labor ideology. This gave southern Democrats and northern Republicans enough common ground to join together to oppose the changes of Reconstruction and eventually bring about its defeat in the southern states.

In the early 1870s the work of James S. Pike, a Republican journalist from Maine, cemented the idea that African Americans in the South were dangerous to the political economy of the United States. Born in 1811, Pike had been involved in politics and journalism since his twenties. Through the 1850s, he was associated with Horace Greeley's *New York Tribune* and became known as one of the nation's leading anti-slavery writers, though he had "a strange indifference, even hostility" toward African Americans themselves. During the late 1860s Pike's attitude toward the Republican Party, especially its representatives in southern states, changed. In March 1872 he published an article about South Carolina titled "A State in Ruins" in the *New York Tribune*. Since Pike had never seen South Carolina, he relied on Wade Hampton for his information. The ex-Confederate general told Pike about "oppressive taxation" and the worsening corruption in state government. According to Pike, the black legislators were a "great mass of ignorance and barbarism . . . guided by unprincipled adventurers from other states, who make use of these freedmen as their agents for the most nefarious acts which were ever committed under the shelter of republican forms of government." Since Pike's article proved popular, Greeley enlisted him to write several more articles about South Carolina in early 1873. This time, Pike visited the state himself, observing the legislature and interviewing people, almost all of them conservative white Carolinians. When these articles, too, were received favorably, Pike decided to expand them into a book. In December 1873, *The Prostrate State: South Carolina under Negro Government* was published by D. Appleton and Company in New York.[3]

The importance of *The Prostrate State* in shaping the way the nation would remember Reconstruction cannot be overestimated. Nearly all the initial reviews of the book were glowing, except those in the African American and labor press. Since Pike had been an ardent Radical Republican, his depiction of the Republican government in South Carolina was accepted as unbiased and accurate. The book arrived at a time when the American public was particularly anxious about the stability of society. In 1870, Americans had watched as France lost a disastrous war with Germany and then saw the rise of the Paris Commune in spring 1871. The Paris Commune and its brief but bloody struggle for existence became an example to Americans of what could happen when workers unfit to govern themselves in a democracy seized power by force. Opponents of Reconstruction quickly adopted the analogy, comparing Republican militias in the South to Parisian mobs. Their fears of social upheaval were only confirmed when the Panic of 1873 led workers across America to strike and protest.[4]

The Prostrate State epitomized the growing critique of African American political participation, and its themes would be repeated without significant challenge for nearly a century by white southerners and other

Americans alike. Pike's book vividly depicts "a society turned bottom-side up," where "the wealth, the intelligence, the culture, the wisdom of the State" had been replaced by "the rude form of the most ignorant democracy that mankind ever saw, invested with the functions of government." The most significant aspect of Pike's overwhelming racism was his continual assertion that African Americans were inevitably ignorant and corrupt. Pike carefully moved an important part of the responsibility away from African Americans, though. According to Pike, "The changes here experienced have been accomplished by outside forces . . . the compulsive power of the Federal authority at Washington." The corollary of this proposition was that "it is a government that the intelligent public opinion of the State would overthrow if left to itself." Pike depicted a society out of kilter, an unnatural product of class legislation rather than the natural result of a free labor system working without improper interference. In the first years after the Civil War, the South had been a laboratory for the free labor ideology, but in *The Prostrate State* it had become an experiment gone terribly wrong and a danger to the rest of the nation. Pike's criticisms were echoed by white Democrats in South Carolina, who held a Taxpayers' Convention in February 1874 to protest to the federal government and the national public against the idea that the propertyless, especially African Americans, should have any political voice; an earlier Taxpayers' Convention in 1871 had complained that "they who lay the taxes do not pay them, and that they who are to pay them have no voice in the laying of them."[5]

The national media reflected the Taxpayers' Convention's success in convincing northerners of the truth of their claims. Thomas Nast, the great illustrator for *Harper's Weekly* who had earlier supported Reconstruction, reflected the new attitude. On 14 March 1874 he published a drawing of the South Carolina legislature that followed the lines laid down by *The Prostrate State* and the Taxpayers' Convention's propaganda. In *The Nation* in April 1874, editor E. L. Godkin published "Socialism in South Carolina." It followed the interpretation set up by Pike, quoting his work at length. "Politics in South Carolina," Godkin argued, "have consisted of determined efforts on the part of a few designing men, with the aid of the negro vote, to plunder the property-holders." White South Carolinians, however, were not content merely to wait for national opinion to swing their way. They began organizing "rifle clubs" (also known as "gun clubs" or "sabre clubs") across the state, cloaking their political purposes in a mantle of sociability. The rifle clubs' true purposes were illustrated in August 1874, however, when gunfights between rifle clubs and black militia occurred in both Georgetown and Edgefield.[6]

Vol. XVIII.—No. 898.]   NEW YORK, SATURDAY, MARCH 14, 1874.   [WITH A SUPPLEMENT. PRICE TEN CENTS.

Entered according to Act of Congress, in the Year 1874, by Harper & Brothers, in the Office of the Librarian of Congress, at Washington.

Thomas Nast's cartoon "Colored Rule in a Reconstructed (?) State," which appeared on the cover of *Harper's Weekly* on 14 March 1874, illustrated the declining national support for Reconstruction in South Carolina.

With public opinion outside the South increasingly opposed to Reconstruction and Democrats in South Carolina mobilizing, Republicans in the state found themselves unable to make significant reforms quickly enough to satisfy their opponents. Governor Daniel H. Chamberlain did work for reform, but his vision of reform still included suffrage for African Americans, and his willingness to support some of the Democrats' demands alienated his core Republican constituency and weakened the party. Democrats realized that they need only continue to work and to wait, not to compromise.[7]

The death throes of Reconstruction in South Carolina began in late 1875 and ended in the spring of 1877. The drama and violence of 1876 would make the events of that year the touchstone of whites' memory of Reconstruction throughout the twentieth century. Reconstruction across the South was already on its last legs. South Carolina's neighboring states had long since returned to Democratic control, with Democrats regaining the entire state government in Georgia and the legislature in North Carolina in 1870. In Louisiana, the White League formed in 1874 to recapture the state through violence. In the Battle of Liberty Place, in September 1874, the Democrats and the White League took over New Orleans for a brief period until Federal troops arrived to support the Republican government. The success of such a strategy inspired white Mississippians to organize and challenge Republicans across the state in the 1875 election. Despite widespread violence and intimidation, the Grant administration allowed the results to stand and another Republican administration had been swept aside in the South.[8]

Prompted by widespread white opposition to the election of two circuit court judges, the state Democratic executive committee chairman announced on 6 January 1876 that the party would be reorganized "from the bottom up, at the ward, precinct, township, and county levels." Immediately, Democrats began to hold small meetings and large rallies across the state. The Democratic Party met for its state convention in May, but at that point many of the delegates doubted their party's strength and still favored cooperating with Chamberlain and the more moderate elements in the Republican Party. Others, such as Martin W. Gary and Matthew C. Butler, advocated a "Straight-out" policy: the Democratic Party should nominate only Democrats and use whatever means necessary to ensure their election. With no consensus, the party decided to reconvene a few months later. The Democrats' indecision was settled by a bloody confrontation in Aiken County in early July that pitted a few dozen of the state's black militia against several hundred rifle club members. Seven militia members were killed—six executed in cold blood—in the Hamburg Massacre, embold-ening Democrats and pushing aside thoughts of political compromise.[9]

When the Democratic convention met again on 15 August, the Straight-out policy had much greater support and was quickly adopted. The party nominated former Confederate cavalry general Wade Hampton for gover-nor. Hampton was considered more moderate than Gary and Butler, and it was hoped that his leadership might appeal to some black voters and also restrain white violence enough to prevent federal intervention. Notwith-standing this patina of moderation, the Straight-out leaders prepared for a campaign based on economic pressure, fraud, intimidation, and enough violence to make the intimidation work. The reorganization of the Demo-cratic Party, initiated the previous January, gave Democrats a statewide network of supporters who had adopted the red shirt as the symbol of the campaign for white supremacy. Gary drew up a "Plan of Campaign" that was distributed to local Democratic leaders. In very specific language, it called on Democrats to use fraud and murder to control the Republican vote. One of the Democrats' principal tactics throughout the campaign was to demonstrate their superiority over Republicans by taking control of their meetings whenever possible. This policy was known euphemistically as "dividing time" and usually meant that several dozen to a hundred Red Shirts would arrive at a Republican meeting conspicuously armed and in-sist that their leader or one of the Democratic state candidates be allowed to address the Republican voters. Sometimes they simply dispersed the meeting by riding, shouting, and firing guns in the air. Since there were as many as 290 gun clubs (now known as Red Shirt clubs) throughout the state, it was difficult for Republicans to avoid them. Meanwhile, Wade Hampton campaigned across the state. Starting in Anderson, Hampton traveled across the northern border of South Carolina to Marion, then across the state through Sumter to Edgefield and down through Barnwell and Orangeburg, ending up in Charleston on 31 October 1876. Elabo-rate celebrations and pageants greeted Hampton all across the state, with "mounted torchlight processions, fireworks, cannonade and speeches by Hampton and lesser Confederate lights calling for resistance and unity among white conservatives." The reason the "nonviolent" approach of the Red Shirts worked so well is that African Americans learned that real vio-lence lay just beneath the surface of these demonstrations of force. Several riots occurred in the weeks of the campaign, taking dozens of lives, and though the federal government finally sent more troops to South Carolina to preserve order, their inability to halt the violence merely underscored the Republican administration's impotence.[10]

The election of 1876 in South Carolina became part of a larger national electoral crisis that was not completely settled until April 1877. After weeks of complex disputes over voter fraud, the Democratic members of the state House of Representatives (the state Senate still had a decisive Republican majority) went to a separate building and constituted themselves as the legitimate House, on the grounds that without their presence, the House meeting in the State House lacked a quorum. The Democratic House became known as the "Wallace House," after its Speaker, William H. Wallace of Union. The Republican House, called the "Mackey House," for Speaker E. W. M. Mackey, held that since the Laurens and Edgefield members did not count, they had just enough for a quorum. The two Houses continued to operate separately for the next several weeks. On 6 December 1876, the Mackey House inaugurated Chamberlain as governor, and the Wallace House inaugurated Hampton on 14 December. Hampton immediately called on his supporters to pay taxes to the Democratic government, not the Republican one. This tactic worked and further weakened Chamberlain's administration.

The results of the 1876 presidential election remained uncertain through the early months of 1877. Disputed election returns from South Carolina, Louisiana, and Florida meant that neither Democrat Samuel Tilden nor Republican Rutherford Hayes had enough electoral votes to claim the presidency. If all the electoral votes from the three states went to Hayes, he would barely win. The parties were deadlocked by mid-December, and by a complex process of negotiations, a special electoral commission decided on Hayes, who was inaugurated on 4 March 1877. After meeting with both Chamberlain and Hampton in Washington, President Hayes agreed to remove Federal troops from South Carolina. Without troops to support him, Chamberlain's administration was sure to collapse. Federal troops left Columbia on 10 April 1877, and on 11 April Wade Hampton took possession of the governor's office of South Carolina.[11]

TWO

WADE HAMPTON'S LEGEND IN BEN TILLMAN'S WORLD

There was nothing accidental nor inevitable about how white southerners remembered Reconstruction. The carnivalesque depiction that James S. Pike, Wade Hampton, Martin W. Gary, and others created in the 1870s to overthrow South Carolina's Republican administration proved just as useful in the 1890s for building a society where powerful white men need never again worry about the aspirations and political power of African Americans and the poor. In the 1870s, lurid tales of a world turned upside down had worked in tandem with the lash and the rifle to secure power, but by the end of the century, hot young blood had cooled somewhat. White South Carolinians sought to naturalize their power by obscuring its violent origins, and they did this by elevating Wade Hampton to legendary status in the final years of his life. Though his own politics were by then an anachronistic irrelevance, the paternalistic leader of the Red Shirts proved an appealing figurehead for a historical memory of Reconstruction that was a critical element in providing moral justification for the Jim Crow system it had helped create.

The 1890s was a period of tremendous political upheaval for the South, bringing in changes as far-reaching as those of the 1870s, but much more durable, and the memory of Reconstruction was an indispensable instrument in effecting those changes. As historian Stephen Kantrowitz reminds us, white supremacy was "more than a slogan and less than a fact," and the 1890s saw that project challenged on a number of fronts. The Lodge Elections Bill was the last great attempt by the national Republican Party to make southern black voters a significant part of its electoral strategy and to keep their needs in its platform. The firestorm of criticism it evoked from white southern elites drew heavily on comparisons to Reconstruction, and this response helped codify and publicly disseminate the white supremacist narrative of Reconstruction given currency by James S. Pike and the political tumult of the mid-1870s.[1]

Across the South, as more farmers fell into tenancy and peonage with the growth of sharecropping and the crop-lien system, their anger expressed itself in an economic and political challenge to the order the Bourbons had created in the aftermath of Reconstruction. Out of that political instability, a new generation of southern politicians took charge, exemplified in South Carolina by the raw and provocative figure of Ben Tillman. Explicitly defining himself in contrast to the genteel, patrician Hampton, Tillman took the measure of his state and realized that white South Carolinians were ready to abandon the Bourbon notion that African Americans could be a part of civic life so long as they were properly managed and led by white elites. By mobilizing those white men who had found themselves on the losing end of the society the Bourbons were creating, Tillman led a movement to cast African Americans out of public life entirely and thereby push aside Bourbons such as Hampton who depended on their control of African Americans for their economic and political power. This generation of Bourbons became redundant, no longer useful as political leaders in a society that was bent on creating de jure and de facto segregation. Yet, men such as Hampton still had great symbolic usefulness, as Confederate leaders who had defended their states from invasion, but also, and at least as importantly, as leaders who even after crushing defeat on the battlefield had the courage to rally a broken people to throw off domination by a conqueror, apostate native whites, and uppity former slaves. To look at it in terms of the leading personalities involved, white South Carolinians wanted to live in the world that Ben Tillman created, but they wanted to venerate Wade Hampton as the founder of that world.

The white supremacist version of the history of Reconstruction assumed its classic form at the very point when southern states were ensuring that the African Americans who had come to know freedom and citizenship during Reconstruction would no longer play a part in the political life of the South. When President Benjamin Harrison intimated that he was willing to protect the voting rights of blacks in the South and Congressman Henry Cabot Lodge began mobilizing support in December 1889 for the Lodge Elections Bill (known to southerners as the "Force Bill"), southern politicians responded by telling a horrible story of what had happened twenty-five years earlier when the federal government involved itself in southern politics. The key provision of the Lodge Elections Bill was that a small number of determined voters in any congressional district could trigger federal investigation of, and hence supervision of, elections. Southern Democrats, especially in areas where the Republican Party had once been strong and still remained viable, were certain to lose political power if this bill became law. They were unable to stop it in the House, however, and it barely passed, on 2 July 1890.[2]

In the midst of this debate, a congressman from Alabama, Hilary A. Herbert, used the powerful and still fresh memory of Reconstruction to argue against any new federal protection for black voters. Born in upstate South Carolina, Herbert had followed the cotton frontier to Alabama as a boy, serving in the Civil War and taking a leading part in bringing Alabama's Reconstruction to an end in 1874. Elected to Congress from Alabama's Second District in 1876, Herbert was part of the Democratic political bloc known in the 1880s as the "Solid South," and he titled the collection of essays he coordinated *Why the Solid South? or, Reconstruction and Its Results*. Although Herbert's biographer claims that *Why the Solid South?* was "rushed . . . to completion" in the spring and summer of 1890 as a response to the Lodge Bill, Herbert had been planning the book for well over a year before that. As early as March 1889, Herbert had been holding informal discussions with other congressmen and senators about the possibility of producing a history of Reconstruction, "written by those who participated in the memorable struggles of that trying era." On 8 April 1889, he sent a circular letter to twelve such men, outlining his plan for the book. Each writer was to "[give] the history of reconstruction & its results in his own state," emphasizing its disastrous financial consequences. Herbert's introduction would outline the argument he suggested each writer make: that although conditions and events during Reconstruction varied from state to state, Reconstruction was an economic disaster for every southern state. Years later, in his memoir, Herbert insisted that *Why the Solid South?* was purely a work of objective historical scholarship and was not meant to serve any political ends, but the elaborate planning evident in the April 1889 letter belies this claim. Herbert knew the conclusions the book's chapters on the various southern states would reach before they were ever written. "Not all of the States were reconstructed under the same laws," he pointed out to his contributors, "but in perhaps every act of Congress dealing with the subject will be discovered the same spirit." *Why the Solid South?* was intended not merely to educate, but to affect contemporary political decisions: "The great lesson which I think our history will teach to thoughtful men is that they should be slow to sanction radical legislation especially when party leaders seek to win them to its support by appeals to passion & prejudice." Herbert sought to make the white supremacist story of Reconstruction more palatable to main-stream America by twining it into the story of the nation's recovery from war. James S. Pike's 1874 book *The Prostrate State* decried the rule of the propertyless over the propertied, and Herbert's volume would vindicate the revolution Pike's book had propelled, reiterating how bad Reconstruction had been, but also showing how the South had thrived in the decade since its end. If the nation wanted to continue its industrial boom, then repeating the radical mistakes of Reconstruction with the Lodge Elections Bill was not the way to do it.[3]

Herbert originally wanted Wade Hampton to write the chapter on South Carolina, but he had to settle for Congressman John J. Hemphill instead. Born in Chester, South Carolina, in 1849, Hemphill practiced law during the early 1870s, served in the state legislature in the late 1870s, and by 1890 had held a seat in Congress for ten years. Hemphill's essay sets out the basic white supremacist narrative of Reconstruction in South Carolina that would dominate public discourse for nearly a century. His story relies on a series of interlocking cause-and-effect structures that follow an inexorable logic, leading to the end of Reconstruction and the return of prosperity to the South. His first proposition is that malevolent federal interference established an illegitimate regime in South Carolina. According to Hemphill, the Reconstruction Acts of March 1867 were conceived in a spirit of vindictiveness and unjustly disfranchised South Carolina's rightful rulers—white men of property. The Constitution of 1868 and the regime it established had no legitimacy that white South Carolinians were bound to respect. Hemphill goes on to explain how the Republican government used the all-black militia and federal force to consolidate its position and perpetrate various frauds and corruptions. In this part of his narrative, Hemphill tells a story of government corruption familiar to Gilded Age readers, making the Reconstruction South seem less exotic. Northern readers of *Why the Solid South?* could allow themselves to be convinced that the issue at hand had little to do with section or race; it was only an issue of "good government" and its obstacles. The next part of Hemphill's narrative recounts the story of the Taxpayers' Conventions of 1871 and 1874. The analogy Hemphill is drawing, while not explicit, is clear. In the 1870s, as in the American Revolution of the 1770s, overtaxed Americans whose interests were not represented in their government peacefully petitioned for redress of grievances. But no one listened, not even when the taxpayers appealed directly to the distant head of the government to plead their case. It was clear that reform would not come from outside. The conclusion of Hemphill's essay echoes the conclusion of all the other essays in

Why the Solid South? and of the book's concluding chapter, "Sunrise": with the providential end of Reconstruction in South Carolina, good (white) government returned, "the resources of the state are being greatly developed; the manufacturing enterprises are multiplying wonderfully, and the people are looking to the future for still greater development of its industries and resources." Herbert's book presented to the general public arguments against federal protection for African American suffrage that would soon be heard on the floor of the Senate.[4]

The debate on the Lodge Bill moved to the Senate in August 1890, but it was postponed until December so the Senate could discuss the tariff question first. By the time the December debate came, the fall elections had shown Republicans that they were losing ground with the electorate, lending the debate on the Lodge Bill greater urgency. As Senate debate on the bill wound toward a close in January 1891, Wade Hampton, South Carolina's senior senator and the man who had led the fight against Reconstruction in 1876, took the floor to oppose it. Although his speech was insignificant at the national level, it gained great symbolic importance in South Carolina as the statesman's last valiant defense of white supremacy. Hampton recognized the significance of this occasion, commenting at the end of his speech, "I feel now . . . that I am discharging, if the last, the highest public duty I owe to my State and to my country." His speech opened with a thinly veiled threat; the bill was "a measure which, in my opinion, is fraught with evil to the whole country and which might bring innumerable woes upon our colored citizens, who have, I am sorry to confess, been too often made the victims of injustices at our hands." His main argument against the Lodge Bill, however, was that it would bring about exactly what it was intended to bring about: African American political participation. Reconstruction, Hampton explained, had been a disaster for (white) South Carolina for just that reason. He scorned the ill-conceived idealism of that period: "In my opinion the voters who in any State represent the best elements, the capital, the intelligence, and the virtue, should govern, despite all fine-spun theories of fraternity and equality, the sacred brotherhood of mankind, and the divine right of universal suffrage!" The (white) South's sacrifices during Reconstruction should thus stand as a lesson to the nation that white supremacy must be maintained. Finally, Hampton cited the South's prosperity in the last fifteen years as another reason to leave well enough alone. By the end of January 1891, the Lodge Bill was dead.[5]

White southerners never wanted to have to worry about congressional enforcement of African American suffrage rights, so several states, starting with Mississippi, decided to revise their state constitutions. The

South Carolina Constitutional Convention of 1895 was not subtle. As historian George B. Tindall pointed out, it "was called for the specific purpose of disfranchising the Negro by evading the Fifteenth Amendment to the federal constitution." The new constitution would replace one created in 1868, during Reconstruction, that had introduced what one later writer would call "the cooties of democracy" into South Carolina's political process. Memories of Reconstruction were invoked all along the way as the constitution was debated. In the movement for white supremacy, "the greatest motivation," according to Tindall, was the "legends of Reconstruction that had been rehearsed in more and more macabre shape with the passage of time."[6] During the campaign to call the convention, in the fall of 1894, Senator Ben Tillman and Governor John Gary Evans both argued that the new constitution was necessary to avoid a return to the conditions of Reconstruction. When a federal lawsuit over the illegal election of delegates threatened to stall the convention in May 1895, Evans responded with a manifesto that combined antebellum ideas of state sovereignty with a rehashing of Reconstruction: "The State was put under martial law, and under the reconstruction acts the ignorant slaves, whose fetters had just been broken, manipulated by carpetbaggers from the four quarters of the earth, were placed in entire control of our State government." The constitution they produced in 1868, Evans argued, was invalid, and "this condition lasted until 1876, when the oppression and misgovernment had rendered our people so desperate that with one impulse they asserted their manhood and overthrew the despotism of the carpetbaggers and resumed control of the State's affairs." The current situation, Evans exaggerated, was becoming as desperate as that of 1876 and might call for the same solutions: "Let the man who undertakes to lead the ignorant blacks against you suffer as he did in 1876." When the business of the convention turned to suffrage, Tillman again returned to stories about Reconstruction to justify what his faction was accomplishing. The handful of black Republican delegates also referred back to Reconstruction, but as a time that showed that blacks and whites could work together in a political system. They lost.[7]

South Carolina was not the only southern state to use the memory of Reconstruction as a tool in the fight to create a less democratic constitution. As C. Vann Woodward noted, "The legend of Reconstruction was revived, refurbished, and relived by the propagandists as if it were an immediate background of the current crisis." Historian Glenn Feldman has identified what he terms the "Reconstruction syndrome" as an important tool used by Alabama's white elites to convince poor whites to vote for a constitution that would ultimately disfranchise many of them. The "Reconstruction syndrome," Feldman argues, was "a psychological response to Dixie's traumatic experience of defeat, abolition, economic ruin, military occupation, and black suffrage" characterized by a number of "stubborn and ingrained components: antiblack, antifederal, anti-outsider, anti-Yankee, antitax, and antiliberal impulses." Supporters of the new constitution argued that it was the mischief wrought by Reconstruction, particularly the Fifteenth Amendment, that made this change necessary: "Are we willing to risk the chances of reconstruction again?" asked one Alabama delegate.[8]

After the completion of disfranchisement in South Carolina with the 1895 Constitution, memory of Reconstruction was used in politics, but in a different way. Up to 1895, references to Reconstruction were used as a means of political mobilization in order to get citizens—of both races and varying political affiliations—to address the political questions still lingering from Reconstruction. After 1895, references to Reconstruction and its overthrow in 1876 came almost entirely from Democrats, who used them as a raw threat and as a self-congratulatory account justifying why the political landscape was as it was and why it must remain that way. The year 1898 saw a brutal repetition of the tactics of 1876. In North Carolina, Democrats were determined to regain control of the state from a biracial coalition of Republicans and Populists. To do this, they whipped up fears of black political power and its threat to white womanhood. Ben Tillman came to give a series of speeches about South Carolina's overthrow of Reconstruction; his listeners donned red shirts and repeated the process. Back in Greenwood County, South Carolina, a local white Republican family, the Tolberts, made one last attempt to lead a biracial Republican Party. Their efforts led to a battle on election day 1898 at the crossroads village of Phoenix, which left one white Democrat and at least eight black Republicans dead. As historian Daniel L. Wilk argues, "It was through the prism of Redemption that many local whites saw the unfolding events in Phoenix." Newspaper coverage of the riot compared it to similar events in 1876 and used warnings about "negro rule" to whip up whites to help root out the Tolberts and their supporters.[9]

Literally in the same week that Ben Tillman and his followers were using memory of Reconstruction to rewrite the state constitution in Columbia, the city of Charleston was welcoming a native son. "Hampton Day," on 14 May 1895, commemorated the hero of Reconstruction, ex-governor and ex-senator Wade Hampton. The event also promoted the visibility and credibility of two recently formed organizations in Charleston devoted to memory. Camp Moultrie of the Sons of Confederate Veterans (SCV) was organized in November 1894 with one hundred charter members. It came out of a restructuring of the Survivors' Association of Charleston, which became Camp Sumter of the United Confederate Veterans (UCV). The same month, the Daughters of the Confederacy was organized in Charleston. The two groups decided to hold a joint meeting with a prominent Confederate hero as speaker to raise money for needy Confederates and their widows and children. Wade Hampton was the obvious choice and he was happy to help "[arouse] the dormant love and memory of the Confederacy and its Heroes, . . . and to awaken the interest, and inform the ignorance of a generation that is growing up, unconscious of the glorious past that it can boast."[10]

The Hampton Day parade in 1895 called to mind certain other parades. With many veterans participating, it evoked memories of 1861 when the Washington Light Infantry marched off to war as part of the Hampton Legion. It also evoked, for many, the parade on 30 October 1876, as Hampton concluded his canvass of the state before the election. But just as the paraders in 1895 deliberately walked in the footsteps of those who had paraded through Charleston's old streets before them, they also sought to scuff out the footsteps others had left, especially footsteps left by African Americans claiming their place in the public streets with events such as the annual parades celebrating Emancipation Day.[11]

The one parade the organizers of Hampton Day would have most liked to forget occurred thirty years earlier as Reconstruction began in Charleston. On 21 March 1865, little more than a month after the liberation of the city, thousands of freedpeople turned out for a parade to celebrate their freedom. Organized by ministers from two of the leading black churches, the parade began with mounted marshals and the 21st Regiment U.S. Colored Troops. A "Car of Liberty" with thirteen girls dressed in white and carrying American flags invoked the Revolutionary heritage of liberty. Groups of tradesmen and members of various societies participated, as did eighteen hundred schoolchildren, all signs of the hope and progress of the race. Most memorable, though, for both the freedpeople and their former masters, were two floats mocking the institution of slavery. The first featured an auctioneer selling a slave family for ridiculously large sums of now-worthless Confederate currency. The second was a hearse bearing a coffin labeled "Slavery." Inscriptions on the hearse stated "Slavery Is Dead" and "Sumter Dug his Grave on the 13th of April, 1861."[12]

The Hampton Day parade, with its cannons, bells, bands, carriages, veterans, decorations, and spectators, brought Hampton's visit and the history he represented to the forefront of people's minds that day. A sizable proportion, perhaps a majority, of Charleston's white population (accounts of the parade make no mention of blacks) involved itself in the parade. Charleston's public schools opened late that day so that all schoolchildren could attend the parade. Indeed, it is difficult to imagine a white Charlestonian in 1895 explaining to a neighbor or family member that he or she would not go out that morning to cheer for Hampton. Likewise, once along the parade route, it would be hard to imagine hearing a boo or a hiss amidst the cheers. The very scale of the parade developed a social momentum that compelled participation. Packed onto the sidewalks, flags waving, the strains of "Dixie" drowned out by thousands of cheering voices, individuals found their identities submerged in a collective expression of welcome for the "typical South Carolinian, the State's savior." The emotional context of such a parade nudged individual and potentially disparate memories toward common ground. Around the city, "the battles that Hampton had fought in peace and war [were] lived over again in a thousand homes during the day" as Charlestonians awaited the evening's ceremonies. The next day, "the outpouring of a people's love at the Academy of Music the evening before, was the talk on all sides," and "everywhere in the street the meeting was talked over and discussed." Large public assemblies such as the parade on Hampton Day prompted people to talk with one another. They talked about their personal lives, the weather, politics. But, above all, they talked about what it was that drew them together that day.[13]

The *Charleston News and Courier's* coverage of Hampton Day made 1876 the center of the story of Hampton's career. The *News and Courier*, the leading newspaper in the state, solicited "articles specially written for the occasion by Confederate veterans or by those intimately associated with the great leader since the civil war," and published several articles about Hampton's Civil War career, emphasizing both his leadership and his personal losses. The longest article, however, was "Hampton as Peacemaker: The Thrilling Story of the Federal Usurpation of Authority in 1876 and How Hampton Restrained the Indignation of the People." The climax of the story was a series of speeches Hampton made to angry crowds in Columbia, calling on them to remain peaceful. The people were indignant that Hampton was not permitted to take office, and the same force that brought Hampton within reach of the governorship threatened to overflow into violence. Had Hampton's leadership failed, or had he lacked the judgment to exercise restraint, the story claims, events in Columbia would have engulfed the nation in a new civil war.[14]

In his speech at the Academy of Music, Hampton insisted that he and

Wade Hampton speaking at the dedication of the Confederate cemetery in Chicago, May 1895.

the rest of the citizens of the state were obligated not to forget the Confederate dead and to make their sacrifice worthwhile by justifying the principles for which they died. Hampton recognized that he was nearing the end of his life, and that this was "the last occasion, in all probability, on which [he] shall ever address [his] fellow citizens of South Carolina in public." As Hampton and others of his generation died off, he worried "that the younger generation who will soon take [their] places here had grown so indifferent to the glorious traditions and memories of the past, and that even the sons of our veterans were becoming forgetful of the undying fame won for our State by their fathers." For Hampton, vindication of the cause for which Confederates fought came not on the battlefields of the Civil War, but in the continuation of that struggle in the years following the dissolution of the Confederacy. Simply championing the soldiers' bravery and loyalty to the cause of states' rights could not justify their sacrifice nearly so well as telling the story of how that sacrifice was eventually redeemed in their own land. "I have felt pride on many a battlefield," said Hampton, "but the proudest day of my life was that on which I announced to our people, on my return from Washington [in April 1877], that the Federal troops would be withdrawn from the State House, and that Carolinians, the rightful rulers of the State, would resume their hereditary authority, so long denied them." In comparison to that proud day, Hampton in 1895 worried that the unity whites achieved in 1876 had disappeared in the political factionalism of 1890 that had put him out of the Senate.[15]

One of the first books about Reconstruction in South Carolina was written by an amateur historian who had ridden with Wade Hampton's cavalry in the Civil War. Edward L. Wells, a native of New Jersey, moved to South Carolina after the war, though his status as a Confederate veteran and a friend of Wade Hampton seems to have insulated him from being termed a "carpetbagger." By the 1880s, Wells was writing for the *Southern Historical Society Papers,* and in the 1890s and into the 1900s, he wrote occasional pieces for the *Publications of the Southern History Association.* Wells's first publication was an autobiographical account of how he came to be a Confederate, and he moved from autobiography to accounts of the Civil War battles in which he had participated under Hampton's command. Wells began work on what would become *Hampton and His Cavalry in '64* in 1896. Hampton gave Wells access to his papers, letters, and battle plans, and this account also relied, as did so many of the time, on Wells's claim to the indisputable authority of personal experience. Wells tried to publish the book with several prominent New York houses, but they were not interested. B. F. Johnson of Richmond agreed to publish it, and *Hampton and His Cavalry in '64* appeared in the spring of 1899. By about April 1900, a second edition was printed. The book was made all the more valuable, as Wells pointed out to his publisher, by the fire at Hampton's house that had destroyed most of the original documents on which the book was based.[16]

When Edward L. Wells wrote *Hampton and Reconstruction* in 1907, he began with an argument for why he was the sort of person best qualified to write such a history. "It may perhaps be said that, granting all so far," wrote Wells, "the account of this period should be written only by one who has grown to manhood since its close, for he would write in a more 'judicial spirit,' as the phrase is, than an older man." But Wells denied that objective distance from his topic was an advantage. Someone older, like himself, who had lived through the events described, could do a better job by relying on memory, since "the keen interest that animates an observer of contemporary events stamps on his mind exact impressions of facts, and these impressions are durable as brass." Wells contrasted these credentials with the rising generation of professional historians whose work was less credible, because "a mere academician, cold, unimpassioned, . . . who undertakes to gather materials from lifeless, moldy volumes . . . is like an artist attempting to make a faithful portrait of a dead stranger by glancing at his corpse."[17]

Actively hostile to the new standards of scientific history, Wells's book has none of the apparatus of scholarship. Although it relies on government records, newspapers, and personal letters, there is no discussion of sources, much less a system of footnotes or other references to direct readers to Wells's sources. Wells blended several types of sources to fit his evidence to his conclusions. As evidence for his claim that "Reconstruction in South Carolina was the same in general scope as in other Southern States, but the effects here were more ruinous at the time, and the injury more permanent, than elsewhere," Wells used examples from Thomas Nelson Page's 1898 novel *Red Rock*. In his discussion of the 1868 Constitutional Convention, Wells did not use any official records, but instead cited a 1901 article in the *Atlantic Monthly* by Daniel H. Chamberlain, the last Reconstruction-era governor of South Carolina. A long quote from James S. Pike's 1874 account, *The Prostrate State*, summarized conditions in the state during Reconstruction, and Wells backed this up by relating a personal anecdote.[18]

Response to *Hampton and Reconstruction* varied according to the expectations of the various audiences who read it. The professional historians took virtually no notice of the book; the *American Historical Review* merely noted its publication. The northern popular press considered it one more in a long line of sectional, partisan histories from southern authors. An exasperated reviewer for the *Independent* snapped, "The author is evidently unaware that the South brought down upon itself the horrors of reconstruction by its stubborn failure to accept the results of the war in its first constitutions." "All of this is interesting reading, no doubt," the reviewer concludes, "but it is hardly to be classified as history." Wells fared much better in the southern popular press. Commenting on the book, a reviewer for the *Columbia State* felt that only a southerner such as Wells could write the history of Reconstruction. "Already," the reviewer wrote, "when the South is but beginning to write out its memories of that period of brutality, the North is trying to forget it or to shift the terrible responsibility for its horrors. It must, therefore, be Southern pens that will write the story of the period of despair."[19]

Wells's work represents a sort of historical writing popular in the late nineteenth century, especially in the wake of the Civil War: rich in anecdote, thin on documentation, more exciting than analytical, and often legitimated by an appeal to the author's own experience. Some historians, dissatisfied with these popular histories, tried to professionalize their discipline and change the way people learned about history. Using scientific methods, it was thought, history could aspire to the same level of accuracy and prestige as science. In the study of Reconstruction, however, the professionalization of history only served to entrench the traditional white supremacist version of history ever deeper, giving it a stronger official imprimatur than before. The details of how this occurred explain much about how historical memory develops and the ways in which a narrative with substantial political and cultural support can resist change by co-opting the epistemological agents of that change.

The professionalization of history was one of many attempts in late nineteenth-century America to increase the power and prestige of various occupations by means of organization and standardization. Crucial to these ventures was the creation of organizations that could regulate membership in the profession according to standardized credentials, provide a forum for communication between members and presentation of new information, and represent the profession to the public. For American historians, this professional organization was the American Historical Association, formed in 1884. The *American Historical Review*, the association's official journal, began publication in October 1895, creating an outlet for the new scholarship produced by these historians. Reading history of the sort produced by professional historians came to require more than just a casual knowledge, limiting the number of people who would appreciate and be interested in the history written by professional historians. In "'professionalized' history . . . issues were much less charged than they were when history was part of general intellectual discourse."[20]

Professional history could have challenged the white supremacist narrative of Reconstruction, but in the end it only reinforced it. The new historical practices devalued the unverified personal recollections that had been the staple of amateur historians such as Wells. By consulting as many contemporary, written documents as possible and critically assessing them to account for the documents' biases and inaccuracies, professional history aspired to scientific objectivity. With these standards, northerners or anyone else could write about southern history with as much authority as any southerner. Being from the South and having lived through Reconstruction was no longer an advantage, much less a requirement, for writing Reconstruction history.

In practice, professional historians told the same story about Reconstruction that amateur historians did, because both groups grounded that history in the beliefs of the time. Ideas first popularized by contemporary opponents of Reconstruction such as James S. Pike became part of the assumptions on which professional historians based their work. The beliefs that African Americans were innately inferior to whites and ill-equipped by nature to participate in democracy, along with white property holders' objections to any sort of land reform or taxation to support expanded government services, were ingrained in most of the first generation of professional historians writing about Reconstruction, shaping the types of sources they consulted, the questions they thought worthwhile, and the answers they were willing to find. Thus, the old white supremacist narrative of Reconstruction gained an entirely new kind of intellectual and cultural authority. In fact, the very lack of controversy (among southern whites) about the historical memory of Reconstruction made it a perfect subject for the new history, since the lack of controversy could be taken for the effects of a consensus based on objectivity. Rather than freeing Reconstruction from white supremacist memory, the professionalization of history bound it ever more tightly to that memory by covering its roots in unreliable, biased evidence with a gloss of scientific credibility.[21]

Even the best-trained historian writing about Reconstruction in South Carolina at this time brought racist assumptions into the framework of scientific history. John Porter Hollis wrote the first academic history of Reconstruction in South Carolina in 1905. He was born in Chester in 1872 and grew up in Rock Hill. After attending Wofford College, a Methodist-affiliated school in Spartanburg, and teaching high school in Rock Hill for a few years, Hollis entered the Johns Hopkins University in 1900. Historians trained at Johns Hopkins and at Columbia University turned out a number of studies of Reconstruction in particular states in the early twentieth century. They were known collectively as the Dunning school, since their work was influenced by Columbia's William A. Dunning, whose essays and 1907 book, *Reconstruction, Political and Economic, 1865–1877,* set the interpretive framework for academic histories of Reconstruction for the next forty years. Hollis completed his Dunning-influenced dissertation, "The Early Period of Reconstruction in South Carolina," in 1905. Rather than being issued by the popular press of a newspaper in South Carolina, like Wells's 1907 book, Hollis's work was published by the Johns Hopkins Press as part of the Johns Hopkins University Studies in Historical and Political Science.[22]

Hollis's discussion of the role of African Americans after 1865 demonstrates that the standards of scientific history did not guarantee balanced, objective history. He produced a study that agreed on all essential points with the works it sought to supersede, because on matters of race he was willing to set aside standards of evidence and rely uncritically on hearsay and oral tradition. Discussing the role of African American troops in South Carolina during Reconstruction, Hollis asserted, "Numerous reports of their atrocious acts are given." He went on to recount specific examples of these reports: "At Anderson it was said that they protected and carried off a negro who had murdered a white man. At Pocotaligo they were declared to have gone to the house of a white man and, after tying him, violated the women." Finally, Hollis tells the story of the death of Confederate soldier Calvin Crozier at the hands of black Federal troops in Newberry. Of these, only the Crozier story is given any documentation whatsoever.[23]

Even when Hollis provided documentation for some of his more racist statements, he did not account for the probable biases of his sources. Again discussing African American troops, he relies on a congressional document for the assertion that "it was alleged that labor was disturbed throughout a large district of the vicinity of a negro garrison, and that there was danger of the colored troops joining the blacks 'in case of insurrection.'" Hollis was dismissive of the idea that African Americans might take part in government. As a footnote to an innocuous sentence about registration of voters in 1867, he cites a derogatory dialect story about ignorant blacks who could not understand what registration and voting meant. The story came from the *New York Herald*, a newspaper that had supported Presidential Reconstruction and had been a consistent antagonist of the Republican Party and African American suffrage. Hollis reminded the reader that the *Charleston Mercury* had described the Constitutional Convention assembled in January 1868 as "the 'Great Unlawful,' the 'Congo,' and the 'Ring-Streaked and Striped Negro' convention." By importing these "common sense" ideas about race into his academic work on Reconstruction, Hollis gave the traditional interpretation of Reconstruction a considerable boost in prestige and professional credibility.[24]

John S. Reynolds's *Reconstruction in South Carolina* (1905) straddled the divide between amateur and professional history, as did its author. Reynolds was "formerly on the editorial staff of the (Columbia) *Register* and editor of the (Columbia) *Evening Record*," and joined the staff of the *Columbia State* as treasurer shortly after the newspaper was founded in 1891. By the time he wrote *Reconstruction in South Carolina*, he was "the supreme court librarian and a distinguished attorney." In some ways, Reynolds hewed to the standards of scientific history. In the author's note, Reynolds vouched for the accuracy of his sources, writing, "Public records have been used wherever accessible. Statements about which there might be a question—especially those affecting the character of individuals—have been carefully verified by reference to such records or to other sources of equal authority." Nevertheless, his book, like Wells's, did not use footnotes or specific citations to sources.[25]

As with Wells's book, response to Reynolds's *Reconstruction in South Carolina* varied according to the audience. George A. Wauchope, a professor of English at the University of South Carolina, reviewed it for the *Baltimore Sun* and concluded that Reynolds had "approached his difficult and delicate task with that absolute impartiality and perfect balance of judgment which characterize the modern historical investigator." Other reviewers were less convinced of Reynolds's "impartiality." Frederick W. Moore, professor of history at Vanderbilt University, reviewing the book for the *American Historical Review*, disagreed: in this "partizan narrative . . . Mr. Reynolds loses sight of the philosophy of history in the combat of opposing parties." William E. Dodd of Randolph-Macon College in Virginia felt that Reynolds "succeeded in a high degree, but not entirely." Reviewers outside of universities criticized Reynolds's objectivity more strenuously, one suggesting that "this history is not judicial," and another arguing that "a judicial method is attempted thruout, tho unfortunately not always maintained." Reviewers were more unified in their criticism of Reynolds for not documenting his sources. Even Dodd's generally favorable review took Reynolds to task: "A serious mistake consists in his failure to cite the authorities used. In a historical work covering so many disputed points no author is safe without his authorities at hand, without giving the exact date, place, and circumstance." Notwithstanding these limitations, Reynolds's book remained "the 'standard' treatment of reconstruction in South Carolina for twenty-seven years."[26]

Reynolds's book marks an attempt to shift the epistemological basis for historical knowledge of Reconstruction. Earlier authors, such as Wells, relied on what philosopher Jean-François Lyotard terms "narrative knowledge." The legitimacy of such knowledge rested within the story itself and its internal coherence with a set of related stories, and in the social authority granted its author to hold and transmit that knowledge (thus the importance of Wells's emphasis on having lived through Reconstruction and having known Hampton personally). Reynolds and other professionalizing historians, however, were trying to push history away from narrative knowledge and toward scientific knowledge. Scientific knowledge could be legitimated by appeals to objective criteria unconnected to the person who held the knowledge, criteria such as the documents upon which Reynolds relied, rather than the oral accounts and personal memories Wells used.[27]

This epistemological shift also explains why Reynolds's work strives for totalization. The person who reviewed Wells's *Hampton and Reconstruction* characterized Reconstruction as something beyond the powers of history to fully apprehend: "It is so huge, so complex, so dark a crime it is probable that its full history will never be written." Reynolds and the project of scientific history had no such worries. "If systematically pursued," suggests Peter Novick in his account of objectivity in history, scientific history "might ultimately produce a comprehensive, 'definitive' history." *Reconstruction in South Carolina* was the first book that presented the entire history of Reconstruction in the state, and it was one of many Dunning-school histories of Reconstruction as it unfolded in particular states. In addition to providing the complete chronological scope of Reconstruction from 1865 to 1877, Reynolds's book is packed with list after list of legislators in sessions of the South Carolina General Assembly and delegates from each county who were present at various meetings. The book's advertisement claimed it was "a treasury of facts from which future historians of the period must draw material," and this was one of its purposes. By using, and often quoting, copious primary sources, Reynolds's book was to be sui generis. A reader need not come to it with any background knowledge of its topic. This would instantly make the works of amateur historians, such as Wells's, obsolete, useful at best as a source for a colorful anecdote or example, but unnecessary to the project of the history of Reconstruction. Reynolds may have agreed with Wells in substance, but not in style. More serious than disagreements between different types of historians who fundamentally agreed on matters of interpretation was the relationship between histories that disagreed on important points: Reynolds's scientific history of Reconstruction was to delegitimize the counter-memory of Reconstruction that existed almost entirely in the form of narrative knowledge.[28]

Wade Hampton died at 8:50 AM on Friday, 11 April 1902, twenty-five years to the day after he had taken office as governor of South Carolina. The very timing of his death seemed to emphasize his role as the savior of South Carolina, rather than his Civil War service. Hampton's last words were "All my people, black and white—God bless them all." "The last word," as German cultural historian Karl S. Guthke has observed, "is the enduring legacy—life transcending itself into artifact, time transcending itself into timelessness." Hampton would have known that his last words would be noted, remembered, and sifted for the truth they contained. Indeed, it was this final statement, in bold type and edged in black, that led the newspaper story announcing his death the next day. By the time of his death, Wade Hampton was more than simply a man with a particular history. "Wade Hampton" was an incipient legend, an imaginative joint creation of the man himself and the culture in which he lived. His last words were his last contribution to that creation.[29]

As news spread of Hampton's death, South Carolinians mourned as they had not mourned since the death of John C. Calhoun fifty years before. The tolling of bells was probably the means by which most South Carolinians first learned of Hampton's death. The city bell in Columbia tolled for a full hour, and the bells of St. Michael's Church in Charleston tolled at noon. Courts adjourned in Richland County and Sumter County. The governor closed the state government. Flags flew at half-mast, and black bunting hung on Confederate monuments. In addition to these public displays of grief, individuals across the state noted Hampton's death. For example, Jane Massey, a widow living in the mountains near Walhalla in Oconee County, noted in her diary a few days after Hampton's death, "General Wade Hampton died April 11, 1902." It is one of the few contemporary news events that ever interrupted her insular account of family, farm, weather, and religion.[30]

Although it does not appear that Hampton's death stopped the spindles in the mills or the plows in the fields, mourning displays in shop windows marked the event even amidst the commercial bustle of South Carolina's cities. America's new urban, commercial culture could easily be adapted as a tool of memory. Displaying goods in show windows created an illusion of intimacy: shoppers could see the objects but could not touch them without purchasing them. A memorial display in a show window, like the ones responding to Hampton's death, would have created a similar illusion of intimacy. A viewer might never have seen Hampton in person, but suddenly he was as real as a pair of shoes or any other object on the other side of the plate glass. In Columbia, three downtown stores had displays in place within a day, each including portraits of Hampton. One placed a portrait of Hampton at the foot of a column, all "draped in white and black." To reinforce the point, a "female figure clad in deep mourning" stood next to the column. The Columbia Book Store had a marble bust of Hampton in its window, and "groups of people were gathered around the window all during [the] afternoon and evening." Show windows in Greenville presented similar displays.[31]

Coming together to mourn, South Carolinians united behind the social memory of Reconstruction that Hampton embodied. In the days following Hampton's death, groups of people memorialized the leader across the state. Confederate organizations such as the UCV and the UDC met and grieved for Hampton. In Newberry, the local UCV camp met in the courthouse on Saturday morning. One local leader gave a short tribute to Hampton and then the group adopted a set of resolutions describing their grief and requesting members to attend the funeral, if possible. The meeting drew members of the UCV camp, but also many who were not members. People as far away as Georgetown, Florence, Charleston, and even Atlanta, who could not attend the funeral on Sunday, heard memorial services for Hampton in their own churches. At Atlanta's First Baptist Church, James W. Austin, originally from Greenville, held a memorial service. Citizens of Florence combined the two, with the local UCV camp leading a memorial service in the Baptist church. Memorial services for Hampton were held in two of Charleston's three principal Episcopal churches, and ministers delivered sermons on Hampton all around the city. In Georgetown, congregants of all denominations met at the Methodist church to hear addresses by three people. Students and faculty of South Carolina College in Columbia gathered on Saturday in the chapel for a memorial service.[32]

Despite Hampton's deathbed request for a simple and unostentatious service, his funeral was a huge event. In accordance with Hampton's wishes, the body did not lie in state at the State House, but several thousand people did view the body at his residence on Sunday before the funeral, which was held at Trinity Episcopal Church, with Ellison Capers, Episcopal bishop and ex-Confederate general, officiating. Around twenty thousand mourners followed the funeral procession from Hampton's home to the church, with organizations of all kinds from around the state represented and even delegations from outside the state. Visitors who could not get close to Hampton's grave during the funeral service itself continued to come to the grave for several days afterward.[33]

Even before Hampton was buried, plans were afoot for a state monument to him. On the day of his death, a man in Union wrote to the editor of the *Columbia State,* suggesting "that the citizens of the State erect an equestrian statue to him to be placed on the state house grounds at Columbia." He further suggested that a committee be established to raise money for the monument, enclosing a dollar toward the subscription himself. Five days after Hampton's death, the UDC and UCV chapters in Columbia met to plan for erecting a monument. Within a few weeks, a joint effort between these organizations and several newspapers had established a subscription fund for the planned monument. As historian Kirk Savage has noted of monuments in nineteenth-century America, public subscriptions like this one served to illustrate that the monument was the spontaneous product of a unified citizenry. "The more widely the monument campaign appealed," explains Savage, "the more enthusiasm it seemed to generate, the more convincingly its public would come to resemble the democratic vision of one people united by one common memory." Some Charlestonians wanted to put the monument there, but most soon agreed that Columbia was the more appropriate location.[34]

Fundraising started almost immediately. In Greenville, for instance, the local UCV camp had contributed one hundred dollars to the fund by the end of April 1902, and the students and faculty of Furman University contributed ten dollars. One of the merchants with an elaborate window memorial after Hampton's death promoted "Hampton Monument Day" at his Greenville dry goods store on 2 May 1902, when 10 percent of the day's sales would be donated to the Hampton monument fund. The monthly meeting of the Washington Light Infantry in Charleston in April 1902 raised one hundred dollars. By early 1903, the governor had appointed a commission to take charge of the monument. It coordinated fundraising efforts, and the South Carolina legislature appropriated twenty thousand dollars for the monument, on the condition that an additional ten thousand dollars be gathered from voluntary subscriptions. Counties contributed widely varying amounts, with two putting in more than a thousand dollars each; Saluda County managed to contribute forty cents. In October 1903, residents of Columbia held a fundraising bazaar in the halls of the state capitol, raising over five hundred dollars in three evenings.[35]

When it came time to design the monument itself, the commission turned to noted American sculptor, Frederick Wellington Ruckstuhl. Born in Alsace in 1853, Ruckstuhl grew up in St. Louis and went to Paris to study sculpture in 1882. He was one of the organizers of the National Sculpture Society in 1892, and following the World's Columbian Exposition in Chicago in 1893, he became one of the primary spokespeople for architectural sculpture. "American architectural sculpture," Ruckstuhl and others argued, "would familiarize people with the best aspects of past and present cultures and would do so on an even greater scale than could a single statue." His figures adorned several public buildings in New York, Washington, and elsewhere. In the 1890s, as an extension of his interest in educating the public through sculpture, Ruckstuhl turned to the bustling business of Civil War memorials. He sculpted the Confederate monuments in Baltimore, Little Rock, and Salisbury, North Carolina, and "Victory" for the soldiers' monument in Jamaica, Long Island, New York. Ruckstuhl also created an equestrian statue of General John Hartranft of Pennsylvania that was unveiled in 1899.[36]

For his equestrian statue of Wade Hampton, Ruckstuhl simply copied his Hartranft statue and changed the face and uniform. Hampton's horse (a stallion) prances with feet lifted high, as the rider sits erect in the saddle with the reins held loosely in the left hand. Hampton's shoulders are thrust back and his chest juts out in an almost unnatural position. His right hand grasps his hat, as his saber remains sheathed on his left side. According to Ruckstuhl, the statue represents "Hampton riding down the line at a review of his troops and saluting them as they cheer him." Hampton's role in Reconstruction, however, was clearly intended to be part of the monument's message. Hampton is dressed in his Confederate uniform, but in a subtle way Ruckstuhl clues the viewer that the Hampton he portrayed was not exactly the Hampton of the Civil War. A photograph of Hampton, taken in late 1864 and later described as "probably the best known of Hampton portraits," shows him in his Confederate uniform with a full beard. On Ruckstuhl's statue, however, Hampton's beard is trimmed into long muttonchops and a bushy moustache, matching a photograph "made in Columbia in the early part of 1876" that was "extensively distributed during Hampton's first campaign for the office of governor of South Carolina." Some who actually knew Hampton made similar observations.

The Wade Hampton monument erected in 1906 on the grounds of the State House, Columbia, South Carolina. (Photograph by author).

Claude E. Sawyer, a member of the Wallace House in 1876, wrote in 1926, "Now we see the equestrian monument of Senator Hampton's head on the shoulders of General Wade Hampton. What a monstrosity! It makes me sick to look at it. I want to see a monument presenting General Hampton as he looked then or in 1865." At the dedication of the monument, on 20 November 1906, a member of the monument commission made the association clear: "We realized that the memory of a chieftain, an illustrious warrior, the hero of an hundred battlefields must find expression in that statue; the Hampton of Reconstruction, the Hampton of '76, the Hampton as Governor and in the Senate of the United States—citizen, statesman, and the leader and the loved of all Carolina's yeomanry must be crystallized and perpetuated in the monument that we build." Even the *New York Daily Tribune*'s account of the monument's unveiling emphasized Reconstruction more than the Civil War and praised Hampton for his restraint after the election of 1876. The form of the monument stressed this quality of restrained power. An equestrian statue is an ideal form to depict a man who exerts control over other men, since the man in the statue is not only poised himself but is controlling his horse as well. The power of the horse magnifies the strength of the man who is able, effort-lessly, to control it. Hampton gently but firmly restraining his mount is visually equivalent to Hampton gently but firmly restraining his red-shirted followers after the election of 1876.[37]

By his own efforts and those of others in South Carolina and in the nation as a whole, Wade Hampton became the central figure in the mythology of Reconstruction. Other southern states had their own heroic Redeemers—Zebulon B. Vance in North Carolina and L. Q. C. Lamar in Mississippi, for example—but none fit the role quite so well as Hampton. His fabulous wealth before the war, his dashing image as a cavalry general, his impoverishment after the war, and his implacable and ultimately successful resistance to Reconstruction all made him the white South's ideal savior. In his later career, Hampton himself worked to solidify this image, yet his legend was never entirely within his control. The Hampton of legend was always both the Civil War cavalry general reconciled with his former enemies and the unreconstructed rebel who saved his state from the horrors of Reconstruction, the champion of white supremacy and the advocate of limited political participation for African Americans. White South Carolinians lionized Hampton, a moderate paternalist on matters of race, but they did so in the society Ben Tillman had created with their votes, a society grounded in a violent, exclusionary white supremacy.

THREE

CELEBRATING THE
RED SHIRTS

After Wade Hampton died, his bronze visage staring down protectively over the capitol he once fought to regain, a more stridently white supremacist memory of Reconstruction came to dominate public life in South Carolina, more in keeping with the new, harsher racial order. Just as the Red Shirts had ridden in 1898, in the flesh in North Carolina and in rhetoric at Phoenix, they would ride in the first decade of the twentieth century, in the pages of a melodramatic novel that became a regional sensation and, aged and gray and in tattered red shirts that had been carefully saved for thirty years, in a series of reunions of the veterans of 1876. And on the eve of a new war, the Red Shirt martyr, McKie Meriwether, the only white casualty of the Hamburg Massacre, would be memorialized with a monument of his own. In the first two decades of the twentieth century, the white supremacist narrative of Reconstruction went from being an effective tool for political mobilization to being an essential component of southern culture, all but unchallenged in the public sphere.

In the early years of the twentieth century, an obscure Methodist minister and writer tapped into a strong local oral tradition about Reconstruction and a new fad for melodramatic historical novels. J. W. Daniel's *A Maid of the Foot-Hills* was never a national bestseller; it was barely known outside the upstate of South Carolina. But in that place, its readers loved it, reading and rereading it in preference to more widely known novels on similar themes, and integrating its details into local tradition about the novel's hero. The book was still popular in the 1930s, and it was recommended reading to those celebrating the state's tricentennial in 1970. Literary critic Jane Tompkins suggests that popular novels have provided "men and women with a means of ordering the world they inhabited," and that by studying them we may discover "powerful examples of the way a culture thinks about itself, articulating and proposing solutions for the problems that shape a particular historical moment." Historian Edward L. Ayers underestimates the power of this new "vicious and bitter literature of racial hatred" penned by Daniel, Thomas Nelson Page, Thomas Dixon Jr., and others. More than simply reflecting the early twentieth-century shift to a new, harsher style of race relations, the particular vision of history presented in Reconstruction melodramas such as Page's *Red Rock,* Dixon's *The Clansman,* and Daniel's *A Maid of the Foot-Hills* helped shape race relations, providing a powerful narrative structure into which the story of Reconstruction could be retold. New times and new social orders called for new fiction, and these stories of Reconstruction came into their own.[1]

After the Civil War, northerners and southerners imagined sectional reconciliation in fiction and, by imagining it, helped to bring it about. Stories and novels about the Civil War described it as a "noble catastrophe" and depicted the Old South as an idyllic setting, a comforting refuge from a present filled with the class tensions, overcrowded cities, and complex problems created by industrialization. A shared longing for reconciliation made the romance an ideal genre in which to reimagine the past in fiction. The romance starts with two opposing and apparently irreconcilable entities. Through a series of complications and tests, the two sides realize they are united by something more fundamental than what divides them. The final reconciliation is typically symbolized by a marriage. In reconciliationist fiction, the complications were the Civil War and Reconstruction, and the marriage was between members of the once-opposed sections, usually a northern man marrying a southern belle. Such works of fiction created a body of myth upon which to create a united nation. By fitting the ruptures of the Civil War, Emancipation, and Reconstruction into a narrative framework in which everything worked out well in the end, reconciliationist fiction comforted and reassured northern and southern readers that the nation was again whole and healthy. The problem that had pitted whites from one section against whites from another section was solved. If the task of historical fiction in the first thirty years after the war was to prove that whites in the North and the South could live together, the new task for historical fiction was to show how whites and blacks were to coexist in the South.[2]

Luckily for the white South, another mode of literature was ready at hand to replace the romance of reconciliation that dominated earlier fiction: melodrama. Literary critic Peter Brooks argues that "melodrama starts from and expresses the anxiety brought by a frightening new world in which the traditional patterns of moral order no longer provide the necessary social glue." The destruction of a traditional, sacred moral order leaves in its wake "radical freedom," in which "all is potentially permitted." Although Brooks argues that melodrama as a mode of literature became important in fiction later in the nineteenth century, all its essential characteristics are visible in the stage melodramas from the early nineteenth century: "an intense emotional and ethical drama based on the manichaeistic struggle of good and evil, a world where what one lives for and by is seen in terms of, and as determined by, the most fundamental psychic relations and cosmic ethical forces. The polarization of good and evil works toward revealing their presence and operation as real forces in the world. Their conflict suggests the need to recognize and confront evil, to combat and expel it, to purge the social order. Man is seen to be, and must recognize himself to be, playing on a theatre that is the point of juncture, and of clash, of imperatives beyond himself that are non-mediated and irreducible." One key to the literary style associated with the mode of melodrama was the use of excess to clarify the conflict between good and evil. In this mode, compromise and reconciliation of the sort found in romances of the Lost Cause were unthinkable. Like the French Revolution, the Civil War and, even more so, Emancipation marked the end of an ancien régime. Reconstruction was a period of "radical freedom" in which individuals and groups had to create a new order for the world. Southern whites proposed a model for this new moral order predicated on racial hierarchy, and that model won out. The task for literature in the final stages of this victory was to craft new narratives about the past so that the telos of history became the Jim Crow world of the present and the future. Melodrama was ideally suited to the task.[3]

The first major southern writer to address Reconstruction in fiction at the end of the nineteenth century was Thomas Nelson Page, the acknowledged literary authority on life in the Old South and author of such bestsellers as *Marse Chan*. *Red Rock: A Chronicle of Reconstruction* appeared first as a serial in *Scribner's Magazine* and then as a book later in 1898, selling 100,000 copies by 1900. The novel fits smoothly into the melodramatic mode, with heroes and villains that are extravagantly good or bad and climactic confrontations. Two features mark Page's novel as a transition between his own older Lost Cause fiction and the newer Reconstruction melodrama. First, all the significant characters are white, casting Reconstruction as less a revolution in race relations than a struggle between whites for mastery of the South. Second, for all the conflict, the story contains relatively little violence, and most of that occurs offstage.[4]

Despite Page's stature as a man of letters and the impressive success of *Red Rock*, it would fall to another southern author, Thomas Dixon Jr., to create the masterpiece of Reconstruction melodramatic fiction. According to Dixon's account, a 1901 encounter with a stage version of Harriet Beecher Stowe's *Uncle Tom's Cabin* outraged him so much that he turned from the ministry and lecturing on the Chautauqua circuit to a literary career, producing the first of a trilogy of Reconstruction novels in 1902. *The Clansman,* published in 1905 as the second of this trilogy, has all the elements of melodrama, a fact not surprising given Dixon's early experience as an actor. The principal hero is Ben Cameron, a young Confederate officer saved from the gallows by the daughter of Austin Stoneman, the leader of the Radical Republicans. Cameron returns to his home in Piedmont, South Carolina, and before long Stoneman and his family move there as well. Unlike Page, Dixon included national political figures as minor characters in his story, the better to show the forces at work in Piedmont, led by Silas Lynch, a mulatto lieutenant governor. Throughout the middle part of the novel, the carpetbaggers and their black supporters repeatedly humiliate the white southern characters. Gus, the Camerons' former slave, becomes an officer in the militia, and this power leads him to rape a young white woman, who then kills herself in shame. Cameron leads the Ku Klux Klan to lynch Gus, and then the Klan drives out the carpetbaggers. Dixon's tale refined the melodramatic story of Reconstruction in several ways. Although Page's villains are local and at best bit players in the politics of Reconstruction, Dixon is able to use Stoneman to depict the threat to the South as both national in scope and local in application. In *Red Rock,* most African American characters are either loyal ex-slaves or gullible dupes of their white leaders, but Dixon creates more dangerous black characters. Figures such as Lynch or Gus have much more depth than Page's automatons, but that only makes them more reprehensible and dangerous. In Dixon's portrayal, African Americans have regressed dangerously into barbarism, justifying their violent treatment at the hands of whites.[5]

Although Page and Dixon paved the way for using the melodramatic mode for fictional accounts of Reconstruction, J. W. Daniel's 1905 novel *A Maid of the Foot-Hills, or Missing Links in the Story of Reconstruction* was closely attuned to local social memory of Reconstruction and managed to strike a chord with its audience. James Walter Daniel was born in Laurens County in 1857. He entered Newberry College in 1874, receiving an M.A.

there in 1879 and a D.D. in 1889. While completing his studies, Daniel pastored several Methodist circuits in Pickens, Greenville, and Anderson counties. He went on to serve at Methodist circuits throughout South Carolina until he retired in 1930. Daniel began publishing short stories at the age of eighteen and in the 1890s wrote two novels, a book about family history, and a long narrative poem based on a Cherokee legend. He also contributed a regular column to the *Southern Christian Advocate*.[6]

A *Maid of the Foot-Hills* has three central characters and a simple plot. Julia Jackson is the daughter of a Confederate veteran who returns to his home in the northeastern corner of Anderson County. Her uncle, Mance Holley, is the hero of the story. The principal villain is Wade Crowe, a local slaveholder who shirked military service during the war and cheated his neighbors in his position of tithing officer or tax collector for the Confederate government. In the aftermath of the war, Crowe allies himself with the Federal troops, especially African American soldiers, in order to protect his ill-gotten gains. Holley's insistence on exposing Crowe's corruption and his proud refusal to submit to the authority of the black soldiers quickly make him an outlaw. When Federal troops murder Holley's brother, he vows to kill one hundred of them in return. African Americans organizing Union Leagues and becoming active in local politics under Crowe's leadership endanger whites, especially white women, and the Ku Klux Klan forms to protect them by lynching would-be rapists and disrupting political activities. The Ku Klux Klan cannot end Reconstruction, though. After a number of depredations by Federal soldiers and the state constabulary and a number of daring escapades by Holley, the year 1876 arrives. All the white men join the Red Shirts, and even Crowe is convinced to rejoin the cause of white supremacy. The African Americans and Republicans are vanquished, Julia marries a minor character, and Holley disappears from the scene.

Daniel's "Mance Holley" is a thinly fictionalized version of a real person from Anderson County. The original for this character, Manse Jolly, lived in the Lebanon section of northeastern Anderson County and served in Company F, First S.C. Cavalry during the Civil War. After the war, he had a brief but busy career as a desperado and killer of Yankee soldiers, freedmen, and Republicans. Jolly left Anderson in the fall of 1866 and went to Texas, where he drowned on 8 July 1869. Although a contemporary account published in *Harper's New Monthly Magazine* mentions Jolly briefly, it is likely that Daniel relied mainly on oral traditions about Jolly still circulating in the Anderson County area. Legends of Jolly remained popular in Anderson County and nearby areas for decades, as demonstrated

Manson Sherrill "Manse" Jolly, photographed during his service with the First South Carolina Cavalry. (Courtesy of Pendleton District Commission).

by the frequent appearance of newspaper articles about Jolly that relied more on interviews with local residents than on documentary sources. Around 1916, an article in the *Anderson Daily Tribune* featured an interview with Manse Jolly's nephew, John L. Jolly. The stories he told have little of the cavalier style of Daniel's novel. According to his nephew, Jolly was an almost emotionless killing machine: "Jolly found two Yankees who had stolen horses from some of his relatives. . . . Taking his two prisoners into the woods, he killed them, then turned the stolen horses over to those who had lost them." Ten years later, one of Jolly's neighbors wrote in a letter about being present when Jolly made a miraculous escape from a church surrounded by Federal soldiers, a scene Daniel had dramatized in his novel (which raises the question of whether Daniel fictionalized a

story from oral tradition or whether a fictional incident entered oral tradition). A pair of newspaper articles in 1932 relied on earlier newspaper
articles and Daniel's novel, but also cited some dozen interviews with residents of Anderson County who gave information on parts of Jolly's career.
As with the nephew's account, the people interviewed in 1932 remembered
Jolly capturing and executing soldiers, five at a time in one instance. Stories about Jolly continued to surface in the local newspapers for the next
several decades, indicating that though people with direct memory of the
outlaw had died, his story lived on.[7]

Daniel's novel, even less subtly than those of Page and Dixon, casts the
story of Reconstruction in the mold of melodrama. Daniel depicts newly
freed African Americans challenging the traditional authority within the
space of the church itself. When the Union League meets "to impress
the negroes with the responsibilities of that kind of citizenship best ca-
pacitated to develop fraud, arson, rapine, and plunder," they do so at the
Old Stone Church near Pendleton. Later, as Federal soldiers become dis-
gruntled with their garrison duty and convinced that white supremacy is
best after all, one tells a story about the captain of a company of Federal
soldiers in Abbeville encouraging a black woman to enter the Methodist
church and sit with the white people. In addition to scenes that show the
sacred order under assault, Daniel uses the mode of excess that charac-
terizes melodrama in order to show the reader clearly which characters
embody good and which embody evil. A group of constabulary comes to
arrest and rob a character who is the quintessence of the simple yeoman
farmer. Julia rides ahead to warn him and the farmer escapes. The constabulary, finding their quarry has eluded them, burn his house and barn.
Then, in case the reader is not quite sure these villains are actually representing the forces of evil, they shoot his dog.[8]

Since he was fictionalizing local history, Daniel tended to stay close
to that history, and throughout the story he is careful not to change the
names of real individuals enough to confuse readers about their actual
identities. Early in the story, Holley encounters a desperado named Texas
Bull. Daniel bases this character on Texas Brown, an outlaw who operated in several upstate counties and who was described by John William
De Forest of the Freedmen's Bureau in an article published in *Harper's
New Monthly Magazine* in December 1868. Another historical figure who
appears in Daniel's book is Joe Crews, a white Republican leader from
Laurens County. In Daniel's novel, Crews becomes "Joe Drews": Daniel recounts Drews's involvement in the 1870 election in Laurens and his escape
from the riot that occurred there. In this case, Daniel's source is almost

certainly a book published in 1879 by a Laurens teacher who had been arrested for Ku Klux Klan activities, but he is probably relying on oral accounts as well, since he grew up in Laurens County.[9]

The 1872 congressional report on the Ku Klux Klan was also an important source for Daniel's novel. In an unwieldy side plot that serves mainly as a vehicle for including stories about the Ku Klux Klan, a minor character leaves Anderson County, where most of the story is set, and goes to York County, where he meets up with the Ku Klux Klan. Klansmen are working against the black militia, which, as Daniel tells it, is busy intimidating white women and children and burning the homes of white people. To put a stop to the black militia, the Ku Klux Klan lynches the captain of one of the militia companies, a black Union veteran named Jim Williams, placing a sign on his corpse reading, "Jim Williams on his big muster." This event is described in detail in the 1872 congressional report.[10]

Common whites throughout Daniel's novel use violence and intimidation to achieve political ends. Violence committed by blacks against whites always provokes disproportionate retaliation by the whites. In a scene echoing Thomas Dixon's *The Clansman* and newspaper accounts of lynchings, a black preacher and politician attempts to rape Julia and is immediately lynched by the Ku Klux Klan. More terrible is the vengeance wrought by Mance Holley for the death of his brother. In the story, black Federal soldiers murder Holley's younger brother. At his grave, Holley vows, "'One hundred of them shall be the penalty.' . . . and it soon ceased to be an item of news that a negro soldier had been killed by the fearless man." This episode is an exaggeration of a story about Manse Jolly that circulated in oral tradition. According to that version, Jolly lost five brothers in battle during the Civil War and swore to kill five Yankees for each of them. Another account credited him with two hundred dead Yankee soldiers and African American Republicans. One account even claimed that Jolly was a charter member of a predecessor to the Ku Klux Klan, founded at Old Stone Church near Pendleton shortly after Lee's surrender in April 1865. According to this story, Jolly's group murdered a Federal officer, Lieutenant Jerome T. Furman of the 33rd U.S. Colored Infantry, in Walhalla. Manse Jolly was hardly the only ex-Confederate guerilla murdering Federal soldiers in the early days of Reconstruction. Perhaps the daring of such attacks helped cement them in local tradition. In Fairfield County, Nick Myers hid out in the swamps and was believed to have killed fifteen or twenty Federal soldiers during Reconstruction, granting him a place in local folklore at least into the 1940s. The early career of the Texas gunfighter John Wesley Hardin also followed this familiar pattern.[11]

In contrast to black violence against whites, Daniel portrays white violence against blacks as legitimate, whether it is inflicted by the regular channels of government and the judicial system or by a self-constituted group representing the white community at large. The Ku Klux Klan killings of a militia leader and a rapist are both depicted as completely justified. At the same time, Daniel downplays the violence whites used against blacks. In an aside, the author writes, "The design of the order was good, and while cruelties may have been perpetrated in the name of the order, the Kuklux Klan was, however, a necessary step toward reform." The portrayal of violence by whites is sometimes muted with humor or a sense of unreality. Holley's murders of Federal soldiers occur offstage. His confrontations with them are exciting but not violent. Holley tricks the soldiers, leading them on chases around the countryside, or else he boldly bluffs his way out of dangerous situations. The effect of these adventures is to portray Holley as a sort of Robin Hood figure, an outlaw who opposes a corrupt and illegitimate usurpation while he waits for the restoration of legitimate rule. Although the Ku Klux Klan does use violence, the real heroes of Daniel's narrative, the Red Shirts, are portrayed as nonviolent, using nothing more than moral force to triumph.[12]

Common whites in *A Maid of the Foot-Hills* create a social life for themselves in the midst of Reconstruction while refusing any sort of social equality for African Americans. In the "Fore-Word," Daniel states, "It has seemed to the author that a correct portrayal of the real spirit of the times, as shown in the humor, amusements, fun, and social enjoyments of the oppressed populace, is necessary to a correct appreciation of the heroic deeds by which the people finally threw off the yoke of oppression and freed themselves from the bondage of thieves and robbers." What Daniel shows in this novel is how common whites could and did create a new social life in a variety of ways and despite repeated efforts by their enemies to disrupt their all-white social events. Immediately after the war, Confederate veterans gather and discuss the war and its aftermath before a church service. At another church service, Holley is forced to flee from Federal soldiers sent to arrest him. When another character has to leave the area, he quickly finds friends and hospitality among the Ku Klux Klan in York County. Social life is again disrupted, but not defeated, when Federal soldiers interrupt a dance, a minor character's wedding, and Julia's wedding by looking for Holley. Each time, Holley eludes them, symbolizing the triumph of whites in creating their own segregated social life and refusing the forced social equality whites thought was the ultimate aim of Reconstruction policy.[13]

According to Daniel, the two things missing from most fiction on Reconstruction were a portrayal of the "grim humor of the oppressed citizens" and a proper acknowledgment of the role of the Red Shirts in the overthrow of Reconstruction. Both omissions focus attention on the actions of individuals at all levels of society, not just the leaders. The melodramatic mode elevates the importance of the individual. "In both its audience and its profound subject," Peter Brooks argues, melodrama "is essentially democratic. It represents a democratization of morality and its signs." Writing about American stage melodramas of the mid-nineteenth century, Bruce A. McConachie identifies one subgenre, the apocalyptic melodrama, which was especially popular with working-class audiences, as dramatizing "a republican revolution of the people against aristocratic oppression aided by providential design and heroic martyrdom," a formula that "emphasized the importance of working-class solidarity to overcome villainy." Daniel's main characters are not the plantation owners who had been Confederate officers, leaders such as Wade Hampton and Matthew C. Butler or the fictional Ben Cameron from *The Clansman*. Instead, Mance Holley and the other heroes of *A Maid of the Foot-Hills* served in the ranks. They return to small farms they work themselves. The large landowner in the neighborhood is Wade Crowe, the villain. By locating heroism not in leaders and aristocrats but in common whites, Daniel sets the stage for the democratization of social memory of Reconstruction. The work of every white man who persevered through the dark days of Reconstruction and wore a red shirt in 1876—not just their leaders—would be worthy of praise and commemoration.[14]

Melodrama "is about virtue made visible and acknowledged, the drama of a recognition," and in the case of fictional accounts of Reconstruction, characters recognize the necessity for unity of all whites in support of white supremacy. We might call such accounts "racist conversion narratives," the inverse of what literary critic Fred C. Hobson calls the "racial conversion narrative" that arises in the 1940s in southern literature. In those, the autobiographer is converted away from the traditions of racial prejudice with which she or he was raised. In the incidents in Daniel's novel, and elsewhere in writing on Reconstruction from this period, individuals tell triumphantly of how they *learned* racial prejudice. Daniel offers many instances of whites who had supported varying degrees of political and social equality for African Americans being convinced, usually by seeing the unfortunate results of those ideas in practice, to support the white supremacy Holley and others advocated. This structure became a stock part of descriptions of Reconstruction. Throughout the novel, white

Federal soldiers become disgusted by the Republican administration they are protecting and begin sympathizing with and secretly aiding Holley. Even Wade Crowe is redeemed. When the 1876 campaign arrives, Holley delivers a specially tailored red shirt to the home of Wade Crowe with the message, "Join us, or you are doomed." Crowe's wife convinces him to wear the shirt and join the other whites in opposing the Republican Party. That Crowe joined the Red Shirts out of fear is less important than the simple fact that he had rejoined the party of white supremacy. In many ways, Mance Holley was the perfect hero for turn-of-the-century whites waxing nostalgic about Reconstruction, an average white man pushed too far who responded with lethal violence against African Americans and outsiders to set society to rights. This championing of the Red Shirts would take a more public, ritualized form in a series of reunions that began in Manse Jolly's neighborhood a few years after the story of his life was published.[15]

In South Carolina, the end of Reconstruction was brought about by the massive mobilization of white Democratic men in Red Shirt units. Historians estimate that at the height of the 1876 campaign nearly three hundred of these units existed, with as many as fifteen thousand men. Even accounting for death and emigration, thirty years later there were still thousands of white men in South Carolina who could claim to have had a part in what their society considered its defining moment. They personally had helped turn the painful defeat of the Civil War and the bitter uncertainties and humiliations of Reconstruction into the promise of the New South. Many Red Shirt veterans were proud of what they had made of their state and welcomed the opportunity to celebrate their accomplishments. The Red Shirt reunions held annually between 1908 and 1911 honored the rank and file of the counterrevolution against Reconstruction, though the organizers of the reunions could never quite decide how to remember the violence of 1876.[16]

Reunions of all sorts were common around the turn of the century. In the broadest sense, they were part of a world of associational life made possible by improved transportation that saw "excursions" by train becoming a popular recreation or that drew members of organizations to cities and towns for conventions and meetings. Reunions, however, were by their nature focused on the past, on a renewal of what had once been close ties. It was in the late nineteenth century that such intimate groupings as churches and families began to hold reunions to bring back together former members who had been swept away on the fast currents of modern life. The Civil War, with its massive mobilization across the country, provided compelling organizational ties that brought former comrades in arms together for reunions across the North and the South from the 1880s up through the early 1930s. The United Confederate Veterans held reunions at the local camp level, but also staged huge gatherings of all their thousands of members in southern cities.[17]

The Confederate veteran reunions were clearly a model for the Red Shirt reunions, but the Red Shirts might never have marched again were it not for the work of Jesse C. Stribling, who combined an interest in his region's past with busy efforts to improve its future. Born in Pendleton in 1844, Stribling enlisted in Rutledge's Mounted Riflemen in 1863. During the mid-1870s, he became an active member of a company of Red Shirts based in Pendleton, serving as the unit's first lieutenant. His interest in history and commemoration led Stribling to serve as the first commander of the Pendleton camp of the United Confederate Veterans when it formed in 1897, and to take a leading role in forming the Old Stone Church Memorial Association, dedicated to preserving the old Presbyterian church near Pendleton where General Andrew Pickens and other Revolutionary War leaders were buried. Not simply stuck in the past, Stribling worked to modernize agricultural practices. From his farm overlooking Eighteen Mile Creek just north of Pendleton, he gained a reputation as a successful livestock breeder, keeping up with the latest advances in scientific farming and building the first silo in the state. This interest in farming propelled him into various agricultural reform movements in the late nineteenth and early twentieth centuries. In the 1890s, Stribling was a frequent contributor to the Farmers Alliance's South Carolina newspaper, the *Cotton Plant,* and as the Farmers Union began to supplant the Farmers Alliance after 1900, Stribling became a local leader in that organization and wrote a regular newspaper column on Farmers Union activities. For Stribling, commemoration of the Red Shirts was part of a progressive, not reactionary, outlook on the world.[18]

In 1908, Stribling decided to hold a reunion of the Pendleton Red Shirt company in conjunction with the Pendleton Farmers Society annual meeting. Invitations were sent to veterans of other Red Shirt companies from the Piedmont as well. The *Anderson Daily Mail* suggested that the "veterans wear their old red shirts, and have another parade, just for the sake of old times." Stribling probably got the idea for the reunion from the renewed interest in the Red Shirts and the campaign of 1876 during the three years prior to 1908. In 1905, John Reynolds's complete history of *Reconstruction in South Carolina* was published, as was J. W. Daniel's novel *A Maid of the Foot-Hills,* which was set in Anderson County and dedicated to glorifying the role of the Red Shirts in the end of Reconstruction. In 1906, the monument to Wade Hampton had been unveiled in Columbia, and in 1907, Edward L. Wells's book *Hampton and Reconstruction* was published.[19]

The central theme of the Pendleton Red Shirt reunion on 14 August 1908, was the restraint the Red Shirts showed in dealing with their enemies. The visible symbol of this restraint was a cannon called the Peacemaker and another cannon used by the Pendleton Red Shirt company in 1876. The Peacemaker had an honored place in the parade at the 1908 reunion. A contemporary newspaper account describing the 1876 campaign explained, "The Red Shirt company carried both these pieces of artillery to a number of negro campaign meetings, and on more than one occasion every preparation had been made to use them. Fortunately the necessity never arose." At a meeting in Anderson the Pendleton Red Shirts succeeded in forcing the Republicans to allow a Democrat to speak: "The day passed off without disorder, but everybody expected a wholesale slaughter." This restraint was what differentiated the Red Shirts from their more violent predecessors, the Ku Klux Klan. The newspaper writer emphasized that the Red Shirts were distinct and different from the Ku Klux Klan, since the Ku Klux Klan wore disguises and operated at night. The Red Shirts, on the other hand, "did not use force, except on very rare occasions, and only when the necessity for force was thrust upon them."[20]

Passing along the accomplishments of the Red Shirts and their ideology to the next generation was an important goal of the reunion of 1908. The reunion's keynote speaker "recounted some of the stirring experiences of the 70's, and urged the young white men now growing up to study the history of those days, and learn of the trials their fathers endured and the struggles they made to insure white supremacy for their children." Children did not merely listen to stories of the old days from Red Shirt veterans. They joined in the activities: boys of the town organized into their own junior Red Shirt company and were given the responsibility of dragging the Peacemaker though the dusty streets of Pendleton in the parade, with sisters tagging along. When a photographer made a souvenir picture of the white-bearded Red Shirt veterans, a few boys crowded proudly into the photograph with their heroes.[21]

The 1908 Red Shirt reunion was such a success that another was planned for 1909 in the nearby manufacturing town of Anderson. Jesse C. Stribling remained involved in the planning and the fledgling statewide organization of Red Shirt veterans that formed after the Pendleton reunion. In Anderson, however, business and civic leaders were the principal force be-

The parade of Red Shirt veterans at Pendleton, South Carolina, on 14 August 1908. (Courtesy of Pendleton District Commission).

hind the 1909 reunion, and they used the event as part of a town booster campaign to gain the support of working-class whites and women for their goals of civic development.[22]

In the first decade of the twentieth century, Anderson was a cotton mill city. In 1907, Anderson had eight mills employing a total of just over three thousand people, one fifth of the town's population. Other businesses were linked to textile interests as well. In addition to the eight textile mills, Anderson had a mattress and bedspring factory, a factory making overalls, and three metal shingle factories, the largest of which, Burris Metal Shingle Company, specialized in roofing for textile mills. The proprietors of many nonmanufacturing businesses had ties to the city's textile mills. One businessman, for example, operated a lumber store and was vice-president of a bank, but he also owned a cotton mill. Moreover, small businesses were increasingly dependent on the trade of Anderson's mill hands, as in 1903 the city established eight and a half miles of trolley lines in the city.[23]

Especially in South Carolina, Reconstruction was an important part of the ideology of leading mill owners, who tended to exaggerate their own importance in its events. Historian Melton McLaurin argues that the southern mill owner "saw Reconstruction as a devastating, traumatic experience, economic and social, in which the South, with tremendous fortitude, had conquered with his leadership, only after years of bitter struggle." In the 1880s and 1890s, Ellison Adger Smyth was the pioneering cofounder and president of Pelzer Manufacturing Company, where generations of mill managers got their start. In 1876, he had commanded the Red Shirt companies of Charleston, for which he earned the lifelong title of "Captain." Textile leader and editor D. A. Tompkins felt Reconstruction was so important that he included an account of it as the preface to his influential 1899 book *Cotton Mill, Commercial Features: A Textbook.* Slavery had distracted the South from developing manufacturing, argued Tompkins, and freedom for the slaves had created anarchy and poverty. "Promptly, however, on the restoration of stable government, a revival of manufactures commenced, which has grown steadily, and is still growing." Comments in the newspapers connected current prosperity, which was self-evidently based on the boom in textiles, to the restoration of white supremacy at the end of Reconstruction. As one newspaper editor wrote, "Without the 'Red Shirts' as fore-runners there could have been no cotton mills in Spartanburg—Northern as well as Southern capital would have shunned investment under a 'Radical' government." By sponsoring a reunion of the Red Shirts, Anderson's mill men could at the same time honor the origins of their prosperity and invite their workers to join in that celebration as both audience and participants. The owners assumed that mill hands, appreciative of the relative advantages mill jobs gave them over African Americans and white farmers, would be happy to claim their share of the credit for the world of white supremacy they had helped create in 1876.[24]

The years leading up to the Anderson reunion of the Red Shirts were full of uncertainty and concern for mill men. In the first years of the twentieth century, the industry had suffered a serious labor shortage. This was good for mill hands, as they moved around to better positions and were able to get higher wages, but it was a problem for their employers, who resorted to recruiting workers from farther and farther away, including many from the mountains of North Carolina and Tennessee. Then, in 1907, the nation experienced the most serious financial panic since the depression of the mid-1890s. Until World War I, textile manufacturers faced "high cotton prices[,] . . . a labor shortage, . . . and stagnant demand." Organized labor in South Carolina textile mills was not much of a threat to mill owners after the defeat of the United Textile Workers in 1901, but the potential for organizing was always there and workers had not completely abandoned the idea. Most significantly, reformers determined to get rid of child labor had been very active. After gaining a small victory with the state's first law on child labor in 1903, reformers created the South Carolina Child Labor Committee in 1905. When a federal child labor law failed in 1907, the National Child Labor Committee, in March 1909, launched an aggressive campaign to investigate child labor in the Carolinas. D. A. Tompkins suspected the investigation was being funded by New England mill owners. The 1909 legislative session saw the introduction of several bills designed to further restrict child labor, limit the length of the work-day, and enact compulsory education.[25]

To mill men, reformers were similar to the forces supporting Recon-struction that the mill men had defeated in order to build the textile in-dustry in the first place. Outsiders who did not understand how things worked at the local level and did not appreciate the paternalism of those in charge wanted to use government power to take power away from those who owned property and give it to those who should be subservient to the property owners. In Reconstruction, those people had been ex-slaves and now they were propertyless textile operatives. McLaurin details this posi-tion: "This view of Reconstruction flattered the owner and ill prepared him for criticism. In this view, he was the savior of the South, the leader who came forward in a time of social and economic crisis to open a road to material wealth and social security for his poverty-stricken people.... Only a Southerner, especially a Southern industrial leader, could under-stand what the South had gone through and what problems it faced. There-fore, no outsider could intelligently criticize the industry he had created. This was especially true of Northerners, who had brought the South to ruin and were jealous of its recovery and industrial progress." Challenges to mill men's power were construed as challenges to the foundations of the social order of the New South.[26]

Whereas the 1908 parade had included Red Shirt veterans with only minimal participation by nonveterans, the parade on 25 August 1909 be-came a much more inclusive event, inviting more whites to celebrate the end of "Negro rule." Initially, the parade was intended to include only vet-erans of the 1876 Red Shirt campaign, but as planning unfolded, invita-tions to participate in the parade were gradually extended to more and more groups in town. When the parade was actually held, it featured ap-proximately two thousand veterans from 1876, along with young boys from the town, Spanish-American War veterans, firefighters, the local mi-litia unit, a mill band, and fifty local women. The Orr Mills band marching along in the parade echoed the brass bands that played in the processions that greeted Hampton in 1876. More important, they modeled the rela-tions that mill men wanted to exist between their workers and their mills. However overworked and underpaid mill hands might be, dressing up in crisp uniforms and playing the latest music on shiny instruments turned them into displays of model workers. More than that, it gave them an op-portunity to be a part of the public life of Anderson, instead of remaining sequestered in the mill villages that ringed the city. At a time when mill hands were generally seen as a social problem, celebrating the Red Shirts was a way for them to enjoy an honored place in public life, at least for the duration of the parade.[27]

The organizers of the 1909 reunion worked to portray a society unified behind the project of white supremacy in 1876, a society in which intimidation succeeded with little need for actual violence, showing that African Americans in 1876, as in 1909, acknowledged their subservient place in society. When Jesse C. Stribling welcomed the Red Shirt veterans to town, he made a joke of their reputation for violence. "Comrades and Red Shirts," he said, "you were pretty hard to control in 1876, but I suppose you are easier held down now, but for fear that there may be an outbreak of the old rampant feeling and patriotism, I feel it my first duty to appoint a sergeant-at-arms, and I now name the high sheriff of the county, W. B. King." "Stand up!" said Stribling to King. "Now look at him and be good!" Stribling admonished the crowd. (They likely listened to him. William B. "Big" King, who stood six feet, eight inches tall and weighed 430 pounds, could chase down fleeing criminals on foot and was generally the terror of the riotous element of Anderson County.) A newspaper editorial mused on how violence in 1876 should be remembered: "The idea should be to impress the dire necessity that existed for doing those things, rather than to glory in the things that were done."[28]

One who did "glory in the things that were done," however, was the reunion's keynote speaker, Ben Tillman. He deliberately moved away from the earlier theme of restrained violence associated with Hampton and toward a glorification of the violent methods of 1876. Tillman's speech combined a disquisition on the threats to white supremacy in contemporary politics and a call to remember how those threats had been met in 1876—through violence. Tillman, who had gained power in 1890 by splitting the Democratic Party, began his speech by calling for whites to stand unified despite President Taft's plan to split the Democratic Party in the South. Tillman then defended his recent speaking tours throughout the North and Midwest, tours that had been roundly criticized by two of his old nemeses, the *Columbia State* and the *Charleston News and Courier*. The message he had been preaching to northern Chautauqua audiences rested on three main points: "the creator made the Caucasian of better clay than he made any colored people"; "we shot them (the negroes), we stuffed ballot boxes, and did all that was necessary to maintain our hold on the government"; and "there was not power enough between Cape Cod and California to make us again submit to negro rule."[29]

Having set up the dangers in the present, Tillman recounted stories of the "struggles of 1876" as a model for solving all problems dealing with race. The "victory of 1876" was "the triumph of the whites over the blacks; of civilization and progress over barbarism and the forces which were undermining the very foundations of our commonwealth." Tillman discussed the question of which of the three leaders of 1876—Wade Hampton, Matthew C. Butler, or Martin W. Gary—deserved the most credit for the victory. He dismissed Hampton as a good-natured, but gullible figure who actually believed that sixteen thousand blacks had voted for him in 1876: "Every active worker in the cause knew that in this he was woefully mistaken." Gary, Tillman argued, deserved more of the credit, since he formulated the plan of fear and fraud that was the basis of the Red Shirt activity. But more than the Hampton's persuasion or Gary's intimidation, Tillman reserved his special admiration for Butler's cold-blooded violence. He attributed the success of 1876 to the fear that Butler had inspired in a series of bloody confrontations with blacks in the year and months leading up to the campaign. Tillman recalled, "Butler, Gary, and George Tillman [Ben's older brother and surrogate father] had to my personal knowledge agreed on the policy of terrorizing the negroes at the first opportunity, by letting them provoke trouble and then having the whites demonstrate their superiority by killing as many of them as was justifiable." The body of Tillman's speech was a detailed account of the Hamburg Massacre on 8 July 1876. He noted with pride that after the whites had overrun the black militia detachment guarding their armory and captured most of its members, he loaned his pistol to the men, who executed seven of the captives.[30]

Held in Columbia in 1911, the fourth reunion of the Red Shirts completed the project of displaying a public unified in support of white supremacy and willing to countenance the violence that had helped create that society. The 1909 reunion had brought workers and women in to the celebration of the end of Reconstruction, offering them the honor of being affiliated with the Red Shirts in return for their endorsement of the world white supremacy created. In Columbia, African Americans became a crucial part of the celebration of the Red Shirts. The participation of black Red Shirt veterans seemed to vindicate Wade Hampton's claim that he had actually won the support of a significant proportion of South Carolina's black citizens in 1876, and it suggested that African Americans in 1911 were content with their lot. This story is seen best through the eyes of the most celebrated of the 1911 black Red Shirts, Joe O'Bannon of Barnwell.

Based on life in Barnwell, O'Bannon's memories of Reconstruction must have included both great hopes and a profound sense of vulnerability born of violence and terror. Before the Civil War, Barnwell was part of the wealthy Black Belt of South Carolina with large cotton plantations.

The novelist William Gilmore Simms lived on a plantation nearby, as did political leaders such as Governor and Senator James H. Hammond and David F. Jamison, who would later be president of the Secession Convention in 1860. O'Bannon's owner was Edwin Augustus Hagood, one of the wealthiest planters in Barnwell District, with real estate worth $35,000 and forty-one slaves in 1860. When war came in 1861, thirty-four-year-old Joe O'Bannon was sent to serve his owner's three eldest sons in the First South Carolina Volunteers. All three were casualties in the Battle of Second Manassas, and O'Bannon returned to Barnwell with his seriously wounded young master. O'Bannon was probably at the Hagood plantation when General Willliam T. Sherman's army pushed through Barnwell County, destroying plantations and giving the town of Barnwell a new nickname: "Burnwell." O'Bannon, along with thousands of other slaves in Barnwell County, was free. After the war, Barnwell benefited from its location near the relatively undamaged city of Augusta, Georgia, and the black-controlled river port and railroad junction of Hamburg, the home of African American political and economic leaders such as Prince Rivers. O'Bannon left his earlier position as a servant and began working as a farm laborer, probably for a younger son of his former master. Whatever changes O'Bannon sought in the new opportunities of Reconstruction, he soon had reason to retreat to the comfort of the familiar.[31]

Barnwell was a fearsome place for African Americans in 1876. The Hamburg Massacre in July happened less than fifty miles away, and many black men were afraid to stay the night in their own homes. In September, the militia stepped in to protect two black men accused of assaulting a white woman near Ellenton, twenty miles away. Within hours, hundreds of rifle club members from around the region poured into the swampy backwaters of the Savannah River, hunting for the outnumbered militia. Confederate General Johnson Hagood, a cousin of Joe O'Bannon's former owner and O'Bannon's near neighbor in Barnwell in 1870, led one of the rifle clubs. Red Shirts killed several dozen African Americans over two days before they cornered the militia. Only the timely arrival of Federal troops prevented a bloodbath, but they were too late to save the life of an African American Republican legislator captured and executed by Ben Tillman's rifle club. Working for the Hagood family but living in Barnwell's African American community, O'Bannon probably heard firsthand accounts of the Ellenton Riot from participants on both sides.[32]

This was the context in which Joe O'Bannon decided to support the Democrats and ride with the Red Shirts. When Wade Hampton came through Barnwell on his campaign tour, O'Bannon put on his own red shirt and rode in the parade that welcomed him to town. He may have de-plored the corruption of the Republican administration and believed that white Democrats could better handle the state's affairs. He certainly had seen and heard about black men and women shot, beaten, driven from home, family, and livelihood for their political actions. In the words of an-other black Red Shirt remembering his own conversion to the Democratic cause, O'Bannon "knowed which side de butter was on de bread."[33]

For whatever reason, O'Bannon decided to support the Red Shirts in 1876, and he decided to attend their reunion in 1911. O'Bannon accompa-nied a group of Barnwell Red Shirts to Columbia to serve as their valet, probably one of many black servants waiting on white men visiting Co-lumbia that week. Black servants were part of the infrastructure of white supremacy, serving whites drinks and meals and also serving as visual symbols of the subservient place blacks occupied in the Jim Crow system. Elderly and dependant on white men, O'Bannon was himself a symbol of what the Red Shirts had accomplished in 1876. When reunion organiz-ers learned that this black servant had been a Red Shirt, they hastened to include him in the ceremonies, finding him a mule to ride and mak-ing a red shirt for him. The *Columbia State* even devoted a whole article to O'Bannon, describing him as "a little feeble, but with a loyal heart still beating in his black breast." The article praised "Uncle Joe" "for the good that he helped bring about [that] is still bearing fruit in the Palmetto State." Laying claim to his status as a Red Shirt veteran earned O'Bannon recog-nition and respect from white South Carolinians he could have achieved in no other way. The attention O'Bannon attracted spilled over to a few other black Red Shirts who attended the 1911 reunion.[34] Surely, white South Carolinians told themselves, if these black men were proud of their role in overthrowing Reconstruction, it proved to the world that the end of Reconstruction had been good for both blacks and whites alike.

Some features of the 1911 Red Shirt reunion must have reminded O'Bannon of the sense of vulnerability he knew from 1876. Governor Coleman L. Blease welcomed the Red Shirts to Columbia, and his speech focused on the most violent aspects of 1876, a complement to Blease's own countenancing of white violence against African Americans. Originally a protégé of Ben Tillman, Blease had gained the governor's office in 1910 by courting the votes of South Carolina's mill hands with a violent appeal to their intertwined senses of masculinity and insecurity over their position in South Carolina's racial hierarchy. In a crowded field, Blease stood out among the other southern demagogues who were his contemporaries for condoning and even encouraging violence against African Americans and for his unswerving support for lynching. In addition to Blease's flamboy-antly violent interpretation of the Red Shirts, the 1911 reunion featured an appearance by men dressed up as the Ku Klux Klan. The white-robed rid-ers who joined the parade down Main Street evoked the heroes of Thomas Dixon's novels as well as the message of violence and vulnerability for black spectators and black participants such as Joe O'Bannon.[35]

The rage for Red Shirt reunions had run its course by 1911, for reasons that are not altogether clear. Organizational weakness may have been one factor. There was never a large, multistate group of Red Shirts, as was the case with the United Confederate Veterans. John G. Mobley of Winns-boro was elected commander of the state organization at the 1910 reunion, and he took the lead in planning the 1911 reunion. Mobley, however, was absorbed in the South Carolina Agricultural and Mechanical Society, of which he was president. The society sponsored the state fair, and Mobley's interest in the Red Shirt reunions may have been overshadowed by his responsibility for this event. In fact, in 1909 Mobley had invited the Red Shirts to hold a reunion as part of the state fair. A poor choice for the location of the 1912 reunion may also have stifled the organization's mo-mentum. At the end of the 1911 reunion, the Red Shirts voted to hold the next reunion in Charleston. None of the organization's top leaders lived there. Moreover, Charleston had fewer members of the organization than did other South Carolina cities and towns. Since the reunions depended heavily on the support of local civic organizations such as the Chamber of Commerce in host cities and the connections of interested Red Shirts to such organizations, choosing Charleston may have doomed the Red Shirt organization and its reunions. But while the reunions of the Red Shirts were a transitory phenomenon, memory of the most violent aspect of the Red Shirts would soon literally be carved in stone on the South Carolina landscape.[36]

In late January 1914, several men with connections to Edgefield County began working to create a monument to one of the heroes of 1876. This monument, though, would not honor a Confederate veteran or one of the political leaders who helped overthrow Reconstruction. Instead, the person to be commemorated was the first white martyr of the 1876 cam-paign, McKie Meriwether, the only white man killed during the Hamburg Massacre. The first sign of interest in creating a monument for Meriwether was a biographical sketch written on 21 January 1914 and published in the *Columbia State* two days later. The author, F. W. P. Butler, wrote it "to en-deavor to stir up some recognition on the part of our legislature to him and his illustrious memory," and suggested "placing a monument over his resting place." On 22 January 1914, J. P. DeLaughter, a representative from Edgefield, introduced a joint resolution to appropriate four hundred dollars to erect a monument to McKie Meriwether. The support for the monument put together by DeLaughter and Butler helped it progress through the South Carolina House and Senate, and the bill was sent to Governor Cole Blease on 28 February 1914. Blease, however, vetoed the bill, returning it to the House with a rather peevish message complaining that the bill misspelled the name Hamburg.[37]

At first glance it seems inexplicable that Blease, who had given a speech at the Red Shirt reunion in Columbia at the beginning of his administration in 1911, would block the creation of a monument commemorating white supremacy. Much had changed since 1911, though, and by 1914, the General Assembly and Blease were at loggerheads. Blease may have vetoed the bill as retribution for earlier political opposition by DeLaughter. It is also possible that Blease was dissatisfied with the person being commemorated. Shortly after he took office in 1911, Blease sent a message to the General Assembly recommending that the state erect a monument to Martin W. Gary on the State House grounds. Gary's "devotion and love for South Carolina was equal, if not superior," Blease argued, "to that of some of those who have been rewarded, either by public office, or otherwise." A House committee considered the suggestion, but found "that it [was] impracticable at this period of the session to take any decided action." Blease probably had not forgotten the slight, and the issue was reawakened while the Meriwether bill was making its way through the General Assembly in 1914. U. R. Brooks, who had written a biography of Matthew C. Butler in 1909, published an open letter to the General Assembly calling for monuments to Butler and Gary. Four years earlier, in his speech to the Red Shirt reunion in Spartanburg, in 1910, Brooks had called on the state to do the same thing.[38]

Meriwether made a more attractive candidate for a monument than Gary. As F. W. P. Butler describes him, Meriwether was young and handsome, "with the easy manners of a country gentleman." He responded to the call and laid down his life to redeem South Carolina. His life was even more of a sacrifice, since he was unarmed when he died: "McKie's gun had become hot from the incessant firing and the brave fellow leaned it up against a pier of the bridge and a bullet from the negro fort hit him in the head and killed him instantly." Gary was another matter. He wrote in his "Plan of the Campaign of 1876": "Never threaten a man individually if he deserves to be threatened, the necessities of the times require that he should die. A dead Radical is very harmless—a threatened Radical or one driven off by threats from the scene of his operations is often very troublesome, sometimes dangerous, always vindictive." This homicidal image fit well with Blease's idealization of the personal, violent defense of white supremacy. However, it was just this encouragement of violence by the governor and his supporters that most enraged and embarrassed his political opponents in South Carolina. They thought it played into the hands of the state's critics and put South Carolina out of step with modern, progressive efforts to efface overt violence from the structures of white supremacy. A monument to Gary would send the wrong message to the state and to the rest of the country.[39]

Blease's veto hardly slowed the plans for the Meriwether monument. The bill's sponsor, who had never made a speech in his two years in the South Carolina House, spoke strongly in favor of the bill, and it passed over Blease's veto by a vote of eighty to four. The General Assembly created a commission to oversee the erection of the monument and directed that it be placed not at Meriwether's grave, but "at some suitable place within the town of North Augusta," the modern town on the site where Hamburg once stood. On 16 February 1916, ex-governor John C. Sheppard presided over an unveiling ceremony for the granite obelisk at the high school in North Augusta. The speaker for the ceremony was Daniel S. Henderson, "the sole surviving member of counsel for the men charged with riot and murder following the famous clash of races at Hamburg in which McKie Meriwether lost his life."[40]

Henderson titled his speech "The White Man's Revolution in South Carolina," and in it he placed the Hamburg Massacre within a continuum of military defense of Anglo-Saxon supremacy that stretched from the American Revolution to the Civil War to the counterrevolution against Reconstruction to the expanding World War that provided the immediate context for his speech. In his rendition, the triumph of white supremacy was the logical, even inevitable, result of a sequence of victories made possible by whites' superior ability and determination. When the day for the hearing on the charges filed against the two white men and against the militia arrived, "crowds of friends and neighbors [of the whites] came." Among them were Ben Tillman's Sweetwater Sabre Club, as well as reinforcements from Georgia. The organizational success of the rifle club paved the way for military success under the leadership of Confederate cavalry general Matthew C. Butler. The battle itself was a mismatch, not so much because of the numerical superiority of the whites or the fact that they had "that Napoleon gun which George Conway brought over from Augusta," as because African Americans were not fit to be soldiers in the first place. This was proven by Henderson's exaggerated claim that "scores of the other side lay stiff in death." Henderson's account gave special emphasis to the trial of those whites who participated in the fight at Hamburg, the part of the story in which he took a leading role. On the day of the bail hearing, the defendants, "in a triumphant procession . . . marched into Aiken, the county seat," where they were met by five thousand mounted men in red shirts and women waving handkerchiefs. All fifty-nine men were bailed out in a show of community support. The judicial triumph made it possible to adopt a Straight-out policy at the State Democratic Convention in Columbia later in the same week, nominate Hampton, and overthrow Reconstruction.[41]

Henderson's speech drew its rhetorical power from its comparison between the American Revolution and the overthrow of Reconstruction. Henderson opened with echoes of the rhetoric of the Revolution by claiming that Meriwether was remembered because "he perished for the cause of liberty." Henderson made the comparison even more explicit a little later on in the speech: "The guns which McKie Meriwether and his companions fired from the abutment of the railroad bridge, down yonder on that hot night, was the token of the White Man's Revolution of 1876, in South Carolina, as much so as the first gun which was fired on the Plains of Lexington in 1775, awakening the Colonies to Arms, and putting down the tyranny of the British Crown. McKie Meriwether died not as a lawless lawbreaker, but as a hero for white independence, and as much a patriot as any Soldier who perished in defense of his country." This comparison positioned Meriwether and the rest of the Sweetwater Sabre Club on the morally unassailable high ground by laying claim to the most potent symbol of righteous political struggle in America. Henderson was hardly the only person to draw such a comparison. In his column in the *Southern Christian Advocate,* J. W. Daniel compared Reconstruction to the American Revolution as well: "Think of the things that have passed over these old roads and trails, they have seen the varied costumes and customs of the people for one hundred and fifty years, witnessed the farces and tragedies that have occurred. They have witnessed battles, murders, mobs, fisticuffs, horse-races, cock-fights, patrols, musters, armies victorious and armies defeated, files of white-gowned Ku-Klux and seemingly interminable lines of Red-shirted cavalry in a cause as just as that for which the patriots of '76 fought. Seventy-six, and then another century marked high noon on the dial of time Seventy-six. What tragedies gathered around these century mile posts! First victory out of poverty and rags, secondly glorious victory out of defeat under the leadership of the brave Confederate General Wade Hampton." By describing the white supremacists as the reincarnation of the Whigs of a century before, Henderson and Daniel implicitly defined their opponents as Tories, Loyalists to a foreign occupying force rather than legitimate members of the body politic.[42]

What makes Daniel S. Henderson's speech so revealing of the shifts in social memory of Reconstruction in South Carolina during the first two decades of the twentieth century is its very ease and confidence. Unlike Pike's book in 1874, or even Herbert's book in 1890, Henderson in 1916 could describe the Red Shirts' attack on the state militia at Hamburg in 1876 not as embattled defiance of the federal government's authority, but as an attempt to uphold the nation's most important principles, comparable to the American Revolution itself. And who was to deny him? As Henderson spoke, the U.S. president was a southerner who spent part of his youth in Columbia during Reconstruction and went on to become one of the historians who castigated the Radical Republicans and their allies. Once in the White House, Woodrow Wilson praised *The Birth of a Nation* and brought Jim Crow to the federal government. Professional historians agreed that Reconstruction had been a mistake, novels presented melodramas of heroic white redeemers and evil carpetbaggers, and the veterans of the 1876 campaign paraded and basked in a state's grateful adulation. Social memory is always contested ground, but by the 1910s, white supremacists living in a society where segregation's grip grew tighter year by year could count themselves winners in the fight over how Reconstruction would be remembered.[43]

FOUR

MEMORIES AND COUNTERMEMORY

By World War I, when Reconstruction was mentioned in public in the South—in the entire nation, for that matter—it was as a warning, what could happen if the wrong people were put in charge. A white supremacist narrative of Reconstruction had been consolidated as one of the tools for building a Jim Crow society in the South, and in subsequent decades, that story became an increasingly central part of the public memory of the South, retold in novels, dominating the landscape in monuments, parading down the streets of the towns and cities. The few whites who had once supported Reconstruction no longer wanted to remember that fact, or to have others remember it either. The historical memory of Reconstruction that saw carpetbaggers as meddling and manipulative, white southerners as righteous and long-suffering, and African Americans as inherently unfit for citizenship was as close to hegemonic as any part of American historical memory had ever been. It seemed an unmovable fact, yet it was not an inevitable fact.

To understand why one historical memory of Reconstruction came to dominate the South requires looking more closely at individuals, at those reading novels about Manse Jolly or cheering parades of elderly Red Shirts. It requires explaining how the public memory of Reconstruction relied upon the construction of memory at the personal level. If we fail to account for the complex process by which lived experience of Reconstruction in all the particularity of an individual life became, over decades, a widely shared common sense about the history of the period, we fail to appreciate the sincerity, power, and tenacity of that historical memory.

At the same time, examining the ordering and transmission of memory at the personal level—what we might call the private discourses of memory—opens up another world entirely, a world where different stories about what Reconstruction meant were possible and, more than possible, were vital to the identity of those who told them. For if a white supremacist narrative of Reconstruction was dominant in public, it could never entirely erase another narrative, one that began without the assumption of racial hierarchy, one that began with the profound reality of Emancipation itself, a countermemory of Reconstruction. Although whites had long since abandoned a countermemory of Reconstruction, African Americans—not all, as the example of Joe O'Bannon demonstrates, but many—held on to a countermemory of Reconstruction that was at odds with the dominant public memory. It was still social memory, to be sure, but it existed, as it had to, well out of sight of the general public, flourishing in just those segregated spaces the Jim Crow system created, where whites were not around to stifle it and shout it down.[1]

The roots of this countermemory go back to Reconstruction itself, and it was squelched only slowly over the next decades, going underground into the realm of private discourse as segregation took hold. We can see that decline in the rise and fall of two holidays intimately connected with Reconstruction for African Americans: Decoration Day and Emancipation Day. The countermemory of Reconstruction emerged back into public view in the late 1930s, as interviewers with the Federal Writers Project began to record the memories of those African Americans who had lived through Reconstruction. Here, we see the kinds of stories that African Americans told among themselves about Reconstruction.

Comparing whites' social memory of Reconstruction and of the Civil War reveals some important points of divergence. In the broadest terms, white Americans, from the North as well as the South, came to agree by about the 1890s on the meaning of the Civil War: it had been an unfortunate waste brought about by zealots on both sides. The war had ended slavery and the danger of secession, and that was good. The South had lost the Civil War, but that loss was ultimately for the best. Of course, a minority of white southerners never reconciled themselves to this view, but they remained well outside the mainstream. Reconstruction, however, became the part of the conflict that white southerners won. By the end of the nineteenth century, white southerners had convinced other white Americans that it had been a mistake to try to integrate African Americans into society as full citizens. Like the defeat of the Civil War, the terrible experiment of Reconstruction had been ultimately beneficial, in that it taught the entire nation this valuable lesson about racial hierarchy and the political order. The overthrow of Reconstruction, significantly called

"Redemption" by white southerners, ushered in a new millennium, a Jim Crow society of segregation and disfranchisement for African Americans and (supposedly) unity for whites across the country. Thus, memory of Reconstruction fit into a broader narrative about sectional conflict and reconciliation from a white supremacist point of view.[2]

The most radical aspects of Reconstruction, however, were much more difficult for whites to assimilate to memory. Reconstruction had the potential to upend two of the foundational beliefs of American society: that white men were superior to African Americans and women and therefore only white men should hold political power, and that only through protecting the sanctity of private property could the legitimate needs of society and its members be met. To be sure, the Radical Republican architects of Reconstruction in Washington remained committed believers in the virtues of industrial capitalism as it was developing in the mid-nineteenth century, but as their policies gave power to black workers in the South, these workers began to push for radical reforms well in advance of those supported by Republican leaders and those historian Nell Irvin Painter has termed "representative colored men." For nearly three years after the Civil War ended, many African Americans hoped, and many whites feared, that there might be significant redistribution of land. Even after this immediate danger passed with the creation of new state constitutions, whites complained that the expanded role of the state in the maintenance of social welfare meant that property was taxed more heavily than before—essentially that wealth was being transferred from those who had traditionally held it to those who had not. The sudden enfranchisement of African American men and their dramatic new role in public life was jarring to whites. Quite simply, not only did many white southerners oppose these changes on grounds of pragmatic self-interest, they simply had no conceptual equipment with which to understand the changes. Reconstruction was, as historian Michel-Rolph Trouillot says of the Haitian Revolution, "unthinkable even as it happened." Belief in white supremacy was self-serving, but we must never fail to appreciate the power of this belief and the sincerity with which it was held, not by everyone, but by most whites. For those starting with such beliefs, there was no way to understand Reconstruction as anything but a terrible, malevolent mistake, the destruction of a sacred, traditional order, and an absolute reversal of how things should be.[3]

Within this framework, then, there was no intellectual space for memories of Reconstruction at odds with the white supremacist memory that came to dominate. But obviously, for those who started out with very different ideas about hierarchies of race and gender and the relationship between property and the social order, very different interpretations of Reconstruction were possible. These we can designate as "countermemories" of Reconstruction, and they persisted in surprisingly vigorous fashion through the entire time that the white supremacist narrative of Reconstruction dominated public life.

Once memory was shaped into narrative, the stories could be told in many different settings to all sorts of audiences. One of the most important contexts in which people heard the stories of Reconstruction was within the family. Whites enjoyed a broad range of occasions, public and private, in which to talk about Reconstruction. Stories of Reconstruction might be recounted at reunions of Confederate veterans in settings that ranged from the tents or other lodgings of the veterans to the formal speeches that were a central part of the reunion programs. Stories of Reconstruction might be passed along in political speeches as well. At all of these formal occasions, narratives would be likely to assume a more standard, canonical form. Since such speeches were thought out well ahead of time and perhaps written and extensively revised, they lacked the malleability of accounts created spontaneously. An account given as a formal speech would also have assumed a more stable form than an account created for a more intimate audience, when the narrator could incorporate audience comments and reactions and modify the narrative in response.[4]

Although oral accounts of Reconstruction provided the foundation for most southerners' knowledge of the period, written accounts were also important and assumed many forms. Many individuals wrote down their own experiences of life during Reconstruction, often setting these personal-experience narratives alongside broader political and social interpretations. Some writers focused on Reconstruction itself, distinct from other periods through which they may have lived. M. L. Bonham's story told about his childhood during the Civil War and used Reconstruction as the setting for his adolescence and growing awareness of the world; the campaign of 1876 was his coming of age. In many cases, episodes dealing with Reconstruction were merely a part of a longer account of an entire life. Reconstruction was but one of many topics covered in James Morris Morgan's memoir.[5]

The audience for written accounts of Reconstruction varied. A number of Reconstruction memoirs were created for family members, usually children or grandchildren. Loula Rockwell Ayers set down her memories of 1876 for her grandchildren, and later the essay was published in *Atlantic*

Monthly. M. L. Bonham wrote his account of the Civil War and Reconstruction, "because my own people seem interested," though it was never published. Organizations, especially the United Daughters of the Confederacy (UDC), prompted other memoirs to be written. At the state level, the UDC initiated a program of soliciting and collecting memoirs from men and women about the Civil War and Reconstruction. On a local level, some individual chapters of the UDC were very active as well. In 1911 the Wade Hampton Chapter in Columbia worked "to get a correct Red Shirt History of the men of '76 from each county."[6]

Much of the discourse about the history of Reconstruction was carried on in the columns of newspapers. Stories about Reconstruction were a constant feature of southern newspapers large and small as long as there were eyewitnesses available to retell their stories. When an old building in Columbia was dismantled in 1927, an elderly man recalled that during Reconstruction a carpetbagger had run a school there. Even as late as the 1940s and 1950s, when "the wearers of the Red Shirt [were] passing—only a few are left," South Carolina newspapers still ran stories about individuals' experiences during Reconstruction. A single newspaper story about Reconstruction would often prompt readers to write in with their own recollections. When the *Charleston News and Courier* ran a story about a Sumter man's experiences during 1876, it led a woman in Marion to tell her story of a treasured table that Wade Hampton had accidentally burned with a cigar while visiting her family's home during the 1876 campaign.[7]

With such significant interplay between oral and written renderings of Reconstruction memory, it is not surprising that some white South Carolinians came to couch their own reminiscences in terms of published accounts. When Sarah Ball Copeland of Laurens described Reconstruction in the 1920s, she began by saying that "Reconstruction was almost worse than war and day by day, week by week, conditions became more intolerable," and then referred the reader to James S. Pike's *The Prostrate State* for further explanation. Similarly, M. L. Bonham told readers of his memoir: "I shall not write of 'Reconstruction,' this is not a political paper. General Pike in 'The Prostrate State' and John S. Reynolds, in 'Reconstruction in S.C.' have informed the world of the conditions which existed in this state during that period." Pike and others discredited Reconstruction for contemporary political ends in the 1870s, but they did more than that. They created the interpretive frameworks to which others would refer as they crafted their own personal memories.[8]

Examining the content of these personal reminiscences reveals patterns that explain how whites remembered Reconstruction. White accounts

generally began by describing a profound loss of control: Federal occupation or the elections following the 1867 passage of the Reconstruction Acts.
"After the war 'the bottom rail was put on top,' the negroes were given the
right of suffrage, which had been taken from the whites," recalled Gasper
Loren Toole of Aiken County, "and this put the control of the government
in the hands of the negroes." The father of novelist Julia Peterkin combined both Federal occupation and black voting in his description of the
beginning of Reconstruction: "In each town a company of Federal troops
was quartered to remind the citizens of Yankee power—how ignorant Negroes were lifted to places of honor, to offices of state, judges, legislators."
In both cases, the chronology of events suggests that whites thought of
Reconstruction primarily as a period when they lost control of the society
in which they lived.[9]

Account after account of Reconstruction centered on profound changes
in social and political status. The higher one's perch, the farther the fall.
White planters such as James Morris Morgan, for instance, found the new
authority that African American magistrates and trial justices exercised
over them excruciating. Morgan grew up as the son of a wealthy lawyer
in Baton Rouge, surrounded by slaves. After Emancipation, he punctu-
ated a command to a black tenant with a casual blow and was astounded
that in the new scheme of things such an action had consequences—and
at the hands of a black trial justice. The sight of African Americans enjoy-
ing luxuries of any kind also drove elite whites to distraction. One of the
"strange sights" Morgan recounted was seeing "a handsome landau drawn
by a spanking pair of high-stepping Kentucky horses and containing four
negro wenches arrayed in low-neck and short-sleeved dresses, their black
bosoms and arms covered with real jewels in the middle of the day, draw
up in front of a barroom on Main Street where the wives and daughters
of the old and impoverished aristocracy did their shopping." Such luxuries had once been a visual marker of planters' status. Now they were a
reminder of how things had changed.[10]

Memories of politics during Reconstruction often focused on the dramatic campaign of 1876, which had dominated news and public discussion across South Carolina. In subsequent years, it took on even greater
significance as it became clear that the 1876 campaign had been a decisive
moment in the overthrow of Reconstruction. What one was doing in 1876
became the sort of historical landmark that Pearl Harbor, the Kennedy
assassination, or the events of September 11, 2001, would be for later generations of Americans. Historian Samuel Schrager argues that events such
as these demand a place in memory. People not only remember events

from the point of view of the groups of which they are members, but those groups themselves require that their members remember events that have a profound effect on the group.[11]

The campaign of 1876, for most whites, served as an exciting counterpoint to the trying years that had preceded it. For M. L. Bonham, as for many white men of his generation, the campaign became a defining experience. The son of one of South Carolina's wartime governors, Bonham joined a rifle club as a young man in the mid-1870s. As he recalled decades later, "I was studying law at Barnwell the year 1876, but after June I did mighty little study. . . . Night and day in our red shirts, we were on the go." Bonham's activities included participating in the Ellenton Riot. He described in detail joining ex-Confederate general Johnson Hagood's rifle club and converging on the scene of the riot, but then he paused, claiming, "This is not the place to enter into intimate particulars of what [sic] serious affray." For Bonham, casting his first vote for Hampton in 1876 marked his transition to "the work of manhood." Bonham went on to become adjutant general and later chief justice of the Supreme Court of South Carolina. A Fairfield County Red Shirt likewise considered the campaign a coming-of-age. "When I became a man," Thomas C. Camak told a Federal Writers Project interviewer, "I put away childish things, joined the Greenbriar Club, in 1876, wore the red shirt of those days, and obeyed the orders of Major Woodward, the leader."[12]

Whites often shaped their memory of Reconstruction to downplay white women's involvement in politics. Most white women portrayed in memoirs avoided becoming directly involved in politics and instead worked for the reestablishment of white supremacy from the safety of their parlors. Someone, after all, had to sew all those red shirts in 1876. Account after account depicts white women reaching the apex of their resistance to Reconstruction by crafting the symbol their husbands or brothers or sons would wear as they did the public work of reestablishing white supremacy. Nearly eighty years later, Loula Rockwell Ayers recalled watching her mother make her father's red shirt, just as she had earlier turned the bed linen into his Ku Klux Klan regalia.[13]

A few exceptions depicted white women inspiring white men directly. The role of Douschka Pickens of Edgefield, riding at the head of a group of Red Shirts, was an example of this. Similarly, Sally Elmore Taylor described the efforts of women in Columbia to organize a parade of women and children during the period of dual government. "When the end neared it came to us like an inspiration that the women might serve a purpose," wrote Taylor in 1906. "That a show of confidence might be made by their moving about [as] though already owning the country." As Taylor described it, the presence of women in the street actions during the period of dual government was of decisive importance in Democrats' efforts to capture the state government.[14]

Group membership, personal identity, and memory are mutually dependent. For southerners in the twentieth century, no set of memories was more important to establishing identity than memories of Reconstruction. Being considered a member of a particular group depended in part on whether one shared that group's historical memory of Reconstruction, and the way one remembered Reconstruction helped to define to which groups one might belong. In these circumstances, white Republicans found themselves in an awkward position. By the twentieth century, there were few good reasons to remind oneself and one's neighbors that during Reconstruction one had been a carpetbagger or scalawag. The things white Republicans had tried to accomplish during Reconstruction had been thoroughly discredited. The party barely survived in South Carolina, and it was easy enough for former members to slip quietly back into the ranks of the Democrats. Originally from New York, Alexander C. Shaffer settled in Walterboro after the Civil War and held positions in local government as a Republican. By the beginning of the twentieth century, however, he told his son "that the most colossal blunder in American history was when the colored men were given the right to vote at the close of the war." Some prominent white Republicans made a habit of speaking of their past only to renounce it. Thomas Jefferson Mackey was one such example. A prominent Republican judge, Mackey switched to the Democrats in the midst of the 1876 campaign. In later years, Mackey told stories about how he had convicted corrupt Republican politicians (conveniently forgetting to mention the numerous allegations of corruption against himself) and assisted destitute Democrats during Reconstruction.[15]

African Americans did not have the option of renouncing or obscuring their political positions during Reconstruction and merging back into the dominant group. Instead, they established and maintained a countermemory that rejected the assertion that Reconstruction had been a terrible mistake. An important strand of this countermemory challenged the dominant narrative directly and, rather than bemoaning the changes Reconstruction brought, celebrated those very changes as evidence of the progress of the race, giving the lie to those who argued that African Americans were racially incapable of citizenship. This celebration of Reconstruction often took place in the context of a broader public commemoration of history from an African American point of view that included celebrations both of holidays of national significance, such as the Fourth of July, and of days important in black history, such as Frederick Douglass's birthday. Two holidays, Emancipation Day and Decoration Day, gave African Americans in South Carolina opportunities to celebrate key aspects of Reconstruction—their very freedom and the claim that African Americans made on the rights of citizenship on the basis of military service in the Civil War.[16]

Emancipation Day in South Carolina was celebrated on January 1st, the date the Emancipation Proclamation took effect in 1863, and the earliest celebrations occurred in Union-occupied portions of the state, even while the war was raging a few miles away. An Emancipation Day speaker in 1902 noted the date's "double meaning" to freedpeople. During slavery, "it was a day of horrors—a day of uncertainty," recalled Thomas E. Miller, "the day upon which sales of negroes were universally made . . . the day upon which husbands were separated from wives, and mothers from children." By the end of the 1880s, Emancipation Day celebrations were common throughout the state.[17]

Emancipation Day parades did not move randomly through space; parade routes often had significance that amplified the assertion of public presence. Columbia's 1892 Emancipation Day parade began at the northwest corner of the State House grounds and passed in front of the capitol, turning left onto Main Street in the shadow of the Confederate monument. From the capitol, where African Americans held an ever-dwindling measure of political power, and under the marble Confederate's gaze, the black marchers headed toward one place where they still had a sense of power and accomplishment, Allen University. Once the parade had reached its destination, orations were the order of the day. Emancipation Day celebrations nearly always included a reading of the Emancipation Proclamation itself, a literal re-creation of the pivotal moment in African American history, the transition from slavery to freedom. When African Americans in Beaufort gathered for Emancipation Day in 1901, they heard Robert Smalls, Civil War hero and Reconstruction political leader, recount the story of the reading of the Emancipation Proclamation there thirty-eight years earlier.[18]

Another celebration with particular significance to African Americans was Decoration Day, which commemorated the fallen Union soldiers. After freedpeople in Charleston went to the Union burial ground at the old racetrack on 1 May 1865, the idea of setting aside a particular day each year to decorate soldiers' graves quickly caught on. In the South, Decoration Day's other name, Memorial Day, soon came to refer to Confederate Memorial Day, celebrated on May 10th in the Carolinas. Decoration Day, May 30th, came three weeks later and was given but cursory attention by most southern whites. Union veterans, though, black and white, gathered from far and wide to decorate the graves of dead Union soldiers in the South, usually under the auspices of the Grand Army of the Republic (GAR), the Union equivalent of the United Confederate Veterans. The GAR maintained a number of posts in the state into the twentieth century, primarily in coastal towns such as Beaufort, Hilton Head, and Charleston, but also as far inland as the Pee Dee region and Columbia. Composed of African American veterans, except for one all-white Charleston post, these GAR posts staged Decoration Day celebrations, arranging a parade through town to the cemetery and bringing in speakers.[19]

As a holiday centered around the ceremony of caring for the graves of Union soldiers, Decoration Day took hold in only two places in South Carolina, Beaufort and Florence. The holiday was occasionally celebrated in Columbia and Charleston, but never with the regularity or enthusiasm it generated at Florence or Beaufort. Occupied by Union forces by November 1861, Beaufort has a national cemetery containing the graves of several thousand Union soldiers, many of whom died in the battles around Beaufort and Charleston. Florence, too, has a number of Union graves because it was home to the infamous Florence Stockade, opened in September 1864 after Andersonville was threatened by Sherman's advance through Georgia. Although the Florence prison was smaller and not as well known as Andersonville, sojourners in Confederate prisons often decided that Florence was worse than Andersonville. Weakened and dispirited by an earlier stay at Andersonville, as many as 2,800 prisoners died at Florence. Since Decoration Day was observed at only a few locations in the South, it tended to draw African American participants from a wide area. Military companies and other groups from Savannah, Charleston, and Georgetown regularly participated in Beaufort's celebration, while the smaller Florence celebration still drew participants from around the Pee Dee region, Columbia, and Charleston.[20]

Speakers for Decoration Day celebrations came from the top ranks of the African American community's leadership. For the first several decades, that often meant prominent Republican politicians. In 1890, the chairman of the Republican Executive Committee in South Carolina, Ellery M. Brayton, spoke to a crowd assembled for Decoration Day at the Beaufort National Cemetery. He connected contemporary controversies over race to the past, noting that the "superstructure of the negro question rests" on "the dreaded State government in the South under Reconstruction." Not very far removed in time from the Republican administrations he had supported, Brayton attempted to defend Reconstruction in order to defuse the vicious racism he saw gaining power in the late nineteenth century. "While there was extravagance and maladministration," Brayton admitted, "there was no viciousness nor malevolence, and if the aggregate of their wrong doings should be compared with that committed by their oppressors, they would not appear at such disadvantage when the balance was struck." Brayton attacked the emerging official memory of Reconstruction head on, averring that those who had overthrown the Republican administration had acted out of viciousness and malevolence rather than any high-minded principles. Any open debate and fair assessment, he argued, would bear this out.[21]

In addition to celebrating the positive sides of Reconstruction in public, African Americans emphasized things such as emancipation, citizenship, and land acquisition in the stories they told in private settings. Interviewers for the Federal Writers Project (FWP), a New Deal relief effort that provided government-funded work for jobless writers and other white-collar workers, recorded this body of oral history in the 1930s. The FWP sent writers out to collect local information that could be compiled and edited at the state headquarters into guidebooks that celebrated American pluralism. The FWP stressed the importance of "ordinary people," and its leaders wanted to write an inclusive history of America based on those whose voices usually went unheard.[22]

African American accounts of Reconstruction began with vivid memories of Emancipation. Mariah Heywood had to wait longer than many for freedom to arrive in Murrells Inlet, on the coast north of Georgetown. "Free everywhere else and we wasn't free Sunnyside till June third or second," she recalled in the 1930s. "Sunday we got our Freedom. Bright day too." Many former slaves remembered freedom so distinctly because they had taken the initiative to bring it about. A slave with the ironic name of William Sherman lived on a Robertsville, South Carolina, plantation. When he could hear the guns of General Sherman's army from his plantation, William Sherman and his cousin slipped away and led several hundred slaves from the neighborhood to the Union lines. The momentous experience of self-ownership was the most important fact of Reconstruction for African Americans.[23]

African Americans remembered situations in which they exercised their new rights and duties as citizens. John I. Young was only ten years old when the Civil War ended, but by the time he was in his late teens he was speaking at Republican campaign meetings in Newberry and Laurens counties. "I got mighty unpopular with de Democrats who lived near me," Young recalled, so he moved to Greenville and became a precinct chairman there, "where a cullud man could speak more freely dan in de country and where nobody told him much about how he should vote." Looking back on his political experience, Young blamed Republican presidents Hayes and Garfield for allowing southern whites "to skin us out of our rights."[24]

Although Reconstruction never worked the revolution in land tenure that African Americans hoped for, some did acquire land, and the experience was an important component of their memory of the transition out of slavery. Born a year before the Civil War, Lawrence Hampton remembered that his grandfather saved money earned during slavery and bought farms for his four sons during Reconstruction. When Dolly Haynes's husband wanted to become a preacher, she worked for three years so he could go to school at Benedict College. "De briars cut my legs an' de breshes tore my skirt, but I tuck up de skirt an' plow right on 'til I bought my little farm." A person who once had not even owned herself, walking over acres that were now hers, the same land, perhaps, she had known in slavery— that sort of discontinuity with the past loomed large in memory.[25]

Publicly commending the good that was done during Reconstruction certainly challenged the dominant historical memory of the period, but there were limits to how far this challenge could go, to how much of the truth of Reconstruction could be told in holiday speeches. Public ceremonial representations of the past in America were powerfully shaped by a narrative of progress that "placed past, present, and future within a single framework, offering a coherent plot within which local residents could interpret their recent experiences and envision their future progress." The hopeful vision at the heart of Emancipation Day and Decoration Day celebrations became less and less realistic as time passed. Decoration Day told a story of how African Americans could be proud of the black soldiers who had saved the Union, obliging that Union to recognize their claims to civil rights. Similarly, Emancipation Day highlighted the progress of the race "up from slavery," to borrow the title of Booker T. Washington's autobiography. But what African Americans desperately wanted had drifted impossibly far from what they could expect, and that disjuncture led to a decline in the two holidays over the years.[26]

The decline of Emancipation Day's optimistic tone is illustrated in a shift in the background of the speakers and their attitudes to Reconstruction. After the 1895 South Carolina constitution decimated the African

American electorate, Republican politicians became much less relevant. It no longer made sense for speakers to use Reconstruction to make a political appeal if their listeners had little political power left to wield. Instead, speakers were more likely to be prominent educators or leaders of important churches. When Rev. William Decker Johnson became president of Allen University in Columbia, he was invited to give the Emancipation Day speech of 1905. Not surprisingly, he discouraged African Americans from pursuing politics and suggested instead, "Let us when we want national recognition appeal to the door of religion. . . . Religion is more powerful than politics and through this channel let us ascend the heights." When Emancipation Day speakers did still speak of Reconstruction, they demonstrated mixed feelings about the period and its significance for present-day African Americans. Rev. E. H. Coit made a tepid defense of African Americans' role during Reconstruction in an 1896 speech. "I am willing to leave the record with the historian to make," Coit said, "provided he will write not with a prejudiced eye." Coit confessed that "the negro has made some, yes, many, blunders in his political adventures, yet I am not willing to admit, unless convinced by reason and common sense that his affiliation in politics, has degraded him or lessened his success or usefulness." He defended the legislative accomplishments of those who had just emerged "from a condition surpassing that of the serfdom of Russia."[27]

A few years later, Thomas E. Miller, former politician and president of the Colored Normal, Industrial, Agricultural, and Mechanical College of South Carolina, took a dimmer view of the African American political experience begun in Reconstruction. Only four years after he had made a last impassioned plea for African Americans' political rights at the convention that formed South Carolina's 1895 constitution and completed the work of disenfranchising nearly all the state's black citizens, Miller had finally given up on the political hopes of Reconstruction. "It is better by far to have no political hope than have one that is predicated upon national aid, national protection or national interference in our behalf," he told listeners. Republicans, even the very children of abolitionists from an earlier era, had abandoned the Fourteenth and Fifteenth Amendments to placate southern politicians and gain their support for American imperialism. Securing new markets for the goods manufactured by northern factories had become more important to Republicans than standing by their former allies in the South. African Americans should stay in the South and rely on the goodwill of their white neighbors, Miller argued.[28]

Carrying meanings that ultimately failed to challenge the emerging Jim Crow society of the South, Emancipation Day celebrations became an established part of life in many South Carolina communities. In the first years after Emancipation, the mere reminder that African Americans were no longer slaves, let alone that they exercised a modicum of political power, was a constant irritant to whites. By the end of the nineteenth century, however, southern whites had generally come to admit that Emancipation had been for the best. A 1904 editorial in the *Columbia State*, titled "The Real Emancipation," illustrated this idea well. "It was not the negroes of the south alone that the war set free," the newspaper argued. "It was the whites as well." Turning to Reconstruction, the editorial continued, "There was presented to both races an equality of opportunity, as the abolitionists desired, but the fanatics of the north in their blind folly could not foresee that an equality of opportunity would be an advantage and a benefit to the superior race—the race which will always be superior." A far cry from the standard complaint about "negro domination," this editorial surveyed the past with a victor's confidence and boasted that there had never been much real competition from such an inferior opponent.[29]

The career of Decoration Day celebrations was controlled less by its African American participants than by the changing attitudes of local whites toward the U.S. military, attitudes that shifted rapidly during times of war. In Florence, the national cemetery was virtually ignored for twenty-five years. Only in 1889 did African Americans begin to gather there on Decoration Day, perhaps partly as an attempt to remind national Republican leaders of their continuing loyalty to the party. The celebration grew in the 1890s, drawing black audiences and speakers. The year after the Spanish-American War, however, the state leaders of the GAR concluded that "on this occasion, for some reason the negroes did not take part in the decorating and it was suggested that the attention of the white people would be appreciated, and that the negroes would be hereafter barred from the celebration if the whites would take an interest in it." There had been interest in such a move as early as 1890, spearheaded by the white GAR post in Charleston, but it was not until wartime that GAR leaders could gather the energy to make a change. Captain James O. Ladd, a white veteran of the 35th U.S. Colored Regiment, presided over the ceremony and then called for the immediate formation of the Florence Gray and Blue Memorial Association. The new association decided to cooperate with local Confederate groups to decorate the graves of both Union and Confederate soldiers in the future. Decoration Day continued to be celebrated in Florence, but under the auspices of the Florence Gray and Blue Memorial Association it was an all-white affair, purged of any memory that African Americans had been Union soldiers during the Civil War.[30]

Beaufort was a center of black political power into the early twentieth century, and Decoration Day there remained an African American affair ignored by local whites, except for former Union soldiers, until World War I. In its heyday, Beaufort's Decoration Day attracted crowds of up to 8,000, but the celebration went into decline in the 1910s. The crowd for the 1913 event was only about 2,100, and 1915 saw even fewer. The transformation of Beaufort's black Decoration Day into the white Memorial Day was driven by the U.S. entry into World War I. The U.S. Marine Corps had established a base on nearby Parris Island as early as 1891, but it was not until 1915 that the base grew into an important center for training recruits. At the height of World War I, over thirteen thousand men were in training on Parris Island, and the increased traffic required more than two hundred new buildings in 1917. Suddenly, Beaufort was once again a town dominated by the U.S. military. The local newspaper did not report any celebration in 1916, but in 1917, Memorial Day, "the first of its kind in Beaufort," was observed, with the marines from nearby Parris Island participating. "The laying aside of old prejudices and ill feeling between the two sections, the north and the south," reported the newspaper, "was stressed by the speakers, and everyone urged his hearers to forget these differences of the past and to stand together as a solid nation in the face of the present world war."[31]

During the 1920s, African Americans struggled to find space in Beaufort's Memorial Day celebrations for the memory of black Union soldiers in the Civil War. In 1920, both black and white speakers addressed the audience during the morning, but few people attended, coming instead to the afternoon exercises at the national cemetery. Beginning in 1921, the American Legion assumed a central role in organizing the celebration, and black participation evaporated. The spirit of earlier Decoration Day celebrations had changed to such an extent that in 1923 the United Daughters of the Confederacy made a wreath for the speakers' stand. The 1925 celebration brought attention back to the Civil War, and "sprinkled in the audience were the few remaining Union Veterans of this section," but the emphasis was on reconciliation rather than Emancipation. The address by Niels Christensen Jr., the son of a white Union soldier who settled in Beaufort after the war, invoked the Civil War, but there was no mention of black Union soldiers. South Carolina's only African American newspaper, however, carried the full text of a speech by a black doctor from Augusta, Georgia, which stressed the importance of the military tradition in African American history. For the next two years, African American participation in Memorial Day celebrations was minimal. Starting in 1928, completely separate celebrations were held. Whites continued to celebrate Memorial Day, while African Americans revived the tradition of Decoration Day. Visitors from the Sea Islands, Savannah, Charleston, and Augusta attended these events well into the 1930s.[32]

    Presenting an African American countermemory of Reconstruction in public discourse faced greater obstacles than mere discouragement, though, for the deepest truths about why Reconstruction had failed could not be portrayed on a parade's banner nor proudly proclaimed from a speaker's platform, at least not by African Americans. Ben Tillman could speak that truth at a reunion of Red Shirts when he boasted of helping kill African American militiamen at Hamburg in 1876. Violence was the part of African Americans' experience of Reconstruction that suffused their countermemory, yet could not be incorporated into public discourse. That absence should hardly be surprising. If, as historian W. Fitzhugh Brundage argues, one of the key functions of these celebrations was to sustain spirits flagging under Jim Crow, frank accounts of beatings, of rapes, of sons shot down in the night, and of fathers' bodies thrown in creeks to rot would hardly have served that purpose. Rather, like stories of lynchings would later do, tales of Reconstruction violence would only have heightened their listeners' sense of vulnerability and their feeling that, as bluesman Robert Johnson would put it, there was a hellhound on their trail. Such violence would clearly be impossible to integrate into a historical narrative about the community's progress. As if all this were not enough, bringing to mind killings and whippings and intimidation would have been incredibly inflammatory, a foolhardy "*j'accuse*" against many of the powerful whites, by whose sufferance African Americans were allowed to celebrate Emancipation Day and Decoration Day at all. In the cruelest of ironies, the very success of the violence whites directed against blacks during Reconstruction created conditions that prevented that violence from being spoken of, at least in public. But as a Haitian proverb reminds us, "The giver of the blow forgets, the bearer of the scar remembers."[33]

African Americans did not forget the violence they experienced during Reconstruction, of course, and they did speak of it in private. Born to freedpeople during Reconstruction, Walter H. Hughes of Columbia recalled that his parents spoke little of slavery. "Most of the talk I heard between Daddy and Mammy was about work and the conditions that bore down on everybody during reconstruction," he noted. These private discourses of violence came to the attention of whites, to the very limited extent that they did, by way of the FWP interviews of the late 1930s. The accounts that these interviewers, most of whom were white, took down echoed the accounts preserved in the congressional investigation of the Ku Klux Klan published in 1872. Even after more than sixty years, the memories of violence at the hands of the Ku Klux Klan and others were still harrowing.[34]

FWP interviewees narrated many of the famous incidents of violence against African Americans during Reconstruction, but they also recorded numerous small incidents and details that never made it into standard sources for the period. Stories from witnesses to the 1871 mass lynching of black militia members in Union and the Ellenton Riot in 1876 made it into FWP files, but so did the casual shooting of a freedwoman by her employer. An eyewitness account of a battle between the militia and the Ku Klux Klan in Chester included the names of several of the Ku Klux Klan members and what they were doing, suggesting the narrator had been present. Ex-slaves, in particular, recalled a time when violence was omnipresent in their lives. John I. Young explained, "I've known men of my race to be taken to de swamp by de Klu Kluxers and shot down for somethin' they never done. All dat one had to do some places to be shot wuz to get into an argument with a prominent white man or to do a little electioneerin' for de Republican party." White folklorist G. Leland Summer interviewed elderly residents of the Dutch Fork section of South Carolina in the 1930s and 1940s and recorded dozens of stories about Ku Klux Klan activities that had never been reported in the original congressional investigation. One former slave described the Ku Klux Klan lining up African Americans on a bridge over Turk Creek and then shooting them, letting their bodies fall into the water below. "Fact is," he said, "dey would not let many of de niggers take de dead bodies of de folks no whars. Dey just throwed dem in a big hole right dar and pulled some dirt over dem. For weeks atter dat, you could not go near dat place, kaise it stink so fer and bad."[35]

In other cases, the violence of Reconstruction could be muted and de-politicized. The son of Prince Rivers, the black militia leader and trial justice involved in the Hamburg Massacre, gave an account of the 1876 fight to a FWP interviewer. Although it might be expected that a story which, as a note attached says, gives a "*good slant* on point of view of Negroes" would describe the violence and its motivation frankly, Prince Rivers's own son seems reluctant to take the side of the black militiamen. At the end of the fight, in this version, "De niggers was routed out on charges by de whites and they come out shootin'. As they run, seven niggers was shot down, dead, and four was wounded." Rivers's son neglects to add that the seven men killed had already been captured. His story concludes, "I can see that de nigger, which had just gained his freedom, was not fit to govern de State." The difference between this account of the Hamburg Massacre and others suggests that the calculated violence of the event was toned down by one of three people: Prince Rivers himself, his son, or the FWP interviewer. The interviewer may be responsible, as he had also written about the 1868 assassination of Republican politician B. F. Randolph, whitewashing the story with the comment that "The carpetbag regime prevailed from 1868 until 1876 when the people of South Carolina, in a heroic campaign, ended the carpetbag–Negro travesty and replaced it with a government of their own choosing."[36]

The looming presence of violence in African Americans' private countermemories of Reconstruction raises the question of what happened to that same violence in whites' historical memory. In public, as we have seen with the Red Shirt reunions and the McKie Meriwether monument, there was an ambivalence about the violence of Reconstruction. When it did become a topic of discussion, it tended to be the violence of the 1876 campaign, a legitimate if regrettable use of force against an enemy who had not figured out when to quit. The violence of the Ku Klux Klan, and especially the systematic rape of black women, was seldom if ever part of whites' public memory of Reconstruction.

How whites recollected the violence they committed as members of the Ku Klux Klan, and how those memories did or did not become part of the stories they told of Reconstruction, is an elusive matter. In some few cases, whites seem to have been fairly forthright in their accounts, or so the evidence of the FWP interviewers would suggest. Two participants in the lynching of black militia members in Union in 1871 told their stories in 1937, while another gave firsthand details of a battle between the militia and the Ku Klux in Chester. Even these cases, however, tend to be the more dramatic incidents, flagrant attacks that were widely discussed at the time and perhaps easier to acknowledge participation in.[37]

Rather more whites, I suspect, downplayed their own involvement in the Ku Klux Klan and the violent acts they had committed. Many cases were probably like that of W. W. Lumpkin. He told his family stories of his youth during the Civil War and Reconstruction, even encouraging his children to stage debates on southern history every Saturday evening. Yet, according to the account of these stories left by his daughter, the sociologist Katharine Du Pre Lumpkin, he never spoke of his involvement with the Ku Klux Klan in Georgia. It was only in the last years of his life, at the prompting of his eldest daughter, that he recorded these memories for the archives of the United Daughters of the Confederacy. A document by

Lumpkin titled "Where and Why I was a Kuklux" tells of violence in a way that strips away its trappings of glory, leaving only bitterness and brutality, stories that were perhaps too much for his children to hear.[38]

Social memory of Reconstruction was segregated in the first half of the twentieth century. The very process by which social memory is built and maintained involves the day-to-day transactions of social life, and the Jim Crow system in the South had segregated most of those transactions. Whites who reveled in the overthrow of Reconstruction had managed by the turn of the century to exhaust not only the opportunities for African Americans to wield political power, but also the opportunities for them to publicly claim the right to wield that power or to recall to public memory having exercised their civil rights during Reconstruction. This was the story whites told themselves about their history in public, and it was the story they repeated in private. Far from being some sort of outlandish idea held only by the undereducated masses, their own view of Reconstruction was the one proclaimed by the most powerful politicians in the nation and printed as truth by professors at the most esteemed universities. The white supremacist narrative of Reconstruction was, as historians have been arguing since the 1940s, wrong in historical terms. With its assumptions of racial inferiority, its casual acceptance of brutality, and its blithe acceptance of a hierarchical world where everyone knew their place, it is a vision of history that nearly all of us now would find wrong in moral terms. But make no mistake—while we may charge those who held these views with historical and moral error, they were not disingenuous. Cynical politicians may have promoted the story for their own ends, but it was a story that was believed, a story that was increasingly easy to believe as people saw it repeated around them in so many forms. It came to be necessary to believe this story, for the white supremacist narrative of Reconstruction was what provided moral justification for Jim Crow. It was not the only thing, of course. Theories of racial degeneration and a generation of crackpot science and sociology supported Jim Crow also. But stories of incompetence, of tyranny, of wreckage and desecration that came from giving African Americans rights and opportunities they neither deserved nor could handle responsibly made a strong argument for fastening on the bonds of a social system that would prevent such mistakes from ever being made again.

The social memory of Reconstruction that would oppose that view, that would see the era without the assumptions of white supremacy, faced an incredible challenge. To call it "countermemory" hardly begins to suggest the obstacles, practical and intellectual, it had to surmount to merely survive, much less to emerge back into public discourse to mount a credible challenge to the white supremacist view of Reconstruction. That counter-memory was itself stunted by the cramped conditions within which it could grow. So little of the story could find a public outlet during the period of segregation. There were no parades of proud, elderly African American legislators celebrating the anniversary of the 1868 constitution. No plaques were placed in courthouses to commemorate a Republican school superintendent who tried to educate little white children and little black children. Mainstream newspapers did not run nostalgic articles about the good old days when the South dabbled with democracy. What did persist in public discourse was a celebration of black soldiers' efforts to save the Union—and after World War I, that celebration was itself seg-regated—and a celebration of freedom, the mere freedom that African Americans got after centuries of toil.

The critical fact of Reconstruction—that African Americans tried to enact the vision of America as a free labor republic and were turned away with violence—could not exist in public for the first several decades of the twentieth century. It persisted in fragmentary form in a variety of private discourses, but it received none of the reinforcement and validation that the white supremacist narrative of Reconstruction did. No wonder some African Americans, such as Joe O'Bannon, instead went along with the dominant historical memory. This core of the countermemory of Recon-struction and a substantive challenge to the white supremacist memory would not emerge until the haphazard probings of the FWP interviews in the late 1930s and the stirrings of a revisionist scholarship originating with black historians and their white allies. Most of all, a fresh, bold assertion of the value of Radical Reconstruction required the work of a new genera-tion of radicals in the South.

FIVE

RECONSTRUCTION AND POLITICS
IN THE ROOSEVELT ERA

The years of Franklin D. Roosevelt's presidency saw the reorientation of politics across the United States, and this reorientation, along with the disruptions caused by the Great Depression and World War II, shook South Carolina's staid political establishment. For old-fashioned white supremacists such as Ellison D. "Cotton Ed" Smith, who became South Carolina's junior senator back in 1908, Roosevelt's New Deal and the political demands his new coalition put on southern Democrats seemed like another attempt by meddling Yankees to upend white supremacy by empowering the wrong sort of people: African Americans and workers. Smith and his allies fought back by mobilizing memories of Reconstruction to convince white South Carolinians to fear change rather than welcoming it, stalling the progress of the New Deal in 1939. Propelled by the momentum of a growing war on Fascism to fight for the "Double V"—victory over Fascism abroad and over racism at home, African Americans began to go on the offensive, prizing open the cracks that had formed in the political system to reclaim the political heritage of Reconstruction.

Despite the tumult of the stock market crash and the gathering Depression, the 1932 election campaign hardly seemed to herald significant change in South Carolina politics. In September 1932 the Republican Party decided to run a candidate for the U.S. Senate for the first time in over forty years and Clara Harrigal became the first woman to run for Congress in South Carolina. Her opponent, the Democratic incumbent "Cotton Ed" Smith, was a twenty-four-year fixture in the Senate. Even though much about Harrigal's candidacy was new, her campaign rhetoric was tried and true. At a meeting in Florence, Harrigal said, "My grandfather was a Democrat and voted thirty-six times in the days of the red shirts. But those days have passed. We need two parties in the state." By 1932, the Republican Party existed in South Carolina only to distribute patronage and send delegates to the national convention. "Tieless Joe" W. Tolbert controlled the party from 1900 to 1940, and although African Americans could be members, they held no power. African Americans could be members of the Democratic Party only if they could provide affidavits swearing that they had voted for Wade Hampton in 1876, a difficult proposition over fifty years later. Even Republicans used the 1876 campaign as a starting point for politics in 1932. Rather than insist that the spirit of 1876 required blind loyalty to the Democratic Party, however, they argued that the true spirit of 1876 involved taking a bold political stance for the good of the state.[1]

A history of South Carolina by newspaper editor W. W. Ball published in 1932 gives a good glimpse of what many conservative South Carolinians thought of Reconstruction. Born in 1868, Ball grew up in Laurens, where his father had been an important figure in the Democratic Party during Reconstruction and the leader of one of the county's squads of Red Shirts. Involved in newspapers in South Carolina since 1890, Ball became the editor of the *Charleston News and Courier,* the state's oldest and most prestigious newspaper, in 1927. From that perch, he exerted his considerable influence on state politics and was active in a variety of historical organizations across the state. After the success of Claude G. Bowers's 1929 history of Reconstruction, *The Tragic Era,* publishers realized that history from a conservative, southern white viewpoint could succeed with the public if it were written in a lively, journalistic style. In early 1931, someone connected with the Indianapolis publishing firm of Bobbs-Merrill suggested to Ball that he write a book about South Carolina. Intrigued and flattered by the idea, Ball agreed, since he had "learned the history [of the period since the Civil War] by ear, chiefly from my father." It would be "a book of sketches, incidents, anecdotes, strung on the thin rope of history." With his daughter as research assistant, Ball spent the next year drafting the book in odd moments stolen from his editorial duties. In addition to his own recollections, his earlier writings on the Red Shirt campaign and Tillman, and newspaper files, Ball called on friends to retrieve details for his story. One acquaintance from York gave Ball information on that county's Ku Klux Klan leader, Dr. J. Rufus Bratton, and promised to get in touch with Bratton's son, who "has a Scrap Book that is wonderfully complete and informing as to the life of his father." Ball's book, *The State that Forgot,* was published in October 1932.[2]

The thrust of *The State that Forgot* is contained in its subtitle: *South*

Carolina's Surrender to Democracy. Thirteen years after World War I had made the world safe for democracy, William Watts Ball remained an unabashed aristocrat. As he explained in his book's first chapter: "My political thesis is that the Federal Government, by means of armed forces, placed South Carolina on the operating table in 1867, that in 1868 the Carpetbaggers made an incision in its body, and, by the constitution they adopted, injected into it the deadly and foreign poison of democracy which, after causing the loathsome ulcers of Reconstruction, subtly spread through the blood-stream of the white people and killed for ever in it the inherited corpuscles of political and social health." The hinge of Ball's story was Reconstruction. In his telling, a worn-out state that had already been forced by the exigencies of war to forget some of its aristocratic habits contracted a fatal case of "the cooties of democracy" with the adoption of universal male suffrage in the 1868 constitution. The rest—demagogues such as Ben Tillman and Cole Blease, the lackluster politicians of the 1920s—was all the inevitable result of this shift to democracy. Ball held no brief for Herrenvolk democracy, either: democracy was democracy to him, in white skin or black, unpalatable either way. The dramatic heart of the story was aristocracy's last great hurrah, the Red Shirt campaign of 1876 as seen though the eyes of an eight-year-old boy. For this chapter, Ball recycled a 1911 paper, "A Boy's Recollections of the Red Shirt Campaign," itself inspired by the 1911 Red Shirt reunion in Columbia and based on a newspaper article Ball wrote in 1905 during the fundraising campaign for the Hampton monument.[3]

Many South Carolinians wrote to Ball praising the book, as did a few individuals from other states. An English professor at the University of South Carolina assigned it to all the students in his South Carolina literature course, and Harry L. Watson, the editor of the *Greenwood Index-Journal,* devoted half a page in his newspaper to Ball's book. The few remaining Red Shirt veterans also enjoyed *The State that Forgot.* An elderly man wrote, "It brings back to memory the days of the red shirt in S.C. I was living near Greenville S C & heard Gen'l Hampton speak to a large gathering. Those were strenuous days indeed."[4]

Rote denunciation of Reconstruction had long been as much a part of political life as stump speeches and barbecue. After the turn of the century, participation in, or at least support of, Hampton's 1876 campaign became a sine qua non of political life, not a campaign issue of its own. During the 1902 race for U.S. Senate, Daniel S. Henderson produced a flyer that cited his legal defense of the Hamburg rioters in 1876 as one reason to vote for him. When John G. Mobley ran for railroad commissioner in

1904, he could not claim such a prominent role in the Red Shirt campaign. Nonetheless, his campaign flyer asserted, "Although a mere boy in '76, he rendered most efficient services to the Democratic party when radical misrule was overthrown and white supremacy reestablished." As a historian noted in 1906, "To have had a hand in that [1876] campaign is to-day a title of distinction in the Palmetto State, an entrée into 'good society,' and that means much to a South Carolinian."[5]

In the 1932 presidential and senatorial campaigns, South Carolina Democrats invoked the legacy of 1876, just as they had for the past thirty years. Some compared 1932 to 1876 to show that yet again a corrupt and incompetent federal government led by Republicans had brought ruin on the South, and only "the spirit of the Red Shirts of 1876" could end "all this misgovernment, racketeering and flaunting of authority by the criminal element." At a campaign rally to consolidate support for Franklin D. Roosevelt days before the general election, former governor John G. Richards called on South Carolina Democrats to display the same "unity of effort" they had in 1876. As a reminder, twenty aged Red Shirt veterans participated in the parade. A week earlier, the Young Democrats of Dillon rode around the county stirring up political interest in the spirit of 1876, though they "[wore] no red shirts, white robes or hoods." These efforts were rewarded when Roosevelt received 98 percent of the vote in South Carolina, the most Democratic state in the nation.[6]

Roosevelt's first term changed South Carolina's political landscape out of all recognition from 1932. Some of the reasons for these changes had been building for a decade and more, but equally significant were Roosevelt's policies and politics. On a national level, the economic effects of World War I and its aftermath had created tremendous demographic change. As the nation geared up for war, African Americans began leaving the South for better prospects elsewhere. In the 1920s, that dynamic continued to operate, boosted by economic problems in the South. Cotton prices had never stabilized after their World War I spike, and the boll weevil had destroyed an increasing proportion of the crop each year, making the entire precarious structure of cotton tenancy increasingly unsustainable. The Great Migration, as this movement became known, shifted approximately 1.75 million African Americans between 1910 and 1940. In the North, these African Americans still faced discrimination, but they were no longer disenfranchised. Unlike foreign immigrants in places such as Chicago, Detroit, or Philadelphia, these new residents usually maintained close connections with their relatives and friends back home in the South, and they remained part of the national political system. Although in the

1920s the federal government showed little interest in using its power to ameliorate the situation of African Americans in the South, the demographic shift of the Great Migration had set up a potentially powerful constituency for change in the South whenever the federal government began to take an active role in the nation's life.[7]

The inauguration of Franklin D. Roosevelt in 1933 broke a decade of lethargy in Washington. Three years of half-measures by Herbert Hoover had done little to solve the problems of the Great Depression, but Roosevelt came into office promising the nation a "New Deal." The suddenness and the extent of federal activity in 1933 gave notice that political realities were in the midst of changing decisively. Although not governed by any one coherent ideology, Roosevelt's New Deal programs and policies all called for the federal government to play a larger role in the lives of its citizens. Power was to shift toward a more centralized federal government in Washington and to citizens who had been marginalized before, left with little control over the decisions that shaped their lives. The losers in this dynamic were the existing coterie of local and state politicians and business leaders who had enjoyed a free rein in the previous decade and a half.[8]

In the first phase of the New Deal, attempts to reform agriculture and industry both tended to destabilize traditional political structures in the South. The Agricultural Adjustment Act (AAA) exerted control over agricultural commodity prices by manipulating the supply side of the equation. The government paid to take land out of production, and though the process was intended to spread the benefits between landowners and tenants, the old patterns of power meant that tenants paid the cost, as landowners pocketed the money. However, even though the AAA did little to improve the status of the South's poorest farmers, it did raise their hopes that the federal government was at least trying to look out for their interests and prompted organization and political action around issues that had long seemed impossible to change.[9]

The National Industrial Recovery Act (NIRA) had less immediate impact on African Americans, but it did provide federal sanction for the formation of unions. More important for African Americans, those implementing the act refused southern whites' demands to include a racial wage differential. The codes that industries would agree to implement in order to stabilize overcompetition had to pay white and black workers the same, although differentials based on region were permitted. The fact that racial wage differentials were defeated owed a little to historical memory of Reconstruction. Robert C. Weaver and John Preston Davis had been educated at the elite Paul Laurence Dunbar High School in Washington, D.C., one of the best educational institutions for African Americans in the country, and there they learned about Reconstruction from history teacher Nevall H. Thomas. When they began lobbying the National Recovery Administration (NRA), the administrative body that implemented the NIRA, in the summer of 1933, "it became crystal clear . . . that the precedents were in the Reconstruction period and that you had to look to the federal government [to improve the economic situation of African Americans] . . . because, of course, by this time all the states in the South had completely disfranchised blacks." The political "restlessness" the early New Deal stimulated in African Americans in South Carolina, though, ran up against barriers that were also inspired by Reconstruction. In 1934, when a group of African American citizens in Columbia attempted to register to vote in the Democratic primary, the party enforced the rule that required all Democratic voters to prove they had voted for the party consistently since 1876.[10]

The NIRA had a much greater impact on South Carolina's white workers and the state's leading industry, textiles. In a response to the problems of overproduction after the end of World War I, textile manufacturers had brought in efficiency experts and had increased workloads. By the end of the 1920s, textile workers were tending more looms and spinning frames for the same pay, a system they called the "stretch-out." Dissatisfaction had led to a wave of violent and unsuccessful strikes in 1929 and low-level disruptions in the years since. The NIRA, with its section 7(a) promising workers the right to organize unions, kindled in textile workers the hope that the federal government and the United Textile Workers of America (UTW) would help them end the stretch-out. Throughout 1934, when it became clear that textile manufacturers were evading the terms of the industry code created under the auspices of the NRA, mill hands organized more quickly than the union could keep up with. A few wildcat strikes in the late summer pushed the UTW into a showdown, and Labor Day 1934 saw the beginning of the General Textile Strike, the largest strike in U.S. history to that point. From Alabama to Virginia, mills across the South stood silent, as nearly half a million mill hands walked out, as many as 43,000 of them in South Carolina. The promise of outside support seemed hollow, as the UTW failed to devote enough resources to the strike, and mill owners and local political supporters were allowed to crush the strike. National Guardsmen herded strikers into concentration camps in Newnan, Georgia, while mill managers shot strikers down in Honea Path, South Carolina, killing six. The strike had collapsed by the end of the month, leaving hundreds permanently blacklisted. In a few locations, such as Tucapau near Spartanburg and Pelzer in Anderson County, the conflict dragged on into 1935, with still more violence in that year.[11]

The unimaginable scope of the 1934 strike provoked almost reflexive responses in South Carolina. Although it did stir up the political activism of mill hands, helping elect former mill hand Olin Johnston to the governor's office a few weeks later, the strike also led others to turn in a more familiar political direction and call out South Carolina's traditional experts at quelling the unruly masses, the Red Shirts. In Orangeburg, the town celebrated its bicentennial in March 1935 with a historical pageant. Since historical pageants tended to portray critical turning points in local history, Red Shirts and the 1876 campaign were a part of most historical pageant scripts in South Carolina in the early twentieth century. The organizers of the Orangeburg bicentennial pageant decided to invite several Red Shirt veterans to take part in the festivities. The thirty old Red Shirts were a huge hit, and the next day they decided to form a statewide organization and hold a reunion in July in conjunction with the local Confederate veterans. A reporter described the scene in slightly dismissive terms: "Men with white hair, grey beards, one with the largest mustache ever seen 'In these parts'; men hard of hearing, with failing eyesight, and tottering steps, but wearing bright red shirts, and seeming full of enthusiasm and happy in spirit." Later in the year, a competing Red Shirt organization sprung up in Greenville, staging a parade that drew as many as two hundred Red Shirt veterans. The Greenville celebration included a bevy of local political luminaries: one former governor, three former mayors, and the current mayor and police chief. Although these Red Shirt parades may have had more symbolic value than immediate political effect, they did serve to remind South Carolinians that in an earlier time the federal government had overstepped its bounds and white South Carolinians had been willing to put on the red shirt (and pick up a gun) to set things right.[12]

Roosevelt's reforms had begun to run into trouble in 1935, with both the NIRA and the AAA struck down by the Supreme Court as unconstitutional. Rather than retreat, Roosevelt instead pressed forward for further change later that year, enacting the Social Security Act, the National Labor Relations Act, and attempts to control large companies and shift the tax burden toward the rich. To carry on with these reforms, Roosevelt needed the backing of a new political coalition. The Democratic Party had long depended on the votes of white southerners and residents of the urban industrial areas of the North and Midwest. To prevail, the Democrats needed new groups of voters. Labor support for the Democratic Party increased in light of the support for workers' rights. The new Democratic coalition would also have to include the African Americans who had left the South during the Great Migration. Roosevelt's dilemma would be how to keep both African Americans and southern whites content in the same party.

In the election of 1936, South Carolina voters expressed their opinions on the New Deal, not in the presidential race, since there was no chance the state's electoral votes would go to a Republican, but in the primary race, where Senator James F. Byrnes was running for re-election. First elected to the U.S. House of Representatives in 1910, Byrnes had gotten to know Roosevelt as early as 1912, and by 1928, Byrnes was urging the New York governor to run for president in 1932. After Roosevelt's victory, Byrnes quickly became the president's leading southern supporter in the Senate as New Deal legislation was being formulated. Because of his close relationship with Roosevelt, Byrnes was able to control many political appointments in South Carolina, and he used this opportunity to bring other New Deal supporters into positions where they could build ever greater local support for Roosevelt and his policies. As New Deal relief programs began to alleviate hardship, most South Carolinians supported Roosevelt wholeheartedly, and they proved it by voting for New Dealers in the elections of fall 1934. As New Deal programs took effect, southerners across the region gave Roosevelt their enthusiastic support. When Byrnes ran for re-election in 1936, he became a local surrogate for Roosevelt and the New Deal. His principal opponent was a popular former mayor of Charleston, supported by South Carolina's senior senator, "Cotton Ed" Smith. Smith resented Byrnes's favored position as Roosevelt's liaison to the Senate and the control Byrnes held over patronage as a result of this relationship. But beyond personal animosities, Smith recognized that Byrnes was an agent of change, a southerner who enthusiastically supported what the New Deal programs were doing to the economy, society, and politics.[13]

Smith demonstrated the opposition of many white southern Democrats to the party's new appeal to black voters with a bit of political theater at the Democratic National Convention in Philadelphia. When an African American minister gave the invocation on 24 June, Smith blustered out of the convention hall, fuming to any reporter who would listen that he was "sick of the whole damn thing" and would not support "any political organization that looks upon the Negro and caters to him as a political and social equal." At a stroke, Smith hoped to make race the only issue in Byrnes's re-election bid. It would no longer be enough for Byrnes to argue that the New Deal had relieved suffering in South Carolina and laid the foundation for a sounder and more just economy; he also had to argue that these changes did not fundamentally disturb the state's racial equilibrium. Since African Americans could not vote in significant numbers in the Democratic primary anywhere in the South, Byrnes need not appeal for black votes directly. He did have to reassure white voters, however, that African American Democratic voters elsewhere in the country posed no threat to white supremacy in the South.[14]

Byrnes's friend, former congressman Asbury F. Lever, provided a strategy. Consulting various histories of the 1876 campaign, such as Alfred B. Williams's *Hampton and His Red Shirts,* W. W. Ball's *The State That Forgot,* and John S. Reynolds's *Reconstruction in South Carolina,* Lever copied excerpts for Byrnes that demonstrated that "General Hampton not only was willing to, but did actually appeal in every County in the State in his memorable campaign of 1876 and in his more formal statements of that time to the negro voter." "If we can appeal to them in South Carolina," reasoned Lever, "why should it be a sin for the Democrats in doubtful States of the North to appeal to them, when it is so important to us of the South that Democratic supremacy and the New Deal principles shall prevail in this country?" As Byrnes traveled around the state campaigning, Lever continued to send him information about prominent white politicians in each locale who encouraged African Americans to vote for Democrats in 1876. Byrnes, however, astutely realized that attempting to answer his opponent on the race issue could backfire, so in his stump speeches Byrnes refused to talk about race at all, relying instead on the accomplishments of the New Deal. "In my campaign," Byrnes said, "I shall appeal to the reason of the voters of this state and not to their prejudices." Others, however, did use Lever's argument. In a letter to the editor of the *Charleston News and Courier,* W. W. Ball's old friend Fitz Hugh McMaster pointed out that one of the delegates in the Democratic convention that nominated Hampton for governor had been African American. McMaster included in his letter Hampton's dying words: "God bless my people,—all, white and black." "A Real Democrat" from Summerville likewise wrote to the *Columbia State:* "Wade Hampton . . . who asked for Negro votes when they were necessary, should be remembered and heeded by the two opponents of Senator Byrnes." If Hampton could accept black voters, then, these New Dealers argued, his latter-day political heirs should be able to do the same, just not in South Carolina. The proponents of this argument never wavered on the principle of maintaining white supremacy in the South. Nonetheless, they challenged the rigid interpretation of Redemption that undergirded the political position of "Cotton Ed" Smith and his generation of southern politicians, the generation that had established and enforced Jim Crow.

Byrnes won the Democratic primary on 25 August 1936 with 87 percent of the vote. Playing the race card had failed because white South Carolina voters were more concerned with the immediate economic threats to their well-being than with abstract threats to their racial privilege.[15]

On the heels of his 1936 victory, Roosevelt worked to solidify the changes in American political economy initiated in his first term. A conservative Supreme Court filled with Republican appointees seemed to be his greatest obstacle, so Roosevelt launched a "court-packing plan," an attempt to amend the Constitution to create new seats on the Supreme Court and mandate retirement. Conservative senators, especially southern Democrats, feared that if this restructuring went through, there would be virtually no limits on the power of the executive branch. They defeated the plan, and the political forces that orchestrated this defeat coalesced into a strong anti-Roosevelt bloc in Congress, though popular support for Roosevelt in the South remained strong. A new recession in the fall of 1937 belied claims that the New Deal had solved America's economic problems and garnered more support for the anti-Roosevelt bloc.[16]

But the New Deal's momentum for change had not been stopped in the South, and the Congress of Industrial Organizations (CIO) made its way south in 1937 to organize the textile industry. Originating in 1935 as an alternative to the hidebound American Federation of Labor, the CIO wanted to organize all industrial workers, not just skilled workers. To do so, CIO unions welcomed members the older unions had ignored, including African Americans, and permitted Communists to be union officials. The CIO's goal of raising wages and improving working conditions for workers in America's mass-production industries meant that it had to organize textile workers in the South so that low wages there could not undercut gains elsewhere. In July 1937, the Textile Workers Organizing Committee (TWOC) began unionizing mills in the South, trying to regain the momentum lost in 1934. Organizers received a warm welcome in South Carolina from Governor Olin D. Johnston. By 1937, Johnston had proven himself a friend to white workers and the CIO, and he did so without lapsing into the racist rhetoric usually expected of South Carolina politicians. When Senator "Cotton Ed" Smith was up for re-election in 1938, Johnston entered the race with Roosevelt's blessing.[17]

Johnston ran on his record as a New Dealer and a supporter of the next phase of Roosevelt's efforts to rework the American economy. His cotton mill background and his political support for labor gave him the edge over Smith among South Carolina's many mill hands, while Smith remained popular among the state's rural voters. Johnston and other critics charged that Smith's refusal to cooperate with Roosevelt in drafting the Agricultural Adjustment Act of 1938 had hurt South Carolina cotton farmers and unfairly benefited midwestern grain farmers. Smith realized that the most effective way to turn the political debate away from economics and cotton and toward white supremacy was to conjure up white supremacy's greatest threat, Reconstruction.[18]

Throughout his Senate career, Smith had used the historical memory of Reconstruction in defense of white supremacy. In 1919, he had warned that granting the ballot to women would admit the legitimacy of the Fifteenth Amendment, breaking down one of the South's barriers to African American voting. In 1935, he had joined Senator Hugo Black of Alabama in a filibuster against the Wagner-Costigan anti-lynching bill, drawing on historical memory of Reconstruction to do so. Black compared the bill to the Fourteenth Amendment and claimed it was a "lineal descendant" of the laws described by Claude G. Bowers in *The Tragic Era.* Smith blamed the problem of lynching on the lingering influence of "the carpetbaggers, the scalawags, and camp followers who, after the surrender at Appomattox, took charge of the finest civilization America ever saw." Earlier in 1938, Smith had been part of the filibuster that defeated the Gavagan-Wagner-Van Nuys anti-lynching bill in the Senate. "The sponsors of this bill," Smith said, "are willing to draw the sectional line once again and to humiliate a whole section of our common country" so the Democratic Party can gain votes. In case his fellow senators were unfamiliar with Reconstruction, Smith gave a short history lesson explaining its relevance to the current debate: "Think of a State . . . seeing her statehouse filled with legislators who could not write their names, her people ruled by carpetbaggers and scalawags, backed up by the military forces of the Federal Government. During that time it was almost worth the life of an individual who would protest, and women were afraid to walk the streets, and certainly were afraid to be about country districts. This element, composed of those who but a few short years previously had been imported from the jungles of Africa, with human passion but with undeveloped human reason, was turned loose in a defenseless community. Naturally they expressed their predominant passion, as they thought they were supported and freed from a retribution that was so terribly visited upon some of them." Smith's speech also testified to the continuing importance of one history of Reconstruction: "I desire to get and read to the Senate a book called The Prostrate State, written by a man named Pike, in which he particularlizes the orgies of extravagance and wastefulness that went on under that régime." The debate over the anti-lynching bill gave

Smith an opportunity to connect federal legislative power, the historical memory of Reconstruction, black political empowerment, and threats to white women and lynching in one elaborate argument. The combination of ideas would prove useful later in the year.[19]

As the Senate candidates traversed the state in the traditional county-by-county stump meetings, Smith worked to turn the debate away from economics and toward white supremacy. Johnston tried to head the issue off by pointing out that the Democratic Party, with the authorization of the South Carolina legislature, had passed a rule restricting primary voting to whites, overturning the Tillman-era rule allowing African Americans who could prove they had voted for Hampton in 1876 to continue to vote in primaries. A third candidate, powerful state legislator and New Deal supporter Edgar A. Brown, likewise tried to deflect the issue of white supremacy, arguing, "The question of white supremacy in South Carolina was settled in 1876 in the days of Wade Hampton." Besides, he pointed out, "you can't eat states' rights and tariffs and you can't live off white supremacy." When Johnston attacked Smith's anti–New Deal stance, Smith responded with a weak defense of his record on economic issues and then turned to the "Negro question, the anti-lynching bill, and states' rights," warning audiences that the Gavagan-Wagner-Van Nuys bill threatened to allow "that unfortunate race [to] overwhelm us as it did in 1876."[20]

The fight between Smith and Johnston in South Carolina unfolded in the context of a larger struggle within the Democratic Party. Opponents of the New Deal such as Smith held considerable power in the Senate and worked against Roosevelt's initiatives. Republicans forged strong alliances with southern Democrats who held the chairmanships of several key committees. Roosevelt decided the success of his programs depended on getting as many of these conservative southern Democrats out of the Senate as possible in 1938. He hinted at his plan to intervene in Democratic primaries in a fireside chat in late June, but the "purge" began in earnest with a speech in Barnesville, Georgia, on 11 August 1938, when he urged voters to elect Lawrence S. Camp as their senator, not the incumbent, Walter George. George responded four days later in a speech at Waycross, Georgia, casting the issue in terms of state sovereignty and comparing the present to Reconstruction: "Are the people of this state or any other state entitled to choose their own servants? Are they entitled to do so? This is not the first time this has been fought out in Georgia. We settled it once before when honesty walked down through the shadow of bayonets held in carpetbag hands and cast an honest vote for redemption in this state." On his way back to Washington from Georgia, Roosevelt stopped in

Greenville to make a short speech that included a cryptic attack on Smith, which many interpreted as a sotto voce endorsement of Johnston. Whatever advantages Johnston may have gained from Roosevelt's blessing, it allowed Smith to further position himself as South Carolina's defender against outside political influence. Smith also excoriated the NAACP's and the CIO's endorsements of Johnston.[21]

The invocation of Reconstruction in campaign rhetoric touched a nerve for many voters. J. F. Geiger of Manning wrote to the editor of the *Columbia State,* "White supremacy in the South is one of the great realities of history. Since 1876 it has saved the civilization of the South when Thad Stevens, Ben Wade and their cohorts were doing all they could to make the South another Santo Domingo." The results of the revolution in Santo Domingo—Haiti—represented the worst political situation a white southerner could imagine: a successful republic of black citizens from which white planters had fled. At a campaign meeting in Sumter, a reporter from the *Columbia State* interviewed an old man who compared that day's political meeting with the ones he had attended as a Red Shirt in 1876. "You folks don't know a thing about politics," he said. "Not one thing. These meetings now, they're tame. I come to 'em mostly to remind me of what used to be. They're all right for stirring us old folks to remember, but you younger folks don't know a thing."[22]

When the primary election came on 30 August, Smith's tactics paid off. Johnston briefly considered using troops to prevent potential voting fraud in Charleston, but decided not to do so. It would only have made Smith's analogies to 1876 seem that much more accurate. In Orangeburg, several hundred men met two days before the primary election to reconstitute an organization of Red Shirts, led by Thomas R. Smith, one of the South Carolina delegates who had walked out of the 1936 Democratic National Convention with "Cotton Ed" Smith. They intended to "patrol every polling place in Orangeburg County." On election day, they put on their red shirts and did just that. As one Orangeburg voter remarked: "I have seen something today at the polls at Branchville that I have not seen in a great many years. The spirit of Wade Hampton was there. There were a lot of men wearing red shirts at the election polls today." Red-shirted men, and a number of women who insisted on sharing the symbol of white supremacy, rode around the rural precincts of the county and carried ballot boxes to the county seat to be tallied. Around eleven o'clock two hundred of these modern-day Red Shirts drove to Columbia for a victory celebration with "Cotton Ed" Smith. As he stood beneath the Wade Hampton monument on the statehouse grounds, clad in his own red shirt, Smith said: "Boys, the symbol you wear tonight is the symbol we hurled to the world. . . . On you rests the responsibility to protect her [South Carolina] from the mongrel breed who would take us back to the horrid days of reconstruction." "We conquered in '76," Smith boasted, "and we conquered in '38."[23]

With "Cotton Ed" Smith surrounded by triumphant Red Shirts under Wade Hampton's statue, those who wanted change might have been forgiven for losing heart. Roosevelt's purge had failed to oust a single southern senator. Southern conservatives were in a better position than ever to thwart New Deal programs that might aid both blacks and whites. There had been no progress on getting an anti-lynching bill through Congress. Nonetheless, the winter of 1939 marked a turning point in southern politics, especially where African Americans were concerned. The NAACP's legal strategy of pushing cases through to the Supreme Court to get the Fourteenth Amendment enforced had begun to bear fruit with the December decision in the *Gaines v. Missouri* case, which said that Missouri had to let an African American student attend law school at the University of Missouri. The founding of the Southern Conference for Human Welfare in November 1938 demonstrated that there were more than a thousand people across the South committed to progressive change. As historian Patricia Sullivan has argued, "The fate of New Deal reform would depend largely on what happened in the South," and the South was beginning to stir in 1939.[24]

In South Carolina, one effect of the 1938 resurgence of conservatism was that local white politicians remained intransigent, often obstructing what federal assistance was available if it might help African Americans. Earlier in the year, the Negro Council of the Greenville County Council for Community Development had lobbied to obtain a city park for blacks and to gain city approval for a federally funded housing project. Other community organizations joined in this effort as well. A Greenville branch of the NAACP was chartered in July, and the Workers Alliance, which represented employees of the Works Progress Administration (WPA) and other public works programs, lobbied for the projects. When the city government rejected both projects, the NAACP decided to help as many African Americans as possible register to vote, in order to elect a more sympathetic mayor in the municipal elections of September 1939.[25]

The president of the NAACP, who led the registration campaign, sought to restore the political power blacks had held when he was a child. Born in Greenville in 1870, James A. Briar came from a politically active family and had been involved with many efforts to improve life for African Americans. "I've always been active in politics," said Briar in 1940, "because my father before me was active in politics." His father, Tom Briar, was a blacksmith who became active in the Republican Party, serving as county chairman in 1876. After Reconstruction, Tom Briar continued his activism. In 1887 he led a short-lived biracial labor organization, and in 1889 he introduced the Colored Farmers Alliance to Greenville. James A. Briar followed his father's lead, though as Jim Crow closed in his opportunities for direct involvement in politics were not as plentiful as those his father enjoyed.[26]

James A. Briar and other activists of his generation link two important periods in African American history. Old enough to remember black political activity during Reconstruction and shaped by fathers who wielded that power, these activists spanned the period historian Rayford Logan termed the "nadir" of African American history. When changes in the political terrain made direct political activism viable again, such local leaders drew on historical memory of Reconstruction as an inspiration and a model for a new round of the freedom struggle. A sociologist in a mill town in the South Carolina Piedmont noted in the late 1940s that "many Negroes refer directly to a former period when relatives held local offices or participated in state politics underscor[ing] the current lack of identification [with local and state government]." In his study of the local leaders of the civil rights movement in Mississippi, Charles M. Payne speculated that traditions of resistance to white supremacy rooted in slavery and Reconstruction were likely to have influenced the civil rights movement in the 1950s and 1960s.[27]

In response to the voter registration drive in Greenville, the Ku Klux Klan launched a coordinated statewide terror campaign in late September 1939 as a lesson to any African Americans bold enough to register (although only a handful had voted in the election earlier in September). Greenville was the home of Fred V. Johnson, chief of staff to the Grand Dragon of the Knights of the Ku Klux Klan in South Carolina, but the first attacks occurred in outlying towns several miles from Greenville. In the small-town South, African Americans traditionally did their shopping on Saturday afternoons and stayed on the streets to socialize well into the evening. On the evening of Saturday, 23 September 1939, ten to fifteen carloads of Klansmen rode into the downtown districts of Fountain Inn and Simpsonville in southern Greenville County. Klansmen beat several black men and women, frisking them and seizing any weapons they found. The hooded, masked men also ransacked a number of black-owned businesses. Three days later, bands of Klansmen visited a National Youth Administration (NYA) camp in Lexington County, near Columbia, and posted signs saying "White supremacy must be maintained." Similar signs appeared that night in Bennettsville, more than one hundred miles away, where Klansmen marched down Main Street and burned a cross.[28]

Beatings and hooded marches were only part of the Ku Klux Klan's strategy; defending their actions to the white public was as important as terrorizing potential black voters.[29] A press release from the Grand Dragon on 2 October 1939 laid out the Ku Klux Klan's case. The Grand Dragon began by assuring the public that he was in control of the Klansmen. He had halted the attacks until he was able to investigate the situation and assure himself that they were justified. The Ku Klux Klan, he argued, was only protecting white citizens from "arrogant and domineering" blacks who were "shooting officers of the law." By stepping in to take over policing duties from the legitimate authorities and protecting whites from armed African Americans, the Ku Klux Klan of the 1930s described its actions in the same terms as had the Ku Klux Klan of the 1860s. As during Reconstruction, African Americans were allegedly flouting racial etiquette by crowding white women off sidewalks, and they were "inspired by influences at Washington and elsewhere." The Grand Dragon also defended the Ku Klux Klan attacks on the NYA camp, complaining that black youth were "living in the greatest comfort at public expense and not working at all." In this interpretation, the NYA became a modern incarnation of the Freedmen's Bureau, supporting shiftless African Americans who should be working for white men instead. The Grand Dragon argued that "almost the same influences which caused the trouble seventy years ago again are at work in our country," and that only the Ku Klux Klan could "[save] this state from negro rule and northern political domination," as it did "during Reconstruction days." In the view of the Grand Dragon, perfect continuity existed between present and past. The fundamental situation could not change, and the races would always be at odds, requiring the intervention of the Ku Klux Klan.[30]

The Ku Klux Klan's actions and their press release, with its claim to legitimacy based on one reading of Reconstruction history, prompted condemnation, much of it from other whites. These critics disapproved of both the attacks and the Ku Klux Klan's interpretation of history. Most of the white press denounced the Klan attacks outright. But in addition to opposing the Klan's violence, many whites opposed their appropriation of the legacy of Reconstruction as a cover for their actions. An editorial in the *Southern Christian Advocate* disputed the Klan's analogy between conditions in 1939 and 1869 and opposed "the terrorizing of a whole community for what may be an isolated infraction of the law." W. W. Ball, editor of the *Charleston News and Courier*, was offended by the Klan's attempt to take credit for ending Reconstruction, a slight to the memory of Wade Hampton's belief in persuasion rather than violence. In 1876, it had been "Hampton's redshirted, unmasked, daylight riders [who] captured the government." Moreover, when the original Klan operated, they had done so in the face of Republican opposition at all levels of government, a far cry from the conditions of 1939, when white Democrats were firmly in control. The *Orangeburg Times and Democrat* argued that while the Klan may have been necessary once, "barring the necessity of redeeming this State from corrupt and inefficient government at the hands of a coalition of white scalawags and ignorant Negroes, there is, and can be, no other excuse for tactics resembling those of the original and revered Ku Klux Klan."[31]

African Americans opposed the Klan and their historical memory of Reconstruction even more vociferously. Unlike white opponents of the Klan, some African Americans did see the modern Klan as a continuation of the original Klan. Soon after the first Klan attacks in Fountain Inn and Simpsonville, a Columbia minister published an open letter to Fred V. Johnson, inviting him to his church to hear a sermon on love. J. Clarence Colclough was the pastor of Sidney Park C.M.E. Church in Columbia and he had served the church for several decades. Born in Sumter County "the very year Wade Hampton became governor of this state," Colclough remembered "Kuklux" from his childhood, "especially about voting time." Like so many African Americans who lived through Reconstruction, Colclough made little distinction between the Ku Klux Klan and other organized bands of white men seeking to do harm to black folks. Colclough's father "rehearsed to us at our fireside how the [antebellum slave] 'patrols were turned into Kuklux.'"[32]

Colclough's narrative was not simply one of black victimization, though. In his version of events, the Ku Klux Klan did "a few wicked stunts until they encountered a few Negroes with guts enough to put a stop to their activities in our county and community." Colclough's entire story centered on black resistance to violence and black accomplishment in the face of violence. During Hampton's time as governor, the Colclough family acquired land, and when Tillman was governor, they acquired more land. Colclough's father told his children, "In spite of the [antebellum slave] patrols we have been freed and in spite of the Kuklux we will remain free." Colclough himself had been terrorized by night riders and claimed, "For three weeks I sat at night with my guns on my lap." A similar spirit animated many of the African Americans in Greenville who led the voter registration campaign. When the Ku Klux Klan came through James A. Briar's neighborhood in November, they did not find him, but they did find armed patrols of young black men ready to defend themselves, and Briar himself carried a gun. Nearly sixty years later, one of those young NAACP members could still point out the streets he and others had patrolled, watching for Klansmen, and the houses in which Briar had hidden.[33]

The 1939 voter registration drive in Greenville ushered in a new phase in the African American freedom struggle in South Carolina. That fall, seven NAACP chapters formed the South Carolina State Conference of Branches of the NAACP, and by the mid-1940s a vigorous organizing campaign built the NAACP into a significant force in South Carolina, with fifteen branches by 1943 and forty-nine by 1946. On a national level, the war restarted the American economy and brought new ideological pressure to bear against racism and domestic fascism. In this newly supportive atmosphere, the NAACP's legal strategy turned to the question of voting, challenging the exclusion of African Americans from Democratic primaries in the South, the only elections that mattered in a one-party system. In April 1944, the Supreme Court ruled in *Smith v. Allwright* that the Democratic primary was an essential part of the political process and therefore could not exclude African Americans. Conservative southerners who had thought their way of life invulnerable six short years earlier were now on the defensive.[34]

The *Smith v. Allwright* decision alarmed white South Carolinians. W. W. Ball saw it as the fulfillment of prophecies he had been making for several years. In a front-page editorial the day the news came out, he suggested that southern states simply abolish primaries, which were "no more necessary to white man's government than they were in 1876 when Hampton and his associates were nominated by convention." A convention, unlike a primary, could easily be controlled by the sort of political elite Ball favored. "If the reconstructed supreme court is bent on Reconstruction in South Carolina," Ball extrapolated, "let it take another step, break into the doors of white men's club rooms, lodges, private homes, lest white men and women meet in them and nominate candidates." Ball saw as clearly as did the NAACP strategists that returning the ballot to black southerners presaged a more thorough attack on Jim Crow, though Ball cast this return to Reconstruction as an inevitable and direct assault on white domestic spaces. The root of Ball's concern was not so much that some African Americans would vote, but that their enfranchisement would undermine the white unity that was the sine qua non of white supremacy. "Scalawags were common in 1870," Ball reminded readers. Since aristocrats such as Wade Hampton no longer ruled the state and kept its politics out of the hands of the common people, "the raw Scalawag material is 20 times in volume now than it was then, and any South Carolinian fancying that no white man would trade with the colored voters in primaries is ignorant of his race." Some white South Carolinians disagreed, returning to the argument that political equality need not entail social equality, which had figured in the 1936 Senate campaign. Robert S. Bailey of St. George wrote, "The negro vote was welcomed by the Democrats of '76 at which time the negroes worship in our churches. They did not then demand social equality—social admixture, and they do not demand it now." Such a view harkened back to Wade Hampton's 1877 vision of a South Carolina in which white men were securely in charge, but where the better class of African Americans would be accorded a limited measure of citizenship. This social arrangement was not the integration and equality African American activists sought, but neither was it the Jim Crow reality that the more extreme leaders of 1876, such as Martin W. Gary and Ben Tillman, had insisted upon and ultimately implemented. Instead, it acknowledged that African Americans serving in the armed forces to defend freedom at home might be entitled to return to a somewhat better situation than the one they left.[35]

The reappearance of Olin D. Johnston in South Carolina politics was an indication of how far the terrain had shifted since the demise of the New Deal. In the six years since he ran for the U.S. Senate as a New Dealer and refused to let the issue of race get in the way of his concern for the economic well-being of white mill hands, Johnston had made a dramatic about-face. When "Cotton Ed" Smith defeated Johnston by appealing to the historical memory of Reconstruction and the visceral power of racism, Johnston, like so many southern politicians before and since, vowed not to be "out-niggered" again. He returned to the governor's office in 1942.

Ten days after the *Smith v. Allwright* decision, Johnston called an extraordinary session of the state legislature to repeal all laws pertaining to the Democratic primary in order to create the legal fiction that the primary was the private function of a private club, over which the state government could exercise no authority. His opening speech suggested that he had learned from "Cotton Ed" Smith how to use the rhetoric of Reconstruction to his political advantage. "I need not remind you," Johnston reminded the legislators, "that where I now stand, on this very platform, once stood two speakers, one of the Wallace [Democratic] house, and the other of the Mackey [Republican] house. Where you now sit, there sat a majority of negroes. What kind of government did they give South Carolina when they were in power? The records will bear me out that fraud, corruption, immorality and graft existed during that regime that has never been paralleled in the history of our state. They left a stench in the nostrils of the people of South Carolina that will exist for generations to come. The representatives of these agitators, scalawags and unscrupulous politicians that called themselves white men and used the colored race to further their own course are in our midst today, and history will repeat itself unless we protect ourselves against this new crop of carpetbaggers and scalawags, who would use the colored race to further their own economic and political gains." In direct response to the 1944 Extraordinary Session, which sought to preserve the remnants of the white primary in South Carolina, a group of African Americans in Columbia founded the South Carolina Progressive Democratic Party (PDP). Led by World War I veteran and NAACP organizer Osceola McKaine and newspaperman John H. McCray, the PDP was an outgrowth of an earlier voting-rights organization, the Negro Citizens Committee of South Carolina, which was itself sponsored by the State Conference of the NAACP. After years of being marginalized by the Republican Party, and with the Democratic Party on the national level reaching out to black voters, McCray and others felt African Americans should create an alternative to the conservative, white organization representing the Democratic Party in South Carolina.[36]

At its first statewide convention in Columbia on 24 May 1944, the PDP charted two possible paths for the party. McCray worried about the distractions that cooperation and compromise necessarily bring and wanted an independent all-black party. McCray's belief that African American political power could rest only on the support of African Americans likely reflected his background, since he was raised in one of the state's few all-black towns. Minister and political leader Richard H. Cain had purchased land in 1871 along the railroad north of Charleston to sell to freedpeople. The town they created—"Lincolnville"—remained under African American political control throughout the Jim Crow era. As a young man just beginning his journalism career in Charleston, McCray had witnessed attempts to take away the charters of Lincolnville and the nearby black town of Maryville. A second attempt in 1936 succeeded in Maryville, but Lincolnville never lost its charter. The town represented one aspect of the heritage of Reconstruction for African Americans: the possibility that they could come together away from white supervision and create a public space controlled by and for African Americans. The advantage that such a space had for a town such as Lincolnville, or a party such as the PDP, is that it avoided the charge leveled by the likes of W. W. Ball that any time

African Americans had political power, they would become the dupes of white scalawags. If there were no whites involved, this could not happen, thus heading off one potential criticism. All-black enclaves also created a counterpublic where African Americans could develop their own institutions and express their own ideas and values without being intimidated or controlled by whites.[37]

McKaine, however, articulated a different path in his keynote speech. He insisted that the PDP "draws no lines of race, creed, sex or social or economic status." The PDP, he suggested, needed to cultivate poor whites as allies in a struggle he viewed as much in terms of class as in terms of race. "Underprivileged white men," McKaine argued, "have been exploited nearly as cruelly by the cynical, visible and invisible rulers of this State, as have the disfranchised and illiterate Negroes." McKaine recounted the achievements of South Carolina African Americans during Reconstruction, "to serve as a background for what we intend to do now, and in the future; to remind you that less than four score years ago, Negroes occupied places of high honor and trust in both the State and National governments." "We are here today," McKaine announced, "to help history repeat itself."[38]

McKaine's vision of a biracial, class-based coalition drew on an alternate strand of the historical memory of Reconstruction. Opposed to both the white supremacist interpretation of Reconstruction and to McCray's emphasis on the formation of black-only institutions and organizations, McKaine urged his listeners to imagine Reconstruction as a time when poor working people of both races had an opportunity to reconstruct southern society along more equitable lines as the power of plantation owners faded. To understand the use of this particular countermemory of Reconstruction, we must follow the development of a radical reinterpretation of Reconstruction that ran parallel to the political changes of the 1930s and early 1940s described in this chapter.

SIX

RADICALS' RECONSTRUCTION

When Osceola McKaine said he wanted "to help history repeat itself" in 1944, he had in mind a particular vision of the history of Reconstruction, one that had been gaining ground for the past decade and that was poised to challenge the historical memory of Reconstruction based on white supremacy. It was, quite self-consciously, a radicals' Reconstruction, a historical memory of the period that accentuated Reconstruction's most radical goals in order to further social and political change in the South and in the United States as a whole. This radicals' Reconstruction was created by the confluence of several developments. Struggles by African American historians to find a place in a segregated profession, a surge of interest in American regions, shifts in international ideologies, and the transformation of the labor movement with the growth of the Congress of Industrial Organizations (CIO) all played a part. Though not all of those whom I see as contributing to the radicals' Reconstruction agreed on their ultimate goals for the nation, I argue that there was enough similarity in the approaches they took to the history and memory of Reconstruction to justify thinking of them as part of what theorist Pierre Bourdieu called an "intellectual field," which "at a given time and place is made up of agents taking up various intellectual positions[,] . . . a network of relationships" between agents who "compete for the right to define or to co-define what shall count as intellectually established and culturally legitimate."[1]

The intellectual field of radicals' Reconstruction intersected and overlapped with several others. It was a key element in the enterprise that historian Jacquelyn Dowd Hall has called the "Southern Front," the project of those who "saw a strong labor movement, an end to lynching, and the reenfranchisement of blacks and poor whites as the key to reforming the South—and a reformed South as the key to economic recovery and, beyond that, to the creation of a social democratic society." The workers in this enterprise included left-led labor unions such as Local 22 of the Food, Tobacco, Agricultural, and Allied Workers of America–CIO, which organized tobacco workers in Winston-Salem, but also student civil rights activists in the Southern Negro Youth Congress and writers, social scientists, and activists based both inside and outside the South. In their analysis, the South was dogged by a long history of racial prejudice, but unlike generations of commentators who had argued that whites and blacks had a natural antipathy based on racial differences, members of the Southern Front saw Jim Crow as a form of "racialized capitalism," in which racial discrimination and subordination was but one tool among many for a ruling class to use to divide and dominate both black and white workers.[2]

Professional historians are part of the radicals' Reconstruction, more as necessary precursors than as active collaborators. The development of an alternative Negro history establishment in the 1910s and 1920s provided a space for systematizing countermemories of Reconstruction that had circulated in oral traditions, and it used them, along with traditional documentary sources neglected by white historians, to craft credible scholarly histories of Reconstruction without the Dunning School's crippling assumptions of racial inferiority and predetermined judgments on the period's tragic errors. Negro history also made these countermemories available to the first white historians who would begin to undermine the Dunning school from within the mainstream of the historical profession, tentatively in the 1930s and 1940s, but with greater confidence and success in the 1960s.

Two other intellectual fields overlapped with the radicals' Reconstruction and also with each other. Quite separate from the essentially bourgeois orientation of the Negro history movement, a distinctive black radical tradition, described by Cedric J. Robinson as being connected to but not reducible to Marxism, also flourished in the 1930s and 1940s. This tradition found its fullest expression in American history with W. E. B. Du Bois's *Black Reconstruction* in 1935, but we can see its ideas in other strains of activism that combined a concern with radical structural change in the nation's economy and politics and an end to racism. The Communist Party also had a complex and often fraught relationship with African Americans and white workers in the South during this period. While often doctrinaire in their understanding of the potential nature of radical change in the South, Communists and a host of fellow travelers played a critical role in forging the new radicals' Reconstruction and using it in their struggles.[3]

To change the South, various supporters of this radicals' Reconstruction had to confront the white supremacist narrative of Reconstruction head-on, and they had to replace it with something more convincing, a story of Reconstruction centered on alliances between white and black working people. To construct this new story, activists drew together elements of the countermemory of Reconstruction maintained by African Americans and analyzed that countermemory in terms of class. This new historical memory of Reconstruction became a tool in the work of dismantling Jim Crow. The radicals' Reconstruction made significant progress, especially in the years bracketing the end of World War II, and for a brief moment southerners could see the convergence of the world they were creating and the stories they were telling about Reconstruction. Progress in challenging Jim Crow legitimated the radicals' Reconstruction in much the same way that the increase of segregation had earlier validated a white supremacist narrative of Reconstruction. But with the sudden upsurge of anticommunism across America, and especially in the South, where anticommunism became an effective mode of fighting against the civil rights movement, the radicals' Reconstruction flickered out, along with the dream of the South it had tried to create.

The white supremacist narrative of Reconstruction rejected outright the two principles of Reconstruction that had been truly radical at the time and remained so in the twentieth century. The first was the rejection of racial and gender hierarchy as an ordering principle for society. The second was that property rights were not absolute and must be subservient to social welfare. Obviously, few supporters of Reconstruction, even the most ardent Radical Republicans, believed wholeheartedly in both these propositions and were willing to act upon them. As historians Heather Cox Richardson and Steven Hahn have both argued, it was not the northern, white architects of Reconstruction policy in the Radical wing of the Republican Party who carried these ideas to their furthest extension; the Radical Republicans were strong supporters of capitalism and private property. Rather, it was rural black workers in the South and their few white allies who combined the two ideas into a powerful and potentially transformative ideology. But whether they were fully accomplished at the time or not, the ideas were being debated and, in attenuated form perhaps, provided the basis for much of the reform of the late 1860s and early 1870s in the South. Conservative southerners took these ideas seriously, even if they were not fully implemented, and their opposition to these ideas grounded their opposition to Reconstruction as a whole.

Southern historian Woodrow Wilson noted in 1901, "Reconstruction is still revolutionary matter."[4]

The new narrative of Reconstruction history I describe with the phrase "radicals' Reconstruction" endorsed both these principles enthusiastically. In casting about for a historical memory of Reconstruction that celebrated, rather than denigrated, the possibility of racial equality, the creators of this radicals' Reconstruction were able to draw on the work of pioneering Negro historians who had been building their histories of Reconstruction around these propositions since the 1910s and by the early 1930s were beginning to influence the mainstream white historical profession as well. Prompted by the Communist Party's attempts to organize southern workers, the radicals could also draw on the less formalized but no less powerful and persuasive body of countermemory that circulated as oral tradition among African Americans. Always a minority position at the time, the aspects of Reconstruction that challenged laissez-faire capitalism were the least hardy in historical memory, and by the 1930s there were only a handful of locations where African Americans who had acquired land during the period could look to their own family histories to see a shadow of that proposition. The hopes that land reform could be carried out on a large scale were never realized, so to the extent that this aspiration of Reconstruction was remembered, it was seen not as a way of thoroughly restructuring or challenging capitalism itself, but as a way for individuals to enter the system as landowners. However, by the 1930s, the proposition that property rights were not absolute and must be subservient to social welfare had gained new adherents among the more left-wing supporters of the New Deal and across a surprisingly broad swath of the population—even in the hidebound South—who were inspired by the Great Depression to reconsider the tenets of the entire capitalist system that had created it and the history of that system.

In 1915, African American historian Carter G. Woodson and friends in Chicago drew upon the support of northern philanthropists and the Tuskegee Institute to create the Association for the Study of Negro Life and History (ASNLH) and the *Journal of Negro History*. Woodson's enterprise drew a long-standing tradition of African American historical writing into the new structures of the historical profession, establishing Negro history as a legitimate subfield and providing support for research and publication. At a time when African American historians could find neither employment nor audience in the white academic world, the

ASNLH became an alternative professional sphere. Whereas Du Bois had attempted to enter the white historical profession and was rebuffed, Woodson gathered together a network of academics at black colleges, ministers, teachers, and black professionals who shared his interest in Negro history and created an organization parallel to the American Historical Association, a counterpublic where Negro history could emerge from its private and local contexts of origin and find a national scholarly audience.[5]

The ASNLH had a precarious financial existence for its first several years, so Woodson turned to the deep pockets of northern philanthropists interested in education. Once Woodson secured a grant from the Carnegie Corporation in 1921, he turned to the Laura Spelman Rockefeller Memorial for more funding to hire a full-time researcher devoted to studying free blacks before the Civil War and the role of African Americans during Reconstruction. Woodson argued for the significance of the project, pointing out that "during the Reconstruction the Negro in his new status became the most important social and political topic before the country." Such a project fit well within the scope of the Laura Spelman Rockefeller Memorial, which devoted part of its resources to remedy "the absence of scientific knowledge concerning the Negro's position in American life and various social, economic, and political forces which surround himself and of which he is a part" by working with "competent Negro investigators." The officers of the Laura Spelman Rockefeller Memorial thought projects such as Woodson's could have a therapeutic effect on race relations across the country. "It is to be observed that this Association [the ASNLH] is not in any way a propagandist one," observed the director of the Laura Spelman Rockefeller Memorial. "[It is] simply endeavoring to determine facts of interest both to whites and negroes with reference to the negroes. On the basis of his facts it is easy to see that much good may result where now there is misunderstanding from a lack of authoritative information." The ASNLH made plans "to arouse interest and to arrange for conducting throughout the country a campaign for collecting facts bearing on the Negro prior to the Civil War and during the Reconstruction period."[6]

The *Journal of Negro History* included some articles about Reconstruction in its earliest years, but it was in 1920 that Reconstruction became an important topic in the journal. The January 1920 issue included over fifty pages of documentation of "Some Negro Members of Reconstruction Conventions and Legislatures and of Congress." This information came from many sources, including proceedings of the conventions and legislatures themselves, newspapers, and letters from participants and observers. Following this data was a brief memoir by "John G. Thompson, the Original Carpet-bagger." In addition to the piece on Thompson, the *Journal of Negro History* solicited from its readers additional information and corrections about its articles on Reconstruction, and prominent Reconstruction political, educational, and religious leaders contributed accounts of their experiences. Woodson introduced the documents, writing, "As future historians will seek for facts beyond those compiled by biased investigators now writing monographs in this field, a few persons realizing the importance of preserving the records in which the actual facts are set forth, are now directing the attention of the country to this neglected aspect of our history."[7]

A $25,000 grant from the Laura Spelman Rockefeller Memorial enabled the ASNLH to hire A. A. Taylor, a young African American historian, in the summer of 1922 to study Reconstruction full-time. A product of the District of Columbia's first-rate educational system, Taylor had studied at the University of Michigan and had worked for the New York Urban League and the Twelfth Street Young Men's Christian Association in Washington, D.C., before joining the faculty of West Virginia Collegiate Institute. There he had met Carter G. Woodson, and soon Taylor was contributing to the *Journal of Negro History*. In 1922, his second article was a reconsideration of the careers of black congressmen during Reconstruction. When Taylor joined the ASNLH as a researcher in 1922, he was able to combine his work and graduate study, completing his M.A. at Harvard in 1923 with a thesis on Reconstruction in South Carolina. The *Journal of Negro History* published his work in two issues in 1924, and the ASNLH's publishing house issued it in book form later that year.[8]

Taylor's history of Reconstruction in South Carolina led the way for future historians to challenge the Dunning school. Building on ideas first presented by Du Bois, but with the institutional support of the ASNLH, Taylor was able to address his work to the community of scholars devoted to Negro history that Carter G. Woodson had slowly built up over the previous decade. In his introduction, Taylor criticized the works written by historians trained at Johns Hopkins and at Columbia, arguing that they were so biased that, "except so far as they contain unconscious evidence, [they] are practically worthless in studying and teaching the history of the reconstruction period." The existing histories of Reconstruction, he argued, focused too much on politics at the expense of all else. They also relied too heavily on an uncritical use of sources created by the contemporary opponents of Reconstruction. Taylor intended to consider a broader array of evidence, and to do so without the racist assumptions that guided the Dunning school.[9]

Taylor put African Americans at the center of the story. He discussed the transition to freedom and the dilemmas the Black Code posed for freedpeople. Turning the conventional narrative of confused and helpless freedmen on its head, Taylor described the freedmen as managing to get by after the war, while "the whites, accustomed to have all their affairs managed by an aristocracy which was then ruined, seemed powerless." One of Taylor's most significant contributions was his analysis of the economic aspects of Reconstruction, especially "the gradual economic development of the State out of the chaos of the transition" to free labor. This was crucial to Taylor's overall recasting of the narrative of Reconstruction, for if the accounts of South Carolina going to complete ruin as a result of freed and enfranchised African Americans were "merely political prate," as Taylor argued, then the overthrow of Reconstruction could not be justified. In addition to economic progress, Taylor highlighted the growth of educational and religious institutions for the freedpeople. In his discussion of politics, Taylor blamed white South Carolinians who "held themselves aloof from the Negroes" for preventing what could have been a more cooperative and less adversarial relationship from forming. The Reconstruction government received credit for its accomplishments, but Taylor acknowledged that corruption was a serious problem; many of the best African American reformers worked against the corruption, however, something earlier historians had failed to note. Taylor justified the rates of taxation during Reconstruction as necessary to support the expanded social functions of a modern government, and he used extensive tables of data to compare South Carolina against other states at that time to show that its situation was not as extraordinary as usually portrayed. When it came to "The Overthrow of the Reconstructionists," Taylor described the 1876 campaign bluntly as a "coup d'état." Taylor understood that the Dunning school had its roots in contemporary partisan depictions of Reconstruction, so he devoted a chapter to showing how the Democratic government used a politically charged investigation of corruption to provide ex post facto justification for their illegal seizure of power.[10]

Taylor's study drew mixed responses. The most favorable came from Walter F. White of the NAACP. Writing in the *New York Herald Tribune,* he praised the book for its careful and unbiased scholarship. Although White admitted that the book would "probably be completely ignored by the white South and North," he hoped it might counter "the stories . . . so familiar to the followers of the Rev. Thomas Dixon and D. W. Griffith." White blamed Dunning-school histories of Reconstruction for the rise of intolerance in America, suggesting that "the whole country has in turn been influenced by the intolerance of the Southern states." Within the historical profession, Taylor's work received limited attention. In a review for the *American Historical Review,* Carl Russell Fish favored the idea of studying Reconstruction from the point of view of African Americans, but criticized Taylor for being too critical of earlier histories of Reconstruction. White southern historians were less charitable. From the University of South Carolina, Yates Snowden later summarized writing on Reconstruction in South Carolina, adding to his correspondent, "I have not mentioned H. A. Taylor's [sic] book on 'The Negro in S.C. during Rec.,' pub'd by the A.S.N.L.H. for it is hardly worth considering."[11]

The first challenge to the Dunning school from white scholars came from two young historians from the Carolinas, Francis B. Simkins and Robert H. Woody. Simkins was born into an old Edgefield family in 1897, graduating from the University of South Carolina just in time to serve in World War I. He completed his M.A. and Ph.D. in history at Columbia University. In 1926 he began teaching at Emory University, and it was here that he met a promising undergraduate, Robert H. Woody. Born in western North Carolina and raised in Kentucky, Woody had arrived at Emory in 1923. Woody was in one of Simkins's classes, and in 1926 Simkins asked Woody to join him in writing a history of Reconstruction in South Carolina. The two spent the summers of 1927 and 1928 researching the book, and Woody used the topic for both his master's thesis and dissertation at Duke University. Woody wrote the chapters on economic and political matters, and Simkins worked on the first years of Reconstruction. In summer 1930 they put the book together and submitted it to the University of North Carolina Press. The readers' reports, coming primarily from South Carolina academicians, were favorable, claiming that the book "contain[ed] much that is new, much that has been neglected and . . . replac[ed] erroneous conceptions along certain lines, with truth." Even the curmudgeonly Yates Snowden expressed his approval, notwithstanding the fact that "some of his [Simkins's] conclusions [about African Americans] would meet with the warm approval of [NAACP cofounder] Oswald Garrison Villard!" The book was published in March 1932 and won the American Historical Association's John H. Dunning Prize.[12]

South Carolina during Reconstruction was a different sort of history of Reconstruction in several important ways. The authors signaled their break with the traditions of the Dunning school early in the preface, saying they would "forego the temptation of following in the footsteps of historians who have interpreted the period as only a glamorous but tragic melodrama of political intrigue." Simkins and Woody's portrayal of African Americans during Reconstruction, while not as sympathetic as in the work of Du Bois or Taylor, was a great step forward compared to earlier histories of Reconstruction written by whites. They criticized rather than justified the Black Code. Where other authors highlighted the threat newly emancipated slaves posed to whites, Simkins and Woody argued that African Americans did not really seek social equality and thus were no threat to whites. The authors were not hesitant to give African Americans credit for significant progress in both religion and education. "The positive contributions of Reconstruction to the permanent life of the state were considerable," they pointed out. The final chapter ended by reassessing the standard interpretation of Reconstruction in South Carolina, point by point. Writers, argued Simkins and Woody, "have painted in deep colors the horrors of the political events of the period, but have given little attention to important economic and social changes. . . . The result is that the white people have come to believe that the horrors and humiliations of Reconstruction were greater than those of the Civil War."[13]

As significant as the content of *South Carolina during Reconstruction* was its methodological innovation, a story told in the footnotes. Earlier histories of Reconstruction had made little use of sources or secondary works by African Americans or northern whites allied to them, but Simkins and Woody "were simply trying to study the material and write what [they] learned." They drew on primary sources, such as memoirs by carpetbaggers, speeches by black and white Republicans, and accounts by northern missionaries, which earlier historians would never have considered worthwhile, since they came from individuals who did not share the belief in black inferiority that underlay Dunning-school histories. Simkins and Woody were familiar with the pioneering work of black historians, including George Washington Williams, Frances Rollin Whipper, Carter G. Woodson, Benjamin Brawley, A. A. Taylor, and Luther P. Jackson.[14]

In the closing pages of their book, Simkins and Woody took a final swing at the legendary campaign of 1876. The mythology of 1876 in South Carolina held that a long-suffering white population finally rose up spontaneously under the almost biblical leadership of Wade Hampton, throwing off the yoke of foreign oppression. The two young historians offered a subtly different view: the campaign had been based on a coolly measured plan, centrally coordinated and controlled, rather than on a pure people's war, as the stories had it. They made this argument simply by reproducing Martin W. Gary's "plan of the campaign of 1876," a strategy document produced early in the campaign that still is shocking in its brutality and frank dismissal of even the formalities of the democratic process. The document was "copied from the original in the possession of Mr. F. B. Gary of Columbia, South Carolina, and is given to us through the courtesy of Mr. Gary and the Hon. John Gary Evans, Spartanburg, South Carolina." Gary's plan was as detailed as any he had made for a military campaign as a Confederate general. In addition to providing instructions for county leaders, it told white Democrats to "feel honor bound to control the vote of at least one negro, by intimidation, purchase, keeping him away or as each individual may determine, how he may best accomplish it."[15]

Some reviewers recognized that *South Carolina during Reconstruction* was a different type of Reconstruction history, the beginning of a revision of the conclusions reached by the Dunning school. As Guion Griffis Johnson put it, "Unlike most students of the Reconstruction period, they have not found it totally bad." "Though written by two Southerners," commented another reviewer, "it is notably free from partisanship, from bitterness and even from that nostalgia which has so often been the refuge of Southern historians." Not only had Simkins and Woody presented an account that reevaluated the political aspects of Reconstruction, they had expanded the scope of their study to include the economic and social realms as well. Historian Howard K. Beale praised the book as "a model for rewriting Reconstruction history," yet scored it for not going further: "The book reveals an underlying philosophy of the propertied white," and "Nowhere is the possibility of social equality for cultivated Negroes seriously entertained."[16]

Southern readers mostly refused to believe that Simkins and Woody had changed the terms of debate on the history of Reconstruction. In an article announcing the publication of *South Carolina during Reconstruction,* for instance, Simkins's Edgefield friend Hortense Woodson played up the authors' connections to Edgefield, South Carolina, and the South, but played down the controversial elements of their history. Her synopsis reads much like any standard Dunning school account, though tucked away in a later paragraph is the warning that "the treatment of men and measures is calculated to arouse comment and perhaps enthusiastic approval or disapproval." Reviews in Raleigh and Richmond newspapers did more than tone down Simkins and Woody's new ideas. They assimilated this new work into the traditional white supremacist narrative of Reconstruction without missing a beat. This story was so entrenched that it would take something much more powerful than the first tentative stirrings of academic revisionism to dislodge it. Deeply held racist beliefs reinforced the white supremacist narrative of Reconstruction, and the white supremacist narrative of Reconstruction in turn validated those racist beliefs. It was almost a closed system.[17]

But white southerners could fly by the nets of the views of Reconstruction they grew up with, as an examination of the roots of Simkins and Woody's revisionism reveals. Certainly, nothing in Simkins's background suggested that he would begin to challenge the white supremacist view of Reconstruction. He recalled: "During my childhood here at Edgefield, the family history was preserved in a few relics, in the tales of the elders, and in a fat scrapbook . . . filled with Victorian fustian gathered from the reminiscences with which the fifty-odd newspapers of South Carolina were loaded during the fifty years following the fall of the Confederacy. A thousand other such families in the state possessed similar books. But such critical disillusionment never entered my mind until, as a young man, I had the experience of being contaminated by the skepticism of Columbia University." Woody explained in later years: "We were simply trying to study the material and write what we learned. . . . I don't think we were consciously looked on ourselves as revisionists, only trying to tell the full story. The fact is that I had never read much of Reconstruction in other states and I doubt if Simkins had. We were probably neither for nor against the Dunning school, just ignorant."[18]

The general intellectual tumult produced by World War I undoubtedly fed into Simkins's willingness to question the version of Reconstruction history he had grown up with and upon which the nation's leading historians agreed, but Simkins's experience at Columbia University was also critical. In the anthropology department, Franz Boas was dismantling theories of scientific racism that were the intellectual underpinning of the world of segregation in which Simkins had grown up. Historian Frank Tannenbaum was writing *The Darker Phases of the South,* indicting the region for such anachronisms as child labor and the chain gang. After Simkins left Columbia, one of his teachers from the University of South Carolina observed that he was "self assertive; has a passion for novelty, and in his desire to free himself from parochialism and 'Southern prejudices' he sometimes, especially in his studies of the negro, 'out-Herods Herod.'" The first part of Simkins's graduate career saw him torn between studying Latin American history with William R. Shepherd and studying the place he knew so well, South Carolina. In 1921 he contributed a two-part article to the *South Atlantic Quarterly* titled "Race Legislation in South Carolina since 1865" (his M.A. thesis), and then followed with a two-part article titled "The Election of 1876 in South Carolina." Simkins turned his energies toward Latin American history next, publishing "Latin-American Opinion of Pan-Americanism" in 1923. The next year Simkins published a biographical sketch of a nineteenth-century Venezuelan leader.[19]

Francis Butler Simkins (left) and Gilberto Freyre (right), taken during Simkins's visit to Freyre's home in Brazil, summer 1924. (Courtesy of Chip Simkins).

A more profound influence on Simkins was his friendship with Gilberto Freyre. This young Brazilian had come to Columbia to study history, and his M.A. thesis, "Social Life in Brazil in the Middle of the Nineteenth Century," introduced a new way of looking at the Brazilian past. Freyre's portrayal of slaves, while patronizing and inaccurate by modern standards, nonetheless did not blame them for the nation's backwardness. He also argued that since the Portuguese had been dominated by the dark-skinned Moors, they did not harbor so strong a prejudice against Africans as North Americans did. Simkins read Freyre's thesis and was "drawn . . . to Brazil, to the Brazilian past, to the mystery of Brazil." In the summer of

1924, Simkins visited Freyre in Brazil to see the country firsthand. When Simkins returned to the United States to take up a teaching position at Randolph-Macon Woman's College in fall 1924, he turned his attention away from Latin America and back to the American South, writing a dissertation on the Tillman movement in South Carolina, which he dedicated to Freyre, "a foreign friend who taught me to appreciate the past of my native state." Freyre's ideas had "revolutionized his approach to the history of his own country," and the result would be seen most clearly in Simkins's study of Reconstruction a few years later. It was southern history, but it incorporated new ideas on race emerging not only from the North, but from south of the South as well.[20]

Simkins's liberalized thinking on race led him to attempt early in his career to bring Negro history to the attention of white historians and the lay public as well. In April 1924 Simkins reviewed Carter G. Woodson's *The Negro in Our History* in the *Columbia State*. "I have long since come to the conclusion," wrote Simkins, "that we as Southerners are too ignorant of the life and achievements of our black citizens, although we often take pride in our alleged knowledge. We know little beyond the everyday achievements of the negro and almost nothing of his inner feelings." Sending Woodson a clipping of the review by way of introduction, the young historian explained, "My object has been to place before a group which knows little of the negro, the white South, a book which I regard as worthy." A few weeks later, just before leaving for Brazil to visit Freyre, Simkins had a conversation with Woodson in Washington, and he hoped he might secure a position as the ASNLH's "agent for research work in the South," a prospect he relished more than teaching. While Simkins's early relationship with Woodson did not result in such an appointment, it established a connection that would prove significant to Simkins's future work and the historiography of Reconstruction.[21]

Rather than a steady rapprochement between white historians and the ASNLH, the next major advance in shaping a black radical historiography of Reconstruction would come through stark intellectual conflict. When Claude G. Bowers published *The Tragic Era* in 1929, the white public heralded it as a masterpiece, but for African Americans, Bowers's book was a "lynching in prose," threatening to increase intolerance and racial animosity at a point when African Americans were gaining a foothold outside the South and building political power and cultural credibility. African America leaders called on their intellectual champion, W. E. B. Du Bois, to revisit his earlier scholarship on Reconstruction and challenge Bowers's misrepresentations. To write a history of Reconstruction, Du Bois sought and received a Rosenwald grant in 1931, but his work on the project began in earnest only in spring 1933 when he returned to Atlanta University as a visiting professor. Like William A. Dunning at Columbia University, Du Bois surrounded himself with a group of graduate students producing studies of particular aspects of Reconstruction that fed into his own work. Several prominent African American intellectuals assisted Du Bois in revising the manuscript in 1934, and it was published in June 1935 as *Black Reconstruction in America: An Essay toward a History of the Part Which Black Folk Played in the Attempt to Reconstruct Democracy in America, 1860–1880.*[22]

Black Reconstruction reflected an evolution in Du Bois's thought on race and history in America and was "his most direct and complicated confrontation with the meaning of historical memory." Although his earliest work had been in the mode of the social sciences, "Du Bois made a gradual but persistent turn away from the scientific empiricism in which he was trained to the poetic sensibilities that characterized so much of his writing after he left Atlanta to edit the *Crisis* in 1910." Du Bois moved toward a form of writing that would challenge the way America's story had been told by using the history of African Americans to expose the fallacies of American triumphalism. By the early 1930s, Du Bois was dissatisfied with the leadership of the NAACP and his own earlier philosophy of the "Talented Tenth," the idea that a vanguard of black intellectuals and professionals could prove to white society that they were worthy of respect and acceptance and thereby pave the way for the rest of the race. The Talented Tenth had done just that in the 1920s, and yet the improvement in race relations that strategy promised seemed as far away as ever. Like many other intellectuals at that time, Du Bois began studying Karl Marx, which helped him feel his way toward a new racial philosophy in a series of editorials in *The Crisis* in 1933. Although Du Bois found much of Marx's thought useful, he thought it needed revision to apply to African Americans. Marx had written about a racially homogenous Europe, but Marxism in the United States would have to consider race to be just as important as, and inextricable from, class.[23]

Unlike the Dunning-school histories of Reconstruction that assumed blacks' racial inferiority, Du Bois's account began with the assumption that "the Negro in America and in general is an average and ordinary human being, who under given environment develops like other human beings." Throughout *Black Reconstruction,* African Americans were the primary actors. They were indispensable to the very civilization of which whites were so proud, for the Atlantic slave trade and the cotton economy it supported were the basis of the Industrial Revolution. During the Civil War slaves helped bring down the Confederacy by staging a "General Strike" and taking up arms for the Union Army, reviving the morale of dispirited white soldiers and civilians in the North. Afterward, freedpeople sought new ways of structuring the southern economy and coming together in political conventions and meetings.[24]

Once African Americans obtained political power in the South, Du Bois claimed, they established a "dictatorship of labor." Led by African Americans, workers had seized the reins of government and tried to create a society that met their own needs, despite white planter opposition. Poor whites, Du Bois argued, initially allied themselves with white planters rather than black workers, until they found that enfranchised blacks could improve conditions for all workers, black and white. Later historians have pointed out that Du Bois's "dictatorship of labor" pushed Marxist interpretation further than the historical evidence could sustain it. Northern Radical Republicans supported the sanctity of private property and capital, and black officeholders in the South were at best lukewarm on land reform. Even though Du Bois's argument claimed more than it could ultimately prove, however, it did introduce new radical ideas about class and race into the intellectual discussion of Reconstruction.[25]

When Du Bois wrote about the Freedmen's Bureau and Reconstruction in the early 1900s, his work made no impression within the historical profession, but by the mid-1930s historians who made the freedpeople the central actors in Reconstruction were able to build upon a growing body of scholarship. *Black Reconstruction* used relatively few primary sources, partly because a black man would have had difficulty gaining access to crucial southern archives in the 1930s, but also because Du Bois was mostly concerned with producing an "aggressive reinterpretation rather than original research." Du Bois relied heavily on evidence in studies by A. A. Taylor, Francis Butler Simkins, and Robert H. Woody to support his reinterpretation. Although later historians would show that African Americans in power during Reconstruction were never as united and high-minded as Du Bois depicted them, historical scholarship on Reconstruction could not be the same after *Black Reconstruction*. The book directly influenced the work of C. Vann Woodward, Howard K. Beale, and others in the late 1930s and early 1940s, helping to shift the historiographic consensus away from the Dunning school. Du Bois's history reached outside the academy as well. A file clerk in Illinois was typical. She requested an autographed copy of the book, to "keep and to use as a symbol to my boys[?] To give them courage to fight on."[26]

Knowing that many potential readers would be inclined to dismiss his work out of hand, Du Bois concluded his historical argument about the nature of Reconstruction with a historiographic argument about the nature of the history of Reconstruction, a powerful chapter titled "The Propaganda of History." White historians had long justified their refusal to consider histories of Reconstruction written by African Americans by describing them as propaganda rather than history, but Du Bois was determined to turn the tables. The history of Reconstruction was "a field devastated by passion and belief," and Du Bois was "aghast at what American historians have done to this field." Du Bois argued that the leading historians of Reconstruction had been blinded by racial prejudice and capitalist ideology, creating a "chorus of agreement" based on biases rather than on sound historical fact. Surveying the course of Reconstruction historiography, Du Bois attacked the flaws of each work, pausing here and there to note the worthy aspects of some. The study of Reconstruction had been hindered not only by white historians' biases, but also by their refusal to consider documentary sources created by African Americans. Poor whites during Reconstruction had been ignored almost as totally as had blacks. Just as white historians had evoked emotional responses from their readers at the supposed horrors of Reconstruction, Du Bois sought to inspire indignation in his readers at the ways in which the very people who were supposed to be dedicated to the scientific discovery of the truth of history had systematically denigrated and demonized one of the episodes in history of which African Americans should be most proud.[27]

Not only had racist histories of Reconstruction given intellectual authority to the inequalities of American society, they had also contributed to an ideology that oppressed people of color around the world. The way historians had studied Reconstruction had corrupted the entire practice of history and its greater purpose: "If we are going, in the future, not simply with regard to this one question, but with regard to all social problems, to be able to use human experience for the guidance of mankind, we have got to clearly distinguish between fact and desire." The propaganda of the history of Reconstruction, the contemporary denial of "these seven mystic years between Johnson's 'swing 'round the circle' and the panic of 1873," when "a majority of thinking Americans in the North believed in the equal manhood of black folk," led directly to the exploitation and brutalization of nonwhites from Africa to India to Alabama.[28]

Du Bois's *Black Reconstruction* was the most powerful manifestation of a Marxist historiography of Reconstruction that attempted to dismantle the white supremacist historical memory of Reconstruction. This body of work focused on questions of labor and capital, thereby moving workers of both races into the center of history, and it demonstrated the viability of aggressively anti-racist historical accounts of Reconstruction. Progressive historian Charles A. Beard had emphasized the economic aspects of Reconstruction, but he paid more attention to northern industrialists than the southerners who worked for them. This Marxist historiography of Reconstruction was not simply the product of abstraction but instead arose directly from the Communist Party's new attention to the South. In 1928 the Communist International reconsidered its understanding of the dynamics of class and race in the United States. While they had formerly written off the South as too precapitalist to sustain a proletariat, much less a revolution, Communists now began to see southern blacks as an oppressed nation within the United States, deserving the opportunity for self-determination, just like colonized people anywhere else. When white textile workers went on strike in 1929, the Communist National Textile Workers Union quickly came south to help lead them, stressing the need to organize black workers as well as white. Communists hoped to use their efforts in the 1929 textile strike and the economic distress caused by the beginning of the Great Depression as a springboard from which to organize white industrial workers and rural black workers across the South.[29]

To spearhead this effort, the Communist Party sent James S. Allen, editor of the International Labor Defense's magazine, the *Labor Defender*, south to Birmingham, Alabama. With its concentration of heavy industry and mining, Birmingham had more industrial workers than other locations in the South, and they even had some sporadic experience in forming interracial unions. Moreover, the city sat in the middle of the Black Belt, the part of the South dominated by black sharecroppers working on large plantations, the main target of the Communist organizing strategy. While the Communists' organizing efforts were centered in Birmingham, Allen himself set up shop a safe distance away in Chattanooga and began publishing a weekly newspaper, the *Southern Worker*.[30]

In addition to bringing southern Communists and their allies news from the region and beyond, the *Southern Worker* had an important educational mission. Allen and other Communist activists knew that the principal obstacle to their success was what had doomed generations of progressive social movements in the South: the ability of white elites to play on the racial hostility between white and black workers. In principle, the Communist Party was devoted to complete equality of the races; a worker was a worker no matter what his or her color. In practice, this was a hard sell in the South. To succeed, Communist organizers had to convince potential members to identify themselves by class rather than by race. They treated exploitation of black southerners as the exploitation of workers, trying to show whites that the racial oppression they had grown accustomed to seeing actually worked against all workers. To this end, the Communist Party and the International Labor Defense mounted a vigorous campaign against lynching, which they linked to other forms of antiworker violence.[31]

Along with concrete actions, such as organizing biracial Unemployed Councils to demand relief and holding rallies against lynching, the Communist Party in the South tried to change the way southerners thought about their own history, as a way of changing their attitudes about race and class dynamics. In the columns of the *Southern Worker,* Allen drew on history to provide inspiration through glimpses of past revolutionary opportunities. An article on the Paris Commune argued that it had helped the later Russian Revolution succeed by "pointing out the way it was defeated and what the workers must do in order to have a successful revolution." Coming closer to home, Allen celebrated the centennial of the Nat Turner Revolt. The revolt failed, according to Allen, because it lacked a "centralized party" to organize it and because it did not have the support of poor whites. Another Communist activist in the South, Otto Hall, memorialized the slave insurrection of Denmark Vesey in the *Labor Defender.*[32]

While these history lessons furthered the Communists' work by showing why past revolutions had failed, they were not nearly so relevant to the obstacles of the 1930s as Reconstruction. Early in the organizing effort, a writer for the *Southern Worker* recognized the power of historical memory of Reconstruction and pointed to *The Birth of a Nation* as a piece of capitalist propaganda. "Its lesson comrades," wrote Harris Gilbert, "is indeed a serious one and one which every class conscious worker should understand and expose." Gilbert was not distracted by the racism (what Communists called "white chauvinism") of Griffith's film. The true villains in the film were the northern capitalists who used the carpetbaggers to trick southern blacks and break the power of southern landlords. Gilbert pointed out that the movie's recent revival across the South was designed to whip up racial prejudice in order to prevent white and black workers from organizing together. Workers should respond by joining the Communist Party and getting rid of "white chauvinism."[33]

The attempt to rethink Reconstruction from a radical point of view was not just an idea imported from New York with the Communist organizers; in fact, some of the very African American workers the Communist Party was trying to organize had long since realized the revolutionary implications of Reconstruction to some degree. A leader of the Share Croppers Union (SCU) in Alabama, Al Murphy grew up hearing about slavery and Reconstruction from his grandmother. These stories, and the inspiration of slave insurrectionists, led Murphy to describe the SCU as "a union of people who had been denied the 'Forty acres and a Mule.'" Another SCU activist, Ralph Gray, grew up hearing stories of his grandfather's bold stance for equal rights while serving in the state legislature during Reconstruction. Surveying the history of these Alabama Communists, Robin D. G. Kelley argues, "Hidden away in Southern black communities was a folk belief that the Yankees would return to wage another civil war in the South and complete the Reconstruction." An important black Communist who grew up in Omaha tied his resistance to racism and his political activism to stories he heard about how his family emigrated from Tennessee after his grandfather defended his family from Ku Klux Klan terrorism with a shotgun.[34]

Homegrown white intellectuals were also involved. Olive M. Stone, a sociologist at the Woman's College of Alabama, helped the Communist Party to organize in the South and change people's thinking about Reconstruction. Born in Dadeville, Alabama, Stone became a mainstay of the Left in Montgomery, leading a Marxist reading group, assisting the Share Croppers' Union, and traveling to the Soviet Union in the summer of 1931. Stone's own research on Reconstruction illustrates the fluid boundaries between mainstream academia and Communist activism and scholarship in the 1930s. Stone's 1929 sociology M.A. thesis on the history of welfare in Alabama revealed to her that the Freedmen's Bureau had supported more whites than blacks in the state. With her interest piqued by this discovery, Stone secured a grant from the Tennessee Valley Authority to hire two researchers to scour the Alabama State Archives for information "for use as background data in my growing interest in civil rights for the Negro farmer. The research focused on Reconstruction and provided dramatic illustrations of the newly freed slaves' hunger for education and enfranchisement." This historical work became the basis of Stone's dissertation in sociology on agrarian conflict in Alabama, completed at the University of North Carolina in 1939. Stone's historical research on Reconstruction brought her to the study of southern tenancy that Rupert B. Vance was leading in Chapel Hill, but she also used that information for more directly activist purposes by providing it to James S. Allen for use in his own writings. Stone's information helped get Allen interested in the history of Reconstruction, and he came to see that history as central to overcoming the obstacles to organizing the South.[35]

By the time Allen finished researching and writing *Reconstruction: The Battle for Democracy* in 1937, a revisionist, revolutionary American history had gotten a boost from another reorientation of Communist policy at the international level. As the threat of Fascism grew in Europe with Germany's aggressive posture and open war in Spain, the Communist International realized that self-preservation demanded cooperation with a broad coalition of anti-fascist groups, even if they did not share the same ultimate goals as the Communists. With this realization, the Popular Front period began in 1935. As party member George Charney recalled, "We were not only Communists, we were Americans again . . . [with] a new consciousness of being American, and we were readily convinced that the two were not only compatible but inseparable. . . . We became Jeffersonians, students of American history, and, as we rediscovered our revolutionary origins, we reinterpreted them in Marxist terms." It was, as Michael Denning has suggested, a "fascination with the grand narratives—the tall tales—of the American past," but unlike much of Depression-era mythologizing, this was American history with a "radical edge." In support of this project, International Publishers, the most important Communist press in the United States, initiated a new series of books in American history in 1937. The first two books in the series were *The First American Revolution* (which confidently anticipated a second one) and Allen's volume on Reconstruction.[36]

In *Reconstruction,* Allen cast Reconstruction as a bourgeois revolution that finalized the destruction of chattel slavery and led to the triumph of an industrial bourgeoisie that was ultimately hostile to the aspirations of the emerging proletariat and the freedpeople. Like Du Bois, Allen insisted on the agency of African Americans, posing them as the "independent allies" of the bourgeousie and the most revolutionary class in the South. Confiscation and redistribution of plantation lands would have "assure[d] the most complete transformation of Southern society possible within the limits of capitalism," but it was defeated, and with it the possibility for lasting democracy in the South.[37]

Deliberately writing against the grain, Allen was keenly aware of the ways in which most historians had distorted the history of Reconstruction, and he leapt to the attack unrestrained by academic detachment. When he turned his attention to the "revolutionary organizations," such as the Union League, that maneuvered for change at the grass roots, Allen began by criticizing "historians with Bourbon sympathies [who] essentially agree in their denunciation of so-called Black Domination and in their glee at the restoration of 'home rule' in the South." He twitted "those specialists who have failed to grasp the grandeur of this popular revolution and have dismissed it with some generalizations about the use of the Negro vote by corrupt politicians." In a passage echoing Du Bois's "The Propaganda of History," Allen argued that "the myth of 'Negro Domination'" was the contemporaneous construction of the Bourbon press, laying the blame at the feet of James S. Pike in a detailed critique of *The Prostrate State*.[38]

Historiography mattered to Allen, not as part of a scholarly debate, but precisely because he was writing history in action. As the editor's foreword explained, "For the most part our historians have hidden the revolutionary content of Reconstruction," rendering it useless as a lesson for current struggles. Allen insisted that "the issues of that revolutionary epoch of Reconstruction still persist—land, suffrage, civil rights—casting their shadow upon the whole country." Changing the way people understood Reconstruction was important as a way of inspiring "the working class and other progressive elements, [so] the Negro people can finish the unfinished tasks of revolutionary Reconstruction and thereby secure for themselves suffrage, civil rights and land." But it was also necessary to fit Reconstruction into a Marxist conception of the progress of history and revolution that could challenge the belief that America was an exception to those world-historical trends. If Reconstruction was, in fact, a bourgeois revolution that shattered the power of a pre-capitalist aristocracy, then it laid the groundwork for a later proletarian revolution, a revolution whose time had come by the 1930s. Southern planters might find it expedient to foster the myth that they lived in a perpetuation of the Old South minus slavery, but in fact they were the operators not of feudal, paternalistic fiefdoms, but of thoroughly modern business enterprises tied to the machinery of industrial capitalism by the tentacles of credit and marketing systems.[39]

Allen's successor as editor of the *Southern Worker* was Elizabeth Lawson, a Communist educator and writer from New York. Her experience in the South in 1931 and 1932 and her work with Allen and other Communists interested in American history were probably the motivation for her 1942 pamphlet on Thaddeus Stevens. Long the whipping boy for white southerners' rants against Reconstruction, Stevens was the quintessential carpetbagger, a fervent believer in racial equality and an advocate of wholesale confiscation of plantation lands for redistribution to freedpeople. At a time when congressmen were the most active obstacles to change in the South, Lawson's biography portrayed the potential for a member of Congress to lead the way in progressive change. As Lawson explained, "Because Stevens' tasks were so well done; because in a later day they were in part undone and must now be shouldered once more; because all that he stood for is today menaced by fascism at home and abroad—the story of Thaddeus Stevens must be told again."[40]

More than any previous event, World War II dragged the South into the modern era. Mobilization for the war picked up people from places where they had lived for decades, generations even, and moved them across the South and beyond. Soldiers traveled the world, meeting and mixing with Americans from other parts of the country and seeing life in foreign countries. Expanding military bases across the South drew in outsiders from the rest of the country at a scale far surpassing that seen during World War I. Southerners moved to cities within the region for work and to the war industries of the Midwest and West. In the war years, a fifth of the South's farm population left the countryside, most never to return, and agriculture changed as the New Deal's acreage reduction programs took hold. Manufacturing, not simply extractive industry and textiles, began to be an important part of the region's economy. The demands of the war finally gave workers the whip hand, and unionization increased proportionately. As veterans began to return, they sparked a movement for political reform. All these changes necessarily affected the way southerners thought, and they affected how they thought about their region's history. A good indication of the kinds of change occurring in southern thought even just before the war broke out was W. J. Cash's iconoclastic *The Mind of the South*. Even previously heretical ideas about Reconstruction that had enjoyed only limited circulation gained increased currency in the atmosphere of destabilization and modernization brought about by the war.[41]

While Allen's history reached the intellectual vanguard of the Southern Front, the "radicals' Reconstruction" project advanced more rapidly by means of popular fiction. Howard Fast was already a successful novelist when he published *Freedom Road* in 1944. Born in New York City in 1914 to a Jewish immigrant family, Fast grew up poor and went to work at age ten. He stayed in school, though, and began to write fiction, selling his first story at seventeen. As he was becoming a professional writer in the early 1930s, Fast grew increasingly interested in socialism and Communism. He published his first novel in 1933 and soon achieved moderate success with historical novels of the American Revolution, culminating in *Citizen Tom Paine*, published in 1943. Fast's early historical novels expressed his belief that America's future could be perfected by an appeal to the values on which the nation was founded. Fast himself noted that his stories "all deal with the struggles of men for freedom." When World War II began, Fast joined the staff of the Office of War Information, where he found himself in charge of writing propaganda for BBC medium-wave radio broadcasts. Influenced by his co-workers at the Office of War Information, Fast joined the Communist Party in 1943. Large numbers of African Americans were entering the armed forces, and Fast's staff researched and broadcast stories to smooth this process. The first reports of the enormity of the Nazis' persecution of Jews made intolerance a pressing concern as well. Fast's predilection for utopian visions of the past, his immediate professional concerns with biracial cooperation, and the influence of Marxist intellectuals led him to turn to Reconstruction as a topic for fiction, and he researched and wrote *Freedom Road* in late 1943 and early 1944.[42]

Like Du Bois's *Black Reconstruction,* Fast's *Freedom Road* focused on the experience of the freedpeople. Gideon Jackson, the main character, had been a slave on the Carwell Plantation in South Carolina. During the Civil War, he had escaped and joined the Union Army. The story begins in 1867 when Jackson is elected a delegate to the Constitutional Convention and learns to read as he helps frame the new constitution. Later, he is elected to the U.S. Congress. Land ownership as the basis for a transformed southern society is as important in the novel as reading and voting. Back at Carwell, Jackson helps convince freedpeople and poor whites to cooperate and buy the old plantation. They establish a cooperative farm there, despite the opposition of white planters. Ultimately, however, the planters use the Ku Klux Klan to terrorize the biracial settlement at Carwell. In a climactic scene, Jackson and his followers at Carwell, abandoned by the Grant administration, die when the Ku Klux Klan besieges their houses.

When Fast wrote about Carwell, he was describing something much more a part of the twentieth century than anything that had existed during Reconstruction. A few cooperative farming ventures had sprouted during Reconstruction, including one on Edisto Island in South Carolina, but they had mostly died prosaic deaths before Reconstruction ended, at the hands of taxes and foreclosures, not heavily armed Klansmen. Fast's vision of the capitalist's plantation appropriated and run by the workers and for the workers bears a resemblance to a handful of experiments in cooperative agriculture in the South. Socialists created Rochdale Farm in Bolivar County, Mississippi, and later Providence Farm in nearby Holmes County in the 1930s as havens for tenant farmers, black and white, broken by the Depression but hopeful for the future. In 1942, Baptist minister Clarence Jordan founded Koinonia Farm, an interracial Christian community in southwest Georgia.[43]

African American characters in *Freedom Road* fight, participate in politics, and cooperate in everyday life with poor whites in the South. This was the exact prescription for change progressives were calling for during World War II. Gideon Jackson had come to Charleston "with the blue uniform and gun in my hand and ten thousand along side of me, singing a hallelujah song." African American soldiers in World War II were proving their abilities as well, and earning the right to demand the same democracy at home that they fought for abroad. World War II saw African Americans push for voting rights in local struggles such as the 1939 registration campaign in Greenville and in the NAACP's legal fight against the white primary. *Freedom Road* depicted the freedmen's tentative forays into political life and their earnest work to make themselves into educated and responsible citizens. The freedmen in the novel's opening scenes were baffled and naive about the most basic details of political activity, yet soon Jackson was speaking in the Constitutional Convention in favor of education and women's suffrage and "absolute equality of black and white at the polls—a forceful prevention of discrimination."[44]

Most far-reaching of the changes Fast envisioned was a South where African Americans and poor whites could bury their old antagonism and unite along class lines. In the novel, Jackson meets a poor white delegate, Clay, and the two begin a cautious friendship. "What do you do when a new world comes?" asks Clay. "You make a piece of it, or you smash it." In an afterword, Fast claimed, "There was not one Carwell in the south at that period, but a thousand, both larger and smaller." Taken as history, this statement is fanciful, an absurd overestimate of the record of biracial cooperation during Reconstruction. The claim has credence, however, as a utopian claim about what Fast thought was possible in the South being reconstructed by the end of World War II at places such as Providence and Koinonia. The kinds of conversations Fast described between Jackson and poor whites, as each slowly overcome old prejudices in order to work together, showed how such relationships could be forged in the 1940s. In the nineteenth century, abolitionists used the biblical Exodus as an allegory for how slaves in the South might find freedom. *Freedom Road* also worked as allegory, setting its story in Reconstruction but concerned less with accurately reflecting the events of Reconstruction and more with using an idealized version of Reconstruction as a path to a better future.[45]

Freedom Road was fiction with a purpose. Fast explained his aim in the afterword. His story was essentially true, he claimed, and after listing some of his sources (including Simkins and Woody's *South Carolina during Reconstruction*), he explained why the story he told had not been told before:

"When the eight-year period of Negro and white freedom and cooperation in the south was destroyed, it was destroyed completely. Not only
were material things wiped out and people slain, but the very memory was
expunged. Powerful forces did not hold it to be a good thing for the American people to know that once there had been such an experiment—and
that the experiment had worked. That the Negro had been given the right
to exist in this nation as a free man, a man who stood on equal ground
with his neighbor, that he had been given the right to work out his own
destiny in conjunction with the southern poor whites, and that in an eight-
year period of working out that destiny he had created a fine, a just, and
a truly democratic civilization." In an article a few months after *Freedom
Road* was published, Fast emphasized the novel's timeliness: "Today, the
Negro is beginning to take his place on the political stage, both as an organized mass from below and a participant in government from above. And
today, more than ever before . . . an organized attempt is being made to
maintain the lie of Reconstruction, the lie which states that during the one
time Negroes were given almost full political rights, they failed, tragically
and completely. Instead of being able to lean on the history of those eight
years, to learn through a study of them, he is forced to engage in a struggle
for the historical truth." According to Fast, what had been hidden by the
white supremacist narrative of Reconstruction was the very example African Americans and whites in the South needed to follow now.[46]

Freedom Road was well timed, and it became Fast's most commercially
and critically successful novel. Plans were made to turn the novel into a
film starring Paul Robeson, but as anticommunism hit Hollywood, this
prospect faded. The national media generally liked *Freedom Road*, fre-
quently acknowledging its political dimensions and mentioning that it
was, for instance, "a useful democratic tract for the times and [for] anyone
who desires racial equality." One critic compared Fast's novel to another famous allegory, John Bunyan's *Pilgrim's Progress*. Reviewers criticized Fast's
characters as oversimplified ("Fast's protagonist is occasionally shadowy,
more a lyric symbol than a realized characterization"). One critic considered this a substantial fault: "It is pious because it assumes that people
are good in proportion as they are oppressed, and it is condescending because, by denying oppressed people human fallibility, it in effect makes
them rather less than human."[47]

Southern reviewers dismissed *Freedom Road* as just one more piece of
Yankee propaganda. A Louisville reviewer called on "competent historians" to refute Fast's tale and noted with alarm "that the words 'carpetbagger' and 'scalawag' . . . appear nowhere in the book." The *Columbia State*

concluded it was "an end product of a typical New York ideology," and the *Raleigh News and Observer* suggested that "this book will find a warm spot in the hearts of members of the NAACP, but it may not set so well with true Southerners." What is striking in these reviews is how they abandon the South's long and largely successful mission of convincing the rest of the nation to accept its white supremacist version of Reconstruction history. An earlier generation of white southerners had insisted that there was a single correct view of Reconstruction—the white southern view— and that the rest of the nation should acknowledge the truth of that view. Responses to Fast's novel lack the vehement confidence of that earlier generation. When the *Columbia State* review describes Fast's novel as a "one-sided story," it implies there is another side. The *Raleigh News and Observer* review ends with the indifferent comment, "Who are we to object to his obviously Northern conception?" Both assessments admit the existence of a "Northern" historical memory of Reconstruction at odds with the views of "true Southerners," and they refuse to fight over the issue.[48]

Some southern reviewers worried that Fast's propaganda might have its intended effect. Writing in the *Sewanee Review,* the conservative mouthpiece of the Agrarians-cum-New Critics, Brainard Cheney classed *Freedom Road* with other "propaganda novels about the South." Cheney traced the current crop of novels to the proletarian literature of the early 1930s, works that used "astounding distortion of the past under the implicit belief that the contemporary end justifies any historical means." Fast and other propagandists, Cheney worried, were trying to "propagate . . . the non-existence of race." A few months later, Louis B. Wright pondered these questions further. As southern whites created fiction that challenged white supremacy, Wright was concerned that people outside the South accepted that fiction about the South at face value—the very process that had helped an earlier generation of fiction spread the white supremacist narrative of Reconstruction to the entire nation. This new view of Reconstruction, though, could cause the country real problems. "The heritage of hate left by Reconstruction must not be unearthed again," Wright argued. Of course, the heritage of white hate of blacks had never been buried, living in the continual glorification of the Ku Klux Klan, the Red Shirts, and other white Reconstruction terrorists. What Wright and others feared was the unearthing of black hatred of whites in response to Reconstruction-era atrocities, a hatred buried out of view of whites for decades, but possibly, they worried, still smoldering. Such rage could manifest itself in forms such as the Detroit Riot of 1943 or instances of "armed self-reliance" as black veterans returned to fight Jim Crow in the South.[49]

The unease conservatives such as the writers in the *Sewanee Review* felt was well founded, for the South was poised on the edge of change as it had not been since the heyday of Reconstruction or Populism. War had strengthened the hand of the labor movement nationwide, and at the forefront was the CIO. Left-led interracial unions organizing whites and blacks, such as the Food, Tobacco, Agricultural, and Allied Workers, had established beachheads in southern industrial centers such as Winston-Salem, and the CIO was preparing a major organizing drive in the South. Throughout the region, African Americans were taking advantage of the Supreme Court's *Smith v. Allwright* decision striking down the white primary to become involved in politics. Returning veterans of both races challenged local power brokers. Decades later, a CIO organizer suggested the scope of change that seemed possible: "If the unions could continue to increase their numbers, if they could forge a stronger unity between blacks and whites, between men and women, among all religious and nationality groups, they could be crucial in moving America down the road that we envisioned: the fulfillment of the social programs of the New Deal, an end to colonialism, and a beginning of free independent nations worldwide. Moreover, if the workers in the South could build this kind of unity in their unions and in their community struggles, they would be able to free themselves from the poverty and the deprivations forced upon them by the Southern elites." One of the barriers to such unity had always been the ability of white southern elites to play the race card, to divide black and white workers by appealing to whites' racism and blacks' fears of that racism and well-founded mistrust of white workers. Defusing that tactic would require, among other things, countering the dominant views of history that supported racial divisions, especially the dominant historical memory of Reconstruction.[50]

The desire to change historical memory as part of a broader effort to effect change in the South animated the Southern Negro Youth Congress (SNYC), which reached its apogee in 1946 with a major convention in Columbia. Founded in 1937, the SNYC grew out of the National Negro Congress and was one of many organizations across the country that mobilized youth for social change. The new organization started out in Richmond and in its first year led a campaign to organize Virginia tobacco workers. Over the next several years, the SNYC worked with other groups on most of the issues facing African Americans in the South: lynching, the poll tax, voter registration, and discrimination.[51]

Reinforcing a radical memory of Reconstruction was one of the SNYC's strategies for fostering social progress. The SNYC's parent organization, the National Negro Congress, had used a radical memory of Reconstruction as one of its tools in attempts to change the culture in which it operated and to promote equality. As early as 1938, the SNYC sponsored a series of lectures in Richmond based on the belief that "the American Negro must remake his past in order to make his future." Roscoe Lewis, a professor at Hampton Institute and state director of the African American section of the Federal Writers Project, spoke on "The Negro and Reconstruction in Virginia." At the SNYC's fourth conference, in 1940, James S. Allen's book on Reconstruction was part of a reading list for delegates, and SNYC leader Esther Cooper Jackson included it on the reading list for a 1945 seminar titled "The Heritage of Reconstruction: Its Effect on Southern Progress," sponsored by the Alabama People's Educational Association. A cultural affiliate of the SNYC, the Association of Young Writers and Artists, sponsored a contest in fall 1944 for artistic responses to Howard Fast's novel *Freedom Road*. The SNYC's last major conference linked its vision of change in the South to the inspiration of Reconstruction. The Southern Youth Legislature held in Columbia in October 1946 drew a thousand delegates who drafted model legislation and discussed strategies for changing the South. On the walls of the main meeting hall hung photographs of African Americans who had served in Congress during Reconstruction. One of the SNYC officers said, "In the rear of this hall we see pictures of those brave men who before us charted a democratic Southland. Let us carry their work before us always—for a historic conference, for the full voting rights of the Southern people, for a peaceful, secure world, for unity of the youth of the world." Howard Fast spoke at the Saturday evening program, and the conference organizers claimed, "We think the shade of Gideon Jackson, the hero of this novel [*Freedom Road*] who became a Congressman during the Reconstruction period, will be sitting among the delegates at Township Auditorium." On the program along with Fast were some of the leading cultural and intellectual figures of the American Left: Paul Robeson, Herbert Aptheker, and Max Yergan. The Southern Youth Legislature's invocation of Reconstruction had a lasting effect on some participants. Jack O'Dell, later an important figure in the Southern Christian Leadership Conference, recalled, "That convention had around the walls the pictures of all the blacks who had been elected during Reconstruction. I had never seen that in my life before. I had three years of college, twelve years of high school and three years of college and I did not know that there had been black congressmen and Superintendents Of Education and mayors of cities during Reconstruction in the south. But they had the pictures of it and that . . . that fascinated me."[52]

The keynote speech of the conference came on its last day, when W. E. B. Du Bois spoke to an overflow crowd at the chapel at Benedict College, Columbia's African American Baptist college. Du Bois insisted that "the future of American Negroes is in the South" and urged young African Americans to "grit your teeth and make up your minds to fight it out right here if it takes every day of your lives and the lives of your children's children." Influenced by the interracial tenor of the moment, Du Bois suggested that African American youth must reach out to the white working class as their natural allies. Like other progressives, Du Bois viewed the current domestic struggle in global terms. The South was "the gateway to the colored millions of the West Indies, Central and South America." Du Bois emphasized the unique moment of opportunity for change and encouraged his audience to be optimistic, determined, and militant.[53]

Not long after the Southern Youth Legislature ended, it became apparent that the United States was moving to the right. In the congressional elections of 1946, Republicans and conservative Democrats took control of both houses. They pushed for a harder line on the Soviet Union, and in the wake of the largest wave of strikes in American history, they passed the Taft-Hartley Act over Harry Truman's veto. This nullification of labor's legal gains cleared the way for state right-to-work laws, pushed Communists out of union leadership positions, and allowed the president broad new latitude to intervene in labor disputes. Truman himself began backing away from the progressive positions he had taken when he assumed the office. He announced the Truman Doctrine on 12 March 1947, warning the Soviets that America would oppose Communism anywhere in the world. To fight Communism at home, he implemented a loyalty program designed to weed Communists out of the federal government. The Communist Party's internal confusion at the end of the war further weakened the Left, as William Z. Foster took over the chairmanship from Earl Browder and the party demanded tighter discipline and emphasized the needs of the Soviet Union at the expense of the more expansive Popular Front approach of the war years.[54]

Progressives felt increasingly out of place in the Democratic Party and worried about the direction in which it was leading the nation and the world. Liberal organizations worried about the toll anticommunism might take on any group tainted by Communism and began to purge their ranks of anyone who might be considered a Communist. One of the most outspoken of the progressives was Secretary of Commerce Henry A. Wallace, who had been vice president under Roosevelt. As he and like-minded supporters grew more concerned about America's rush toward a possible atomic war and the home-front attacks on labor, they combined to form the Progressive Citizens of America in late 1946. Wallace announced his candidacy for president on the Progressive Party ticket in December 1947.[55]

The one area in which the federal government was taking progressive action was civil rights. As the Cold War began, the South's continuing denial of civil rights for African Americans was a source of embarrassment for the United States and an important element of Soviet propaganda. The immediate aftermath of World War II gave critics of the United States plenty of targets. White southerners had attacked black veterans returning home, in the worst outbreak of racial violence since the bloody summer of 1919. Several people were lynched, including two couples shot at Moore's Ford, Georgia. A black veteran riding a bus was blinded by a South Carolina policeman, and in February 1947 another veteran was lynched in Greenville, South Carolina. The state's governor, Strom Thurmond, supported the investigation into the lynching and tried to secure a conviction. The jury took less than five hours to acquit the thirty-one white men charged with the crime. Truman had already formed the President's Committee on Civil Rights the previous December, but after the verdict regarding the lynching of Willie Earle, he took an unprecedented step by speaking to the NAACP annual conference and putting the federal government squarely behind civil rights. The committee's report, *To Secure These Rights,* came out on 29 October 1947, and Truman made a major speech in February 1948 endorsing its recommendations and promising to implement them.[56]

The federal government's newfound commitment to civil rights was too much for many southern Democrats. On 20 January 1948, in his inaugural speech upon being sworn in as governor of Mississippi, Fielding Wright threatened to bolt the party. Democrats in other southern states haltingly broke from the national party, hoping to throw the fall presidential election into the House of Representatives, where they could demand that the civil rights plank be weakened as the price of their support for Truman. A group calling itself the States Rights Democrats convened in Jackson, Mississippi, on 10 May 1948 to lay out their positions. Mississippi governor Fielding Wright and South Carolina governor Strom Thurmond both compared the federal government's commitment to civil rights to the days of Reconstruction. Within a few more weeks, states' rights supporters realized that they would not be able to win concessions on the civil rights plank from within the national Democratic Party, and many bolted to offer their own party with its own slate of candidates. The presidential election of 1948 was a four-way fight, with Thomas Dewey for the Republicans, Harry S. Truman for the Democrats, Strom Thurmond for the Dixiecrats (as the States' Rights Democrats became known), and Henry A. Wallace for the Progressives.[57]

The white South's reaction to Wallace's tour through the South in late August 1948 would have looked familiar to anyone old enough to remember South Carolina's 1876 campaign. In town after town, Dixiecrats and other opponents of the Progressive Party heckled Wallace and drowned out his speeches. They mobbed his car, beating it with sticks and baseball bats. Protestors threw tomatoes and rotten eggs. With the progressive organizations and CIO unions in the South falling apart, Wallace could not raise enough support to mount a credible campaign, and the chaotic campaign tour was but a visible manifestation of structural weaknesses in his cause in the South.[58]

The Dixiecrats, meanwhile, used the parallel to 1876 in their campaigns. Thurmond drew on his Edgefield roots to cast himself as a modern-day Red Shirt ready to defend the South against a repeat of Reconstruction. He found support from the South Carolina Division of the United Daughters of the Confederacy. Since 1944, the UDC had been working to restore the Edgefield mansion Oakley Park, former home of Martin W. Gary, the architect of the 1876 Red Shirt campaign. The November 1947 national convention of the UDC made this project a priority, hoping to raise enough money from the membership to turn the decrepit old building into a "Red Shirt Shrine." Thurmond took time out of his honeymoon to stop by and speak to the convention, and he and his new bride visited Oakley Park in early 1948. As the UDC campaign to restore Oakley Park continued and the presidential campaign heated up, Mrs. J. R. Carson reminded readers of the *United Daughters of the Confederacy Magazine* of the importance of Oakley Park and the Red Shirts by recounting the story of Reconstruction and the 1876 campaign, with a particular emphasis on Gary's role. Linking this story to contemporary concerns, she closed by observing: "This restoration . . . will also serve to point out the fact that there are still governmental rights which belong to the individual States of a Federal Union, and that there is a certain sphere of authority in which these individual States may act without interference from the Central Government." Elsewhere in South Carolina, the Abbeville County Woman's Division of the South Carolina Democratic Party held a "States' Rights tea," with refreshments and stories from elderly members with first-hand recollections of Reconstruction. When election day came, Thurmond went to cast his vote in Edgefield, probably already realizing that his attempt to throw the election into the House of Representatives was going to fail. As he walked up the courthouse steps to the polling place, with his young bride on his arm, he wore a "bright red tie reminiscent of the Red Shirt organization that helped drive out the carpetbaggers in capturing the state government for the white Democrats in 1876"—a more hesitant invocation of the Red Shirt heritage than "Cotton" Ed Smith's confident speeches ten years before.[59]

The 1948 election has been encapsulated in an image of a jubilant Truman holding up a newspaper that announced "Dewey Beats Truman," a classic American triumph of the underdog. Although Truman did manage a very skillful win in difficult political circumstances, the real underdogs of America lost. The threat of Soviet expansion into Europe hardened American foreign policy and initiated a standoff that would last the rest of the century. That threat also proved a potent weapon for conservatives. In the South, where the potential for change had been tenuous in the first place and dependent on an unusual congruence of circumstances and the energy and optimism of many, anticommunism became a way of stifling dissent and substantive change and drawing the boundaries around what sort of civil rights reforms would be within the realm of the possible.

The extent to which anticommunism short-circuited a radical revisioning of Reconstruction is documented in a book that isn't. What might have been one of the great southern novels of Reconstruction sits on no library shelves and earned neither critical praise nor fame for its author. Never published, Katharine Du Pre Lumpkin's novel *Eli Hill* occupies two folders in a cardboard carton in the Southern Historical Collection at the University of North Carolina at Chapel Hill. In its typescript pages lie a story untellable, or at least unhearable, and Lumpkin's correspondence tells of how that novel came not to be and the fate of the radical vision of Reconstruction that seemed to hold such promise in the 1940s.[60]

When she began writing *Eli Hill,* Lumpkin was already a renowned writer. Growing up in South Carolina, she inherited the Lost Cause ideology that suffused her father's life and their household. Interracial work with the YWCA in the 1910s and 1920s and graduate study in sociology slowly broke down her old ideas about the South and about race. Lumpkin detailed her family's history in *The Making of a Southerner,* including her father's activities as a member of the Ku Klux Klan. History, according to Lumpkin, was a powerful and seductive force, but not immutable. Individuals were shaped by the history they were taught, but they could learn better, and so could their society.[61]

Lumpkin discovered the story of Elias Hill in the *KKK Hearings* as she researched *The Making of a Southerner* and was fascinated by it, spinning fiction over the facts she found to create a complete narrative. Lumpkin's fictional character was born a slave in York County, South Carolina. Paralyzed from a young age, Hill was unable to work, and he was made free and literate by the Civil War. As Reconstruction progressed, he was initially reluctant to get involved with politics, preferring to stay aloof in his role as a minister. But his religious activities led him to teaching, and teaching led him to politics. Hill supported the militia, drawing the wrath of the Ku Klux Klan. He considered emigrating to Liberia, but testified before the congressional investigating committee instead. In the end, Klansmen assassinated Hill, and with him died a vision for a South where African Americans could extend their rights. Howard Fast ended *Freedom Road* with the apocalyptic destruction of Carwell, to emphasize that it was neither black incapacity nor the impossibility of biracial cooperation among the working class that had doomed the utopian Reconstruction experiment, but rather the powerful violence orchestrated by the rich. Lumpkin's novel, however, held out hope. The preacher at Eli's funeral compared him to Moses, who never saw the promised land with his people, suggesting that Eli's people might eventually triumph.[62]

Unlike white supremacist novels of Reconstruction and unlike *Freedom Road,* Lumpkin's *Eli Hill* was a fully realized tragedy rather than mere melodrama. Although earlier novelists had been content to build good characters and evil characters and then watch them crash into one another, Lumpkin wrote of "the human heart in conflict with itself." At a turning point in the story, Eli refused to use his literacy to help his neighbors read and understand the Black Code. In this case, the conflict between Eli and his community was rooted in a conflict in himself. He wanted to be a part of the community, but he also wanted to avoid anything that would bring dangerous attention from whites. Even the conflict between African Americans and whites was more subtly conceived than in earlier novels about Reconstruction. "The difficulty is," Lumpkin explained, "that both sides held a most passionate conviction that what they sought and did was right." When Eli Hill finally succeeded in transforming himself into a leader of his people, he found that forces beyond his control prevented him from transforming his society. By the time Lumpkin finished with the novel, she, too, had come to realize that the process of personal transformation leading to societal change she described in *The Making of a Southerner* was unlikely to take root in the South in the immediate future.[63]

Lumpkin completed *Eli Hill* as the Cold War was beginning, unfortunate timing that ultimately doomed the novel's chances for publication. She offered it to Alfred A. Knopf in May 1949, but it was refused. Later that year, Houghton Mifflin awarded Lumpkin a literary fellowship to work on the novel, and she began to negotiate with editor Craig Wylie over revisions to the manuscript. Aside from the usual concerns with the craft of fiction, Wylie's persistent criticism of *Eli Hill* was its characterization of the conflicts during Reconstruction. Wylie conceived of the theme of the novel as "the difficulties which a moderate position involved during the Reconstruction Period," illustrated by the conflict between Eli and John Temple, a white judge who tried to restrain the Ku Klux Klan and also tried to convince Eli and other African Americans to stay out of politics. As the Cold War and the accelerating civil rights movement polarized the world and the country, Wylie saw a potentially valuable lesson in this story of Reconstruction. "One of the greatest problems of our own day," he suggested to Lumpkin, "is just that of the intelligent moderate man trying to maintain his position."[64]

Lumpkin could not agree. She conceived of her novel as the "obverse" of *The Making of a Southerner,* an attempt to explain "the struggle of men against the bondage of White Supremacy" from an African American point of view. Although he was killed, Eli succeeded in this struggle precisely because he refused to allow white supremacy to circumscribe his aspirations and actions. Lumpkin's story was "not a parallel struggle of two men, Eli Hill and John Temple, both men of good will who seek, so to speak, the same general end, a course of moderation in turbulent times," but "one of fundamental conflict of aim between the two men and their two peoples." White supremacy was an absolute position that at its most benign might have "modified its rigors slightly for the occasional individual." "A middle ground solution," argued Lumpkin, "would have meant that the white side gave up its aim of 'White Supremacy,' while the Negro side became content with a slow and gradual realization of full equality."[65]

For almost two decades, intellectuals and activists on the left tried to use a radical vision of Reconstruction as a model and inspiration for the changes they tried to bring to the present. Casting aside the racist assumptions that had allowed the nation to reconcile the divisions of the Civil War and Reconstruction at the expense of the rights of African Americans, these writers reclaimed the emancipatory possibility of Reconstruction. CIO organizers hoped they could form biracial alliances of workers of the sort they imagined had been possible during Reconstruction. Southern progressives hoped that by carrying through on some of the projects and promises of Reconstruction they could renew democracy in the South and the nation. So much had seemed possible when the Southern Negro Youth Legislature met beneath the pictures of Reconstruction legislators in October 1946, but by the time Lumpkin began writing *Eli Hill* in November 1948 the dream of refashioning the United States on the basis of workers' rights and racial equality was beginning to retreat before the forces of Cold War anticommunism and white southern reaction to the federal government's commitment to civil rights for African Americans. Henry A. Wallace's presidential campaign for the Progressive Party had collapsed, CIO unions purged Communists from their leadership under the pressure of the Taft-Hartley Act, and the House Un-American Activities Committee began a more active phase with high-profile investigations of Communists in Hollywood. The infrastructure that had supported a radical revisioning of Reconstruction was falling apart, and the proponents of this historical memory were being discredited and pushed to the margins of public life.

SEVEN

THE STRANGE CAREER OF THE
SECOND RECONSTRUCTION

The Cold War put an end to the "radicals' Reconstruction," the attempt to use a biracial, class-based understanding of Reconstruction as a historical model for reshaping the South, but it did provide the engine behind a different sort of civil rights movement. In the context of the struggle against Soviet totalitarianism, Reconstruction was refigured as an era when America's basic premises of freedom were half-heartedly tried in the South, only to be crushed by the power of racism and the cynical abandonment of idealism. Redeeming the promises of equality embedded in the Reconstruction amendments became an important way of understanding the emerging civil rights movement as a "Second Reconstruction." As the civil rights movement gained momentum after the 1954 *Brown v. Board of Education* decision, it eventually restructured social reality across the South to the point that the white supremacist narrative of Reconstruction no longer worked; it lacked basic explanatory power to account for the world around it. A new generation of revisionist historians played an important role in bringing this idea of a "second Reconstruction" out of the libraries and into the streets, leaving the Red Shirts relegated largely to the realm of museums and nostalgia.[1]

For the first few decades of the twentieth century, popular writers and the most highly esteemed academics had constituted a mutual admiration society when it came to writing the history of Reconstruction. Though their methods may have diverged as the historical profession matured, their messages were in harmony: Reconstruction had been a vindictive mistake that served only to prove the racial incapacity of African Americans to participate in democracy. By the 1940s, however, the drift of the professionals' approach to Reconstruction was moving away from the white supremacist narrative. This is not to say that most members of the public dutifully took note of what the cutting edge of historical scholarship had to say and modified their historical memories accordingly. Rather, the evidence suggests that popular thinking among southern whites remained rooted in the white supremacist narrative of Reconstruction. This was not, as Pierre Nora has described in France, a case of history simply replacing memory as a means of relating to the past, but rather a case of history attacking memory and, as liberal historians of the South set their scholarship to work undermining segregation, attacking the world that memory had made.[2]

The 1930s saw the publication of the most significant book for the shaping of social memory of Reconstruction in South Carolina since James S. Pike's *The Prostrate State*. A newspaper editor named Alfred B. Williams had begun his career with the plum assignment of following Wade Hampton's campaign as it canvassed South Carolina in 1876. Fifty years later, as the state celebrated a half century of white supremacy, Williams dug into his memory and the newspaper files to re-create the campaign for modern readers. In thirty-two weekly installments published in the *Columbia State,* Williams told the story of the 1876 campaign, of bold men in red shirts, of Hampton's indomitable spirit, in a breathless, "you were there" style. The public loved it. Readers wrote in with their own memories to amplify Williams's account. After Williams died in 1930, friends and admirers redoubled their efforts to get his writings collected and published in book form. The result, in 1935, was *Hampton and His Red Shirts: South Carolina's Deliverance in 1876,* praised by both the general public and an older generation of professional historians. E. Merton Coulter of the University of Georgia, reviewing Williams's book for the *Mississippi Valley Historical Review,* explained that the rifle clubs "beat down the opposition—but always just within the law." ("A few bloody riots were precipitated," he conceded.) Indicating just how closely a work of popular history could mesh with professional historians' opinions on Reconstruction, Coulter's review cheerfully concluded, "Though there are no scholarly devices such as footnotes and bibliography, there is no reason to doubt the reliability of this work." After all, Williams was there himself, he supported white supremacy, and the story he told fit the accepted framework.[3]

Coulter himself published the last major entry in the Dunning-school catalogue twelve years later with *The South during Reconstruction, 1865–1877* (1947), the first of Louisiana State University Press's History of the South series to appear. Coulter, a North Carolinian whose grandfather was tried during Reconstruction for Ku Klux Klan violence, grew up immersed in the world of Thomas Dixon, Confederate veterans, and first-hand accounts of Reconstruction. As his earlier evaluation of Williams's book might have anticipated, Coulter did not incorporate the new ideas of Francis B. Simkins and Robert H. Woody, W. E. B. Du Bois, or Howard K. Beale, whose 1940 article "On Rewriting Reconstruction History" marked the clear beginning of a revisionist school of Reconstruction historiography. Beale, who himself had written a study of Andrew Johnson's presidency from a Beardian perspective in 1930, championed the "young historians, most of them Southerners" who were beginning to revise the Dunning school view of Reconstruction. Six decades after Reconstruction ended, Beale asked, "Is it not time that we studied the history of Reconstruction without first assuming, at least subconsciously, that carpetbaggers and Southern white Republicans were wicked, that Negroes were illiterate incompetents, and that the whole white South owes a debt of gratitude to the restorers of 'white supremacy'?" Coulter, on the other hand, felt that the old view had a few more years of life left in it. Coulter announced at the beginning that in his book "Southerner" meant "white" and that the "well-known facts of the Reconstruction program" were not to be challenged. In fact, rather than focus primarily on the upheavals of the period, Coulter insisted that much of life in the South (the white South) had carried on as usual, so he decided to portray, "with all the political and constitutional abnormalities of the times, the ordinary activities of the people, as they sowed and reaped, went to church, visited their neighbors, sang their songs, and sought in a thousand ways to amuse themselves." By focusing on white southerners' attempts to maintain a social existence undisturbed by Reconstruction attempts to renovate social structures, Coulter's 1947 academic study echoes one of the key themes of J. W. Daniel's 1905 novel *A Maid of the Foot-Hills*. For Coulter's efforts, J. G. de Roulhac Hamilton, one of William A. Dunning's students and founder of the University of North Carolina's Southern Historical Collection, had high praise. He fully supported Coulter's refusal to kowtow to historical revisionism, which was "an apparent attempt, at this late date, with all available evidence to the contrary, to substitute for historic fact the outworn, disproved, and rejected falsehoods by which partisan, self-seeking, and often corrupt politicians, together with ignorant fanatics, moved by sentimental but spurious humanitarianism, supported the infamy of the carpetbag régime in the lately seceded states." "The work," Hamilton concluded, "is a consummation devoutly to be praised."[4]

Not everyone was as impressed as Hamilton with Coulter's book. Writing in the *Journal of Negro Education*, John Hope Franklin took Coulter's book apart in a review slyly titled "Whither Reconstruction Historiography?" echoing the title of a recently published pro-segregation book, Charles Wallace Collins's *Whither Solid South? A Study in Politics and Race Relations*. In the most gentlemanly manner, he began by citing the many positive reviews Coulter's book had enjoyed. Then Franklin set to work, questioning Coulter's sometimes sloppy reasoning, his biased use of biased sources, and "his rather systematic effort to discredit the Negro in almost all phases of life during the Reconstruction." Ultimately, Franklin concluded, Coulter's work "is as valuable in the history of history at it is in the history of the Reconstruction."[5]

Another historian with little patience for the persistent white supremacist narrative of Reconstruction masquerading as proper history was Francis B. Simkins. As a recognized expert on Reconstruction and on South Carolina, in the 1930s and 1940s he often had opportunity to comment on books on these topics. Simkins admitted that Alfred B. Williams's book "deeply impresses that small army of persons who cherish the South Carolina tradition," because "awkward details of bloodshed, political frauds, and race hatred are subordinated to a colorful central theme." The book suffered from "the severe prejudices which invariably characterize the uncontaminated South Carolinian." Two laudatory books on Wade Hampton were published at the end of the 1940s: Manly Wade Wellman's biography, *Giant in Gray*, and Hampton Jarrell's *Wade Hampton and the Negro: The Road Not Taken*, which argues that Hampton proposed a moderate racial policy during Reconstruction that was, unfortunately, ignored, leading to conflict and violence. Simkins criticized Wellman for not making "a distinction between the Wade Hampton of the undying legend and the Wade Hampton of the contemporary records." Such sorry history offended Simkins because he saw clearly its effects: "The masses of white Southerners accept these judgments as axiomatic. . . . The wickedness of this [Reconstruction] regime and the righteousness of the manner in which it was destroyed are fundamentals of his civic code. Such a condemnation or commendation justifies the settlement of questions of the immediate past and are invoked to settle issues of even the remote future."[6] History that merely perpetuated threadbare myths seemed increasingly irrelevant to liberal historians facing a challenging postwar situation of their own, but that historical memory remained extremely popular with many less liberal people in the South outside academia.

Developments both within the federal government and from civil rights organizations in the late 1940s and early 1950s portended real change in the status of African Americans in the South, and those who supported the status quo again responded by invoking fears of Reconstruction. The Truman administration was committed to supporting civil rights, most dramatically announced in the 1947 report *To Secure These Rights* and in the desegregation of the military the following year. In 1950, the NAACP made a tactical decision to go beyond trying to desegregate bits and pieces of the educational system and equalizing facilities and teacher pay. Instead, they would tackle head-on the central issue, the constitutionality of educational segregation in the public schools, arguing that it violated the Fourteenth Amendment. The assault began with a test case from South Carolina, *Briggs v. Elliott.* Rev. J. A. DeLaine of Clarendon County led the local NAACP and got twenty plaintiffs to sign on to the case, which went before federal court in Charleston in November 1950. One of W. W. Ball's correspondents observed in 1948, "It seems the Carpetbaggers again are in the saddle, or on the Bench," showing that the Red Shirts were needed again as they had been in the writer's childhood. South Carolina's governor, James F. Byrnes, warned that the federal government of the 1950s would likewise fail to accomplish "what a Carpetbag government could not do in the Reconstruction period." In Mississippi, Alfred H. Stone, who had been writing on the "Negro problem" for decades, wondered if Truman, "as a Confederate soldier's son, knows the meaning and significance of one of the most expressive words in the English language—scalawag." Stone felt compelled to write about "A Mississippian's View of Civil Rights, States Rights, and the Reconstruction Background" because "the younger generation of Southern people, as a rule, have no more technical knowledge of the details of the history of which we are writing than have the people of the same age in other sections of the country." A recounting of the horrors of Reconstruction was therefore necessary, "particularly for the benefit of those who are so ignorant and so blind as to attempt to re-enact any of its features." By the early 1950s, forces that had been in alignment for decades had begun to move away from one another. Politicians from outside the South were concerning themselves in the racial affairs of the South, many of the South's citizens and spokesmen remained committed to the idea of a world shaped by the white supremacist narrative of Reconstruction, and prominent historians, even southern historians, had begun to question the dominant Dunning school interpretation of Reconstruction.[7]

C. Vann Woodward, who would go on to become the leading historian of the South in the twentieth century, developed in the 1930s into one of the region's leading dissidents and could be counted as an early member of the Southern Front, though he would probably have eschewed the label.

Born in Arkansas in 1908, Woodward left the small town behind in 1928 to finish his last two years of college at Emory University in Atlanta, the headquarters of the New South. In the city, Woodward sought out those who went against the grain of the segregated South, encountering Will Alexander, the leader of the Commission on Interracial Cooperation. Woodward crossed the color line to build friendships with people at Atlanta University, including J. Saunders Redding, then an instructor at Morehouse College. After graduating from Emory in 1930, Woodward taught freshman English composition at Georgia Tech for a year, before heading to Columbia University to earn a master's in political science. In New York, he met Langston Hughes and immersed himself in the Harlem Renaissance scene. Moving further afield, Woodward traveled through Europe in the summer of 1932, including a visit to the Soviet Union. Back in Atlanta in the fall of 1932, Woodward threw himself into more interracial activism, this time becoming involved in the defense of Angelo Herndon.[8]

Woodward's involvement in the Herndon case holds important clues for both his later attitudes toward southern history and his involvement in radical causes. Herndon was "a young black Communist charged with violating a Reconstruction death-penalty statute against inciting to insurrection," as Woodward recalled years later. The incongruity of it all— an antiquated statute invoked in the 1930s to suppress dissent—alerted Woodward to how false understandings of history and facile comparisons of the present to the past could sustain injustice, and it suggested the possibility that the clear-eyed study of the South's history could be a means of reforming the region. Woodward's response was to become involved in one of the organizations defending Herndon. In the process, Woodward became caught up in Communist factional squabbles and, with the impetuosity of youth, inadvertently insulted Will Alexander. Though the rift was quickly set right, the experience seems to have taught Woodward to look askance at radical organizations such as the Communist Party. His biographer John Herbert Roper notes, "The Herndon appeal marked the line between dissidence and radicalism for Woodward . . . who declined to answer the call of radicalism at the crucial moments" in the future— though this evaluation discounts some of Woodward's future support of radical causes. Although Woodward's fraught connection with radicalism had much to do with his intellectual judgments and a nature that inclined toward what his Arkansas neighbors might have called "contrariness," we should not discount the personal side of this stance, especially as the personal costs of radicalism would be brought home to him again two decades later.[9]

By 1934, Woodward had decided to turn his dissidence in the direction of history. "By thus writing history that mattered," Roper argues, "by offering perspective and understanding that he hoped would make an actual difference in society's response to racism and injustice, he could perhaps resolve the nagging dilemma produced by the competing claims of reform and scholarship." He planned to write a collective biography of southern demagogues, but eventually decided instead to focus on Tom Watson, the Georgia Populist leader who later became a supporter of lynching and the Ku Klux Klan. With the manuscript on Watson well under way, he arrived in Chapel Hill in 1934 to attend graduate school in history at the University of North Carolina. The university was already the leading center of liberal thought in the South under the leadership of president Frank Porter Graham. Scholars such as Howard W. Odum, Rupert B. Vance, and Howard K. Beale were changing the way the South was studied and thought of, while William T. Couch at the University of North Carolina Press was publishing adventurous studies that wrenched the idea of the region out of the "Sahara of the Bozart" mode. Once at Chapel Hill, Woodward quickly found his way to the center of radicalism, Milton Abernathy's bookstore. Along with Olive Matthews Stone, also a graduate student at Chapel Hill by this time, Woodward got involved in defending textile workers charged with dynamiting a mill in nearby Burlington during the General Textile Strike in September 1934. In the early months of 1935, Woodward organized several meetings of the Workers Defense Committee, and later that year he was involved with the Southern Committee for People's Rights.[10]

Woodward's dissertation, completed in 1937 and published as *Tom Watson, Agrarian Rebel* in 1938, exemplified the sort of engaged scholarship to which Woodward was committed. The book's topic and approach set Woodward apart from most other historians of the South at the time. "A consensus did prevail among historians in the 1930s, a uniquely broad consensus that papered over the breaks and fissures and conflicts in Southern history with myths of solidarity and continuity," Woodward recalled, and such a consensus seemed to him little more than a cynical apologia for the status quo, the sort of manipulation of history for nasty political ends he had seen in the Herndon case. Historians had neglected Populism, since it was a clear example of indigenous southern dissent against the post-Reconstruction order; unlike Reconstruction, the agrarian rebellion could hardly be blamed on carpetbaggers and northern reformers. To take up Watson's critique of the economic and social failures of the Redeemers was something akin to heresy in the 1930s, but even worse was Woodward's praise for Watson's commitment to racial equality and political cooperation. Just as interesting to Woodward, though he never explained it to his satisfaction, was the shift in Watson's thinking around the turn of the century as he lapsed back into an even more vitriolic racism than that from which he had emerged during his period as a Populist leader, a failure that could perhaps serve as a warning to the tentative interracialism of Woodward's day. Woodward considered continuing his scholarly interest in American radical leaders by writing a biography of Eugene Debs, but he abandoned the project when he learned that sufficient primary sources would be hard to come by (and perhaps in response to a colleague's unsubtle suggestion: "Lay off of Debs. You must be a red, or a Communist— or maybe an anarchist or something").[11]

The decade after Woodward published *Tom Watson, Agrarian Rebel* was a busy one, with war adding to the usual chaotic peregrinations of the fledging academic. After a few years writing military history for the Navy, Woodward arrived at Johns Hopkins University in 1946. Here he continued the work he had postponed during the war: writing a history of the New South from 1877 to 1913 for the Louisiana State University Press's History of the South series. As he worked on this project, he found himself sidetracked by what he was finding about the Compromise of 1877. This material eventually took shape as the book *Reunion and Reaction*, published in 1951. Rather than seeing the Compromise of 1877 as a high-minded move toward sectional reconciliation based on abandonment of Reconstruction's misguided efforts at reform in race relations, Woodward told a story of backroom deals inspired not by noble desires to reunify the nation or even to protect beleaguered white southerners, but by the desire to make a quick dollar on railroad speculation. It was "a defiant announcement of adherence to some then-quite-unfashionable tenets of economic interpretation and a lingering attachment to a much denigrated historian [Charles A. Beard] who had gone out of fashion." Woodward's *Origins of the New South, 1877–1913*, also published in 1951, transformed the study of the region, and like *Tom Watson, Agrarian Rebel*, it challenged the hagiographic depictions of Bourbon leaders, showing at every turn how the elite manipulated racial feelings to serve class purposes, though unlike in Marxist accounts, Woodward's working-class whites were no heroes. There were no heroes in the South during this period, except perhaps a few liberals who tried to resist the growth of Jim Crow and inequality.[12]

Woodward's scholarship in the early 1950s on the South was partly a result of his "aversion" to the "so-called consensus school of historiography," and it put Woodward in a delicate position as anticommunism began to exert greater pressure on intellectuals and educators. The leading historians of the immediate postwar period, men such as Richard Hofstadter, Louis Hartz, and Daniel Boorstin, reacted to both the temper of their times and what they saw as the excesses of their historical predecessors. Rather than continue the Progressive history of previous decades that saw history as the "enduring struggle between 'the people' and 'the interests,'" the consensus historians looked at what brought Americans together, not what tore them apart. As a result, they tended to emphasize common ideals and minimize conflict between different parts of American society. According to a 1959 critique of this trend in historiography, the consensus historians "took the United States' apparent economic abundance, political stability, and domestic tranquility during the postwar years as a vantage point from which to examine the long course of the nation's history," finding the "origins of America's essential liberal, democratic, and 'homogeneous' character."[13]

In this context, Woodward found a new way of accommodating the competing demands of reform and scholarship, one that maintained his stance of dissent while backing away from radicalism. Woodward's involvement with the Communists during the Herndon defense had taught him an important lesson about the personal costs of radicalism, and McCarthyism reinforced that lesson. At Johns Hopkins, Woodward had become a close friend of political scientist Owen Lattimore, one of the leading experts on China. Like Woodward, Lattimore had never been a Communist, but he did adopt dissident positions that anticommunists felt were too sympathetic to the Communist government of China. Called before the Senate Internal Security Subcommittee (SISS) in 1951, Lattimore "gamely tried to confront the SISS with its own shortcomings—its use of material out of context and its uncritical treatment of [anticommunist] witnesses." This approach did not save him from being indicted for perjury, tying him up in court until 1955 and wrecking his career. Woodward, informed by this drama as well as his observation of the results of extreme ideologies in Europe during the war, found that his interest in his youthful flirtations with radicalism had evaporated, though his insistence on the importance of dissent and his commitment to social reform remained intact.[14]

In 1952, Woodward, as president of the Southern Historical Association (SHA), had the opportunity to rethink his old ideas about reform and scholarship and reformulate them for the new time in which he found himself. Writing his presidential address in October 1952, Woodward saw the field of southern history, the SHA as an organization, and even the nation at an important turning point, the sort of turning point that figured prominently in the histories he wrote. The SHA, formed in the heyday of regionalism in the mid-1930s, had been around for nearly two decades, but by the early 1950s the nationalizing effects of World War II and the nationalistic effects of the Cold War had discounted the importance of regionalism. The stirrings of the civil rights movement, and especially the embarrassment that racism caused the nation in the international propaganda struggles against the Soviet Union, had left the South looking more backward than ever. The year 1952 did not seem a propitious time to be studying the history of a region that apparently was consigned to the dustbin of history. Yet as Woodward looked around, he began to think that the region's history had something important to offer the nation after all. Taking a cue from Reinhold Niebhur's recent book *The Irony of American History,* Woodward titled his SHA talk "The Irony of Southern History."[15]

The main ideas of "The Irony of Southern History" were that the South's experience with defeat and failure was more like the experience of the rest of the world than the bluff triumphalism of America's national legend, and that the nation could learn valuable lessons from the history of the South. After opening with a subtle but powerful indictment of the contemporary suppression of dissent, comparing McCarthyism to the South's rabid defense of slavery in the antebellum decades, Woodward pointed out that unlike the nation as a whole, the South had experienced "military defeat, occupation." Woodward saw irony in the results of the Civil War and Reconstruction: "As usual, it is only after the zeal of wartime idealism has spent itself that the opportunity is gained for realizing the ideals for which the war has been fought. When the idealistic aims are then found to be in conflict with selfish and pragmatic ends, it is the ideals that are likely to be sacrificed." Excessive moralism in politics, whether it was southerners defending slavery, Radical Republicans trying to push rapid change on the South, or Cold Warriors uncritically insisting on capitalism's manifest destiny, was best avoided. Speaking as McCarthyism was ruining careers and lives, Woodward urged southern historians to point out to the nation "the futility of erecting intellectual barricades against unpopular ideas, of employing censorship and repression against social criticism, and of imposing the ideas of the conqueror upon defeated peoples by force of arms." The alternative to this foolish and destructive idealism, Woodward thought, was a sober, realistic course of moderation. Seeing how Germany and Italy drifted into Fascism in the 1930s, how the Soviet Union under Stalin had drifted into totalitarianism, and how attacks on dissent in the Cold War period were accelerating, Woodward was, like many, mistrustful of all forms of idealism, certain that they could lead only to extremism. Woodward insisted that reform was still necessary in the South, but by the early 1950s he was insistent that the reform needed to be essentially moderate. No more for him the Southern Front's idealistic attempts to fundamentally transform the region.[16]

Woodward continued his commitment to combining scholarship and reform the next year, when he and John Hope Franklin worked with the legal team from the NAACP on briefs for the *Brown v. Board of Education* case. A complex fight over the history of Reconstruction had emerged at the heart of the *Brown* lawsuit in 1953. By late 1952, *Briggs v. Elliott* had been appealed up the court system and had merged with three other cases, from Virginia, the District of Columbia, Delaware, and Kansas, under the name *Brown v. Board of Education of Topeka, Kansas*. After initial arguments were made, the Supreme Court returned the case in June 1953, to be reargued later that year after a number of historical and practical questions had been answered. In particular, the justices wanted to know whether the Fourteenth Amendment had been intended to apply to public education when it was framed and ratified. The historical team found conflicting evidence, so they took a more expansive view of the question of intent and the history of Reconstruction. Relying on the reports of Woodward and Franklin, which argued that "the original equalitarian intentions of the post–Civil War amendments had been eroded in ensuing decades," the NAACP legal team cast Reconstruction as a thwarted attempt to realize America's highest ideals. The vision of racial equality in the Fourteenth Amendment was not, as historians had been arguing for over half a century, a misguided mistake better left forgiven and forgotten, but an unfulfilled promise and, crucially, part of the nation's organic law that could not be ignored. As research coordinator John A. Davis commented, "We rejected the conventional Columbia [Dunning] school of thinking on Reconstruction and its aftermath. . . . We were saying to all of them, 'No, goddammit, now you're going to have to face the truth.'" The argument, of course, was ultimately successful, with the Supreme Court ruling on 17 May 1954 that the *Plessy v. Ferguson* doctrine of "separate but equal" had "no place" in "the field of public education" and that "separate educational facilities are inherently unequal."[17]

The announcement of the decision in *Brown* fulfilled the hopes of the NAACP and its supporters, but it caught many white southerners by surprise. Still, observers looking around the South in the summer of 1954 saw signs that whites might acquiesce to this new "law of the land," and they may have, had more of their leaders, or even their president, said that this was the thing to do. Instead, the silence of good men gave space to those who were determined to resist the Supreme Court's edict, as their ancestors had resisted Reconstruction. Not surprisingly, many segregationists responded by comparing the Supreme Court's decision to Reconstruction and naming those who supported it carpetbaggers and scalawags. The chairman of the Louisiana legislature's Joint Legislative Committee to Maintain Segregation proposed emergency measures to defy *Brown*, arguing, "A vote against these bills . . . is an open invitation to the carpetbaggers, scalawags and National Association for the Advancement of the Colored People to integrate our schools." A Charleston attorney and former politician declared, "The authors of this latest outrage are as deeply imbued with hatred for our Southern customs as was Thaddeus Stevens." Nonetheless, he remained confident and defiant, using the memory of Reconstruction to frame a call to action: "Reconstruction days were harsh, but, notwithstanding the scalawags, the carpetbaggers and the federal bayonet, the basic principles for which the South fought were not destroyed. Today, we face a similar challenge. Perhaps, if we have the strength of character, exhibited by the generation preceding, the dawn of a new 1876 will arrive."[18]

In the summer after the *Brown* decision was announced, C. Vann Woodward prepared a series of lectures that would have a significant effect on how participants in the civil rights movement conceived of the history of the institutions they sought to change and how they saw their movement within the broader sweep of American history. The lectures were delivered at the University of Virginia in November 1954 and published the following year as *The Strange Career of Jim Crow*. As did most of Woodward's scholarship on southern history, this book emphasized the importance of disjunctive change in history, rather than the forces of continuity. In this case, he examined the "twilight zone that lies between living memory and written history," where "mythology" breeds, the myth that segregation was a timeless aspect of the South and not susceptible to change. Instead, Woodward argued, race relations had been relatively fluid from the end of the Civil War through the years after Reconstruction, only hardening into the patterns of Jim Crow with the unrest stirred up by the agrarian crisis and the Populist movement. "Southerners," he pointed out, "have less reason to expect the indefinite duration of any set of social institutions," including segregation. If indeed segregation was not some permanent feature of southern life, but something that had been constructed under specific historical circumstances, then it could, under new historical circumstances, be dismantled. In fact, that project had been well under way since the end of World War II. It was, Woodward claimed, a "New Reconstruction."[19]

Surveying the contemporary scene, Woodward took the idea of the burgeoning civil rights movement as a "New Reconstruction" out of the hands of the segregationists who had first used the comparison as an attack and set it to work for the civil rights movement instead. Ever since southern whites had used the story of Reconstruction to help put Jim Crow in place, they had interpreted any attack on the system as a "New Reconstruction." The idea itself was nothing new. Woodward was not even the first historian to compare the postwar civil rights movement to Reconstruction. The credit for that goes to Francis B. Simkins, who, in a 1951 review of Hampton Jarrell's *Wade Hampton and the Negro* in the *Mississippi Valley Historical Review,* commented that because of the violent racism of Ben Tillman and Martin W. Gary, "South Carolina won an evil reputation which, in the times of Judge Waties Waring [a federal judge in Charleston who became an outspoken supporter of civil rights in the late 1940s], justifies the threat of a second Reconstruction." Woodward's innovation was in reversing the moral valence of the "New Reconstruction." Signaling his complete break with the Dunning school, Woodward refused to beat around the bush: there was a new Reconstruction happening, it was a better one than the first, and it was more likely to succeed. For one of the nation's leading historians of the South to make such a statement— himself a southerner and speaking in the South—put the public on notice. From now on, those who maintained the white supremacist narrative of Reconstruction would do so with the wind of historical scholarship in their teeth, not at their backs.[20]

Woodward elaborated on his idea of the "New Reconstruction" in a 1956 article for *Commentary.* The parallel to the present was one with which any staunch segregationist would agree: "Reconstruction affords the most extreme example in our history of an all-out effort by the majority to impose its will upon a recalcitrant and unwilling minority region." Woodward emphasized the positive aspects of Reconstruction in even clearer terms than he had in 1954, claiming that "in spite of the bad name Reconstruction has earned, an enormous amount of idealism and noble motives went into its making." But despite the extreme lengths to which the "Northern reformers" had been willing to go to implement those ideals, their eventual "apathy and indifference" doomed their attempts to reform the South. From here, Woodward's story grew more pessimistic, as he pointed out that the white South in the 1950s had more resources with which to resist change than it had in the 1860s. But there were also more reasons to hope in the 1950s, as the South's position grew more politically isolated, as dissent against segregation grew among southern whites, as churches took a positive role, and as African Americans became more powerful. However, the New Reconstruction would not succeed quickly: "*Undesirable or not, gradualism is an inescapable fact and a basic character-istic of the New Reconstruction.*" As Woodward had argued four years ear-lier in "The Irony of Southern History," one of the failings of the original Reconstruction had been the gap between "idealistic aims and pragmatic consequences." In the *Commentary* article, Woodward suggested that one of the pragmatic, if unpalatable, truths was that the civil rights movement would have to proceed slowly if it were to succeed.[21]

The 1957 paperback edition of *The Strange Career of Jim Crow* incorpo-rated a new chapter that elaborated on Woodward's ideas about the "New Reconstruction," first presented in *Commentary,* and it was this edition that entrenched the idea of the "New Reconstruction," or, as Woodward was now calling it, "Second Reconstruction," in the vocabulary of the civil rights movement. Two years can be a long time, though, and the South of 1957 was a different place from the one where Woodward had initially crafted the lectures. The Montgomery bus boycott had seen the emer-gence of a dynamic leader in Rev. Martin Luther King Jr. and a new role for the black church in the freedom struggle. Segregationists had mobi-lized, reviving the Ku Klux Klan and creating a network of slightly more respectable Citizens Councils across the South to lead "massive resistance" against integration.[22]

The federal government took another step toward ending Jim Crow when Congress passed a civil rights bill. By creating a division of the Jus-tice Department responsible for civil rights, it ensured that southern states would no longer be able to bury civil rights violations in the shadows, as they had with the wave of racial violence at the end of World War II or the violence after the announcement of the *Brown* decision. Now, violations of civil rights would be a federal issue, and it was clear that the federal gov-ernment would be more vigorous than before in pursuing these matters. For several southerners, the prospect of federal intervention in something that had been a state matter since the 1875 Civil Rights Act had been ruled unconstitutional by the Supreme Court raised the specter of Reconstruc-tion. Georgia senator Richard Russell focused his opposition on the pos-sible use of the military to enforce civil rights, warning that "if this bill is used to the utmost, neither [Charles] Sumner nor [Thaddeus] Stevens, in the persecution of the South in the 12 tragic years of reconstruction, ever cooked up any such devil's broth as is proposed in this misnamed civil-rights bill." He threatened a repeat of the alliance that had brought down the first Reconstruction: "The South was finally freed of the bayonet rule of reconstruction days through the efforts of northern men. There was less bitterness and hate between the soldiers than between the civilians in the War Between the States. Northerners who had been subjected to the waving of the bloody shirt came South in the forces of occupation. They found the truth about the South, and their hearts were touched with compassion at the treatment accorded their late enemies during the reconstruction era. It was really the veterans of the war and those who served in the forces who occupied the South for 12 years who finally broke the chains forged for the South by Sumner and Stevens." It fell to Olin D. Johnston, now a U.S. senator, to take the comparison of the Civil Rights Bill of 1957 to its absurd postwar conclusion: "I should say it is more dangerous and more far-reaching than the old reconstruction-era force bills that followed the War Between the States. . . . It sets a precedent of placing the Attorney General of the United States in the same position that Hitler was placed by similarly patterned encroaching legislation passed in Germany during the 1930's." Though it is generally true that comparing one's opponent to Hitler is a sign of argumentative desperation, by the end of the year, southern senators' warnings about federal use of military force would seem less of an exaggeration.[23]

The political opportunism of Arkansas governor Orval Faubus turned what might have been an uneventful integration of Central High School in Little Rock in 1957 into a constitutional and military crisis that marked a shift in the nature of the civil rights movement. The sort of genteel gradualism Woodward had hoped for was not in the cards, as the backlash against the *Brown* decision gained a momentum of its own. Rather than comply with a court order to allow African American students to attend the high school, Faubus called out the Arkansas National Guard to prevent the school's desegregation. State force had been deployed in direct defiance of federal law; the southern strategy of massive resistance was calling the federal government's bluff on the issue of civil rights. When it became clear that Faubus was ready to let a white mob use violence to keep the nine African American students out of Central High School, Eisenhower sent in paratroopers and federalized the Arkansas National Guard. With federal troops occupying Little Rock, segregationists saw their predictions of another Reconstruction fulfilled, of a federal government drunk with power enforcing its will on the South at the point of a bayonet. As a writer in Little Rock's *Arkansas Gazette* put it, "In one sense we rolled back our history to the Reconstruction Era when Federal troops moved into positions at Central High School to uphold the law and preserve the peace." The Citizens Councils, through articles such as "New Reconstruction Compared With Old" and speeches such as "A Comparison of Attitudes during Reconstruction I and II," exhorted members to fight desegregation.[24]

The Little Rock crisis had many repercussions for the civil rights movement; for the historical memory of Reconstruction in the South, it meant that the old white supremacist narrative was transformed at a fundamental level. In the past, whites determined to keep Jim Crow had called on a historical memory of Reconstruction that gave that social system moral legitimacy. But this historical memory was only ever a species of belief, agreed upon and maintained by a group of people, but not as clearly based on the real world as, for instance, the belief that America had fought Germany in World War I. One of the things that made the white supremacist narrative of Reconstruction so durable, so easy for so many people to believe for so long, was that it had great explanatory power. The South was as it was largely because of its history, and the foundational event in that history was the destruction of the idyllic Old South, the purgatory of Reconstruction, and the Redemption that had brought about the Jim Crow South of today. But by the 1950s that old story no longer explained the world in which white southerners found themselves living. Change was coming, and welcome it or resist it as they may, most white southerners at least realized this inevitability. The white supremacist narrative of Reconstruction was no longer functional, which is not to say that, like a dream, it vanished in the light of this new day. The historical memory remained for many years, even remained a prominent part of public memory for at least a decade, but with its change of status came a change of tone. The white supremacist narrative of Reconstruction changed from a confident jeremiad to an elegiac recollection, often skirting dangerously close to nostalgia and sentimentality. The Little Rock crisis, along with the flurry of racial violence between 1954 and 1957 that included the Emmett Till lynching, also exposed the extreme violence and chaos that massive resistance could unleash, a potentiality abhorrent to many southerners and at least distasteful even to many who still supported segregation. The violence with which white supremacists defended segregation once evoked memories of the heroic days of Wade Hampton. After Little Rock, it was more likely to draw comparisons to Soviet tanks rolling through Hungary.[25]

The transformation of the white supremacist narrative of Reconstruction into a museum piece and the turn of some southern officials away from violent resistance to desegregation converged in South Carolina late in 1957 when the Red Shirts tried, one last time, to ride to the rescue. In December 1957, George C. Tinker of Fort Mill, South Carolina, applied to the South Carolina secretary of state for a charter for the Association of Red Shirts, a group that would "organize citizens . . . into a benevolent, fraternal order based on Southern traditions, such as segregated schools, churches and societies." To his surprise and disgust, the state denied the application, citing many letters it had received protesting the new organization, not because it supported segregation, but because Tinker's group would tend to bring into disrepute the memory of Wade Hampton and the original Red Shirts. Unlike earlier supporters of Jim Crow who had called on the memory of Reconstruction with the confidence that most of the white public agreed with their view of history and its contemporary relevance, Tinker found himself isolated. Insisting that the state's leaders had turned their backs on history and stifled the memory of Hampton, Tinker placed himself in the oppositional position of trying to preserve an endangered heritage from destruction. "We realize," he wrote, "that there are many public officials now and in the past who might be embarrassed if the people of South Carolina became acquainted with the principles established by Wade Hampton and the Red Shirts as they will be surprised to learn that the past officials of their great state had permitted many of the principles of Wade Hampton and his Red Shirts gradually to be erased."[26]

Tinker's indignant appeal to South Carolinians' reverence for Hampton and his principles was not enough to win approval for his organization, but the reason had more to do with the long-standing ambivalence about the violence of Reconstruction than any lack of knowledge of Hampton or lack of commitment to segregation. In the 1876 campaign itself, Democratic leaders knew they walked a fine line between using enough force and violence to win, and using too much and bringing down disastrous federal intervention. This theme was dramatized in an 1895 newspaper article published on the "Hampton Day" festivities that recounted how Hampton had quelled the crowds in Columbia after the election of 1876, preventing violence that would have resulted in a renewed civil war. In recollections of Reconstruction such as the 1908 and 1909 Red Shirt reunions, South Carolinians vacillated between celebrating the results of the violence used and regretting the necessity of using violence and the detrimental effects it had on society. The paradox faces every political movement that comes to power by violent revolution: if violence can once overturn a government and put a new one in place, the people living under that new government must always know that more violence could again turn the wheel of revolution. This paradox helps explain why those who held power in South Carolina were so ambivalent about remembering the violence of the overthrow of Reconstruction. On the one hand, they wanted to project a belligerent image to the rest of the nation in order to deter outsiders from attempting to meddle in southern racial politics. On the other hand, too much emphasis on the violence that brought them to power would undermine the myth that Jim Crow was a natural state of affairs and embolden those who might want to take power in future.[27]

This dynamic was at work again in the 1950s as die-hard segregationists resisted federal attempts to integrate schools and support African Americans' civil rights. In December 1956, hooded men flogged a white man from Camden after he was accused of supporting integration. When a judge urged the grand jury to indict the men accused of the flogging, he couched his comments in this dynamic. After criticizing the Supreme Court for usurping power that should be left in the hands of the states and local communities, the judge argued that the sort of violence the Camden man had suffered would "aid only the 'scalawags and carpetbaggers' who were seeking to bring about another Reconstruction." The argument against the Association of Red Shirts in 1957 took a similar form. As with the controversy over the Ku Klux Klan attacks of 1939, white leaders in South Carolina feared that unruly lower-class supporters of segregation could upset the delicate balance as much as militant African Americans or overbearing federal authorities. The editor of the *Greenville News* expressed this view, denying the validity of Tinker's claim to Hampton's legacy: "General Hampton did not condone secret societies and hooded bands who rode by night and used terror to accomplish their ends. The red shirt worn by his followers was a conspicuous badge of their affiliation, their beliefs and policies. . . . The Ku Klux Klan by any other name, even if the members refrained from hiding their faces, would be just as bad." After all, "the maintenance of segregation is a matter of public policy in South Carolina" that was best left to the duly constituted authorities. If the Red Shirts were to ride again in South Carolina, it would be only as a historical reenactment, not to re-create the history of 1876.[28]

CONCLUSION

In the 1980s I spent quite a bit of time in Greenville, South Carolina, driving along U.S. Highway 29 on my way to Denny's or the International House of Pancakes to drink coffee and pass the time with friends. Of course, we never called the road "Highway 29"; it was "Wade Hampton Boulevard." Thinking back now, after nearly a decade on the lookout for mentions of Wade Hampton in all kinds of sources across the twentieth century, I am pretty sure that I had no idea who Hampton was back then, except perhaps a vague idea that he was some sort of Confederate general and that one of my friends was distantly related to him. Was he the messianic leader who had rescued my state and my race from unspeakable degradation and to whom we should all be eternally grateful? Not so far as I was aware.

How could someone who had grown up mostly in South Carolina by the late 1980s be so completely oblivious to something that earlier generations in the state had taken for granted: the idea that the history of Reconstruction was relevant—and not only relevant, but essential—for understanding the world. What had changed from 1957 to 1987?

As we have seen throughout this account, to endure and thrive, historical memory of Reconstruction had to be functional. Any given variety of the story had to line up with the social reality in which it existed. The white supremacist narrative of Reconstruction provided a solid explanation for why and how the Jim Crow society had come about, why it had to come about, and why it had to be sustained. The "radicals' Reconstruction" story worked to the extent that it explained the history of why working people were kept down in the South and provided a lesson for what to do about the situation. The breakdown of segregation, through a combination of effective African American activism and a reassertion of federal authority, destroyed the credibility of the white supremacist narrative of Reconstruction. Simply put, no historical memory of Reconstruction seemed generally relevant after the end of the civil rights movement.

Part of the reason for this is that, in some important senses, the civil rights movement succeeded. The Civil Rights Act of 1964 and the Voting Rights Act of 1965 were major accomplishments that changed the face of daily life across the South. They were in many ways the fulfillment of promises made during Reconstruction, the effective enforcement of the Fourteenth and Fifteenth Amendments. In a world where African Americans voted, dined, went to school, worked, and generally got on with the business of life on an equal basis with whites, the white supremacist narrative of Reconstruction was suddenly defunct. One of the implicit promises in that narrative was that if its lessons were heeded, then the Jim Crow conditions it had helped create would endure. Any complex of historical memory that serves to underwrite a social arrangement is millennial in this way; it contains the story of the ending of history. But the white supremacist narrative of Reconstruction ultimately had not prevented change from coming. On a more pragmatic level, it suddenly became politically inexpedient to crow about how your grandfather had chased African Americans away from the polls in 1876 if you needed the votes of those same African Americans' grandchildren in 1966.

The civil rights movement, though, was not an unqualified success. It is by now a commonplace to note that after the two landmark pieces of legislation, the Civil Rights Act of 1964 and the Voting Rights Act of 1965, Martin Luther King Jr. and other observers realized that more was needed, that with de jure segregation defeated, the new enemy was poverty and an inequality that knew boundaries of neither region nor race. As King began to confront poverty and to criticize the imperialism of American foreign policy, he became more aware of the obstacles that his program faced. As the supporters of the radicals' Reconstruction had realized thirty years before, King came to understand that in order to build the sort of social justice he sought, based on a biracial alliance of working people, he, too, had to overcome the power of the white supremacist narrative of Reconstruction. He grappled with this in the speech marking the end of the 1965 march from Selma to Montgomery. Basing his historical comments on C. Vann Woodward's *The Strange Career of Jim Crow*, King presented a slightly muddled version of late nineteenth-century southern history. Conflating Reconstruction and the Populist era, King nevertheless pointed to the threat that a potential alliance between blacks and poor whites posed to white elites. In one of his last major speeches, in January

1968, King celebrated the centennial of the birth of W. E. B. Du Bois. The largest part of King's speech on Du Bois's legacy was about the importance of *Black Reconstruction*. "He virtually, before anyone else and more than anyone else, demolished lies about Negroes in their most important and creative period of history," said King. "The truths he revealed are not yet the property of all Americans but they have been recorded and arm us for our contemporary battles." King saw that Du Bois's attack on the white supremacist narrative of Reconstruction had been necessary not just for the success of the civil rights movement as it had taken shape under King's leadership thus far, but also for the continuation of that project in the Poor People's Campaign that King was busy planning even as he gave the speech in Carnegie Hall. Du Bois had "revealed that far from being the tragic era white historians described, [Reconstruction] was the only period in which democracy existed in the south. This stunning fact was the reason the history books had to lie, because to tell the truth would have acknowledged the Negroes' capacity to govern and fitness to build a finer nation in a creative relationship with poor whites."[1]

In South Carolina, the white supremacist narrative of Reconstruction made its last major appearance in public memory in 1970 during the state's tricentennial celebration. In addition to commemorating the colony's origins at Charlestowne in 1670, the tricentennial promoted and sponsored a variety of historical activities across the state. A number of county historical societies, local museums, and other communities got involved with house tours, exhibitions, historical pageants, and other events. Reconstruction was not a central part of every community's presentation of its past, but where it did appear, the story tended to be the tried-and-true saga of carpetbaggers, scalawags, and heroic Hampton. Nowhere was this more true than in Anderson. More than most places in South Carolina, Anderson had always based much of its civic identity around its resistance to Reconstruction, from Manse Jolly's murderous rampages to the opening of Wade Hampton's 1876 campaign. The highlight of Anderson County's tricentennial celebration was the reenactment, on 2 September 1970, of Wade Hampton's parade through the town on 2 September 1876. Just like old times, "the Red Shirts rode again," and the speaker, General William Coleman, commander of Fort Jackson and an Anderson County native, "recalled the Red Shirt movement of 1876 in which South Carolinians wrested control of the state government from Reconstruction radicals" before going on to "review the progress of the state and nation since 1876, touching on the rapid industrial growth and thriving agricultural progress that have marked the past few decades." With these themes—which could almost have come straight from John J. Hemphill's essay in the 1890 political tract *Why the Solid South?*—Coleman's speech could have fit as easily at Anderson's 1909 Red Shirt reunion. On a lighter note, the "Cultural Heritage Day" program featured a version of Shakespeare's *As You Like It* adapted by local writer Milton A. Dickson to a setting in Anderson County in 1876.[2]

The celebration of Wade Hampton and the end of Reconstruction in Anderson had as much to do with timing as location. On the Monday before Wednesday's parade, Anderson County's public schools had finally integrated. In September 1969, the Supreme Court had ruled in *Alexander v. Holmes County Board of Education* that "all deliberate speed" finally meant "now." The school districts in South Carolina and other states across the South that had still, by one means or another, postponed integration by maintaining dual school systems and giving parents "freedom of choice" about where to send their children had to integrate. Although under considerable pressure to shut down the schools altogether, Governor Robert E. McNair conceded, "When we run out of courts and time, we must adjust to the circumstances." Racial tension continually threatened to boil over into violence, but South Carolina's schools reopened on an integrated basis that fall. In some ways, the organizers of Anderson County's tricentennial tried to present the county's Reconstruction history in a racially sensitive manner. Mary Dodgen Few, the chairman of the Anderson County Tricentennial Committee, wrote the biography of Wade Hampton that appeared in the souvenir booklet and emphasized his kindly attitude toward "the Negro, who was ever his friend," and his last words, "God bless all my people, black and white." Nonetheless, parading Red Shirts down the street two days after black and white children first attended school together could only have been a finger in the eye to those who looked forward to a new era in race relations.[3]

The 1976 national bicentennial had a different tone in South Carolina than the state tricentennial six years earlier. As historian John Bodnar has noted, the bicentennial was designed with a therapeutic effect in mind. After the divisive effects of the civil rights movement, the Vietnam War and the antiwar movement, and Watergate, the nation needed an opportunity to come together and feel good about itself. Participation by all minority groups was encouraged at the highest levels, and the South Carolina American Revolution Bicentennial Commission (SCARBC), the state body responsible for coordinating the bicentennial, was fairly diligent in carrying out that directive. In May 1975, the SCARBC held a meeting specifically to "[provide] greater minority involvement in the Bicentennial activities of the state," and the commission added an African American member. The SCARBC promoted a "do-it-yourself" program at the local level, partly because the state legislature was not willing to spend more money after so recently laying out twelve million dollars for the state tricentennial. The local events marking the Bicentennial, then, would seem to be a good reflection of local public memory, albeit with the guiding hand of state and federal authorities supporting the idea that minorities be included in the planning and that programs be aimed at inclusivity and harmony. Of the many programs and descriptions of historical pageants, commemorations, and events, hardly any even mentioned Reconstruction, much less glorified its overthrow. The "spirit of '76" in South Carolina finally seems to have referred to the idea that "all men are created equal" and have the right to "life, liberty, and the pursuit of happiness."[4]

A story about social memory in the South could hardly have such an upbeat ending. If the 1970s saw the end of the white supremacist narrative of Reconstruction in public memory in South Carolina, the late 1990s saw its spasmodic return, though now occupying a position well out of the mainstream. The South Carolina League of the South appears to be the most active proponent of a newly invigorated demonization of Reconstruction, though now couched in terms of opposition to all federal authority and without the overt white supremacy of earlier generations (they welcome members of all sorts who share their goals). Founded in the early 1990s, the organization promotes the idea that since federal authorities have abandoned the nation's Christian roots, "secession is the best way to restore good government to the South" (because, presumably, it worked out so well the first time). The South Carolina League of the South took an active part in the debate over removing the Confederate flag from the capitol building in Columbia in 2000 and has enjoyed considerable growth since. Present-day supporters of the League of the South can even get involved by applying to become Red Shirts. According to the organization's Web site, this latest incarnation of the Red Shirts "seek[s] to advance the cultural, economic, political well-being and Independence of all South Carolinians by all honorable means. . . . They wear Red Shirts, and gather at special events to demonstrate their determination to force cultural and political changes. They hold Red Shirt rallies, pickets, and assemble at meetings held by various government entities from the state level to the smallest community."[5]

This most recent crop of Red Shirts, though, clearly represent a tiny minority and seem to be very aware of the difficulty they face in presenting their view of history to a public that has in that same period made great advances in bringing a more accurate understanding of Reconstruction into its public memory. In the 1990s, this took the form of attempts to publicly praise the role and accomplishments of African American leaders during Reconstruction, an approach perhaps more in keeping with Carter Woodson's early Negro history mode of highlighting black "contributions" to American history than a sophisticated analysis of Reconstruction, but an advance of some sort nonetheless.

One important early marker of this transition occurred in the mid-1980s, when the history of South Carolina that students learned in the public schools changed. For generations, students in South Carolina learned the history of their state from books written by Mary C. Simms Oliphant. Revising a state history originally published by her grandfather, the novelist William Gilmore Simms, in 1860, Oliphant's *Simms' History of South Carolina* was published in 1917 and revised, slightly, for decades. Not surprisingly, it presented a white supremacist version of Reconstruction that was current in 1917 but badly outdated by the 1980s. The new textbook, *South Carolina: One of the Fifty States,* by Lewis P. Jones, presented a very different view of Reconstruction. Jones commented in a newspaper article announcing the new textbook: "Much of the grief of South Carolina in the last hundred years has come from its own misunderstanding of its history. For a state with so much decency, it should have been spared that." Such changes were not immediate, and nearly twenty years later, a newspaper columnist would still plead to the public, "Let's avoid making the same mistake our ancestors made in teaching South Carolina history." Criticizing the effects of Oliphant's "very unreconstructed view of Reconstruction," the writer called for support for a Republican legislator's bill that would give special attention to the civil rights movement and Reconstruction in the history lessons South Carolina students learned.[6]

In the late 1990s, the positive accomplishments of African Americans during Reconstruction began to gain a place in public memory in South Carolina, though not without controversy. This progress can be tracked in small ways in the pages of the state's newspapers. In 2001 the *Greenville News* pointed out that "'Carpetbaggers' changed Greenville in the 1870s"—for the better. The year before, the *Columbia State* published an article on little-known black legislator Alfred P. Moore of Fairfield County and his granddaughter, who wanted "to make sure her own descendants knew about him." Public recognition of Jonathan J. Wright, who in 1870 became the first African American appellate judge in the nation's history, raised more of a ruckus, especially among the self-appointed defenders of South Carolina's "heritage." When the state Supreme Court decided to display a portrait of Wright, one critic howled over the "historical revisionism," since Wright served in "the years of Reconstruction, during which South Carolina was occupied territory." Relying on Alfred B. Williams's account from 1926, the writer repeated the long since discredited assertion that Wright "was a drunken, dissolute and weak individual with only a cursory knowledge of law."[7]

In Kingstree, the county seat of Williamsburg County between Sumter and Orangeburg, the local historical society erected a historical marker in 1998 honoring Stephen A. Swails, a black carpetbagger. Since Swails was a veteran of the 54th Massachusetts Infantry and the first African American commissioned officer in the U.S. Army, it was only fitting that the ceremony was held on May 30th, the old date of Decoration Day. Born in Pennsylvania and spending his early adulthood in Cooperstown, New York, Swails settled in Williamsburg County during Reconstruction, working for the Freedmen's Bureau and serving in the state senate. He remained in Kingstree practicing law until his death in 1900. At the dedication ceremony, Congressman James Clyburn spoke, a fitting tribute from the man who became, in 1992, the first African American to represent South Carolina in Congress since Reconstruction.[8]

Plans were made in the early twenty-first century for a commemoration of Reconstruction in South Carolina on a much larger scale, in the form of a national park at Beaufort. Senator Fritz Hollings and Congressman Joe Wilson introduced bills in Congress in 2003 that would initiate the study of several sites in the Beaufort area, including Penn School, a freedmen's village, and the site of a Freedmen's Bureau office, that could serve as the basis for a new national park with Reconstruction as its theme. The bill had passed both House and Senate by summer 2003, but authorization for the $300,000 needed to carry out the study was slow in coming. What one supporter called "the Confederate problem" took its toll, but it seems likely that the pressing budgetary needs of another war and another reconstruction were probably also factors. In a world infinitely more globalized than during the 1870s, the historical memory of this new war and new reconstruction may become as important to Americans as historical memory of Reconstruction ever was for South Carolina.[9]

Finally, an indication not only of the power that memory of Reconstruction had, but of hope that countervailing memories of the period might eventually settle into some sort of reconciliation. In 1979, a confrontation between members of the Communist Workers Party and the Ku Klux Klan in Greensboro ended in shooting and five deaths. The Klansmen, who had done the shooting, were never convicted, and as with many incidents of racially charged violence in the South, an uneasy silence settled over the Greensboro Massacre. In recent years, though, the Greensboro Truth and Reconciliation Commission was set up, on the South African model, to try to get people to talk openly about what had happened twenty-five years earlier and put to rest some of the long-standing tensions. One of the first people to testify in the commission's open public hearings was Gorrell Pierce, in 1979 the Grand Dragon of the Federated Knights of the Ku Klux Klan, though he was not present at the shooting. Pierce started off his testimony by recounting his own upbringing and how stories he heard from his family set the stage for his future political commitments: "And on those porches, the talk by the elderly people—these were people that came before the radio or the TV—and on Sunday evenings they dipped snuff and they talked about the Civil War and Reconstruction and how things used to be. And I would travel, when I got big enough to travel on my own, from porch to porch to hear more. . . . The older people spoke about Reconstruction and how the Klan overthrew the Reconstruction government. Of course, we all know it was a horrible bad time for anybody, black or white, poor or rich. There wasn't anybody rich, except for the carpetbaggers. So as I got older and loved history, it was easy for me to study North Carolina history, easy for me to study southern history, and down this road I went. And had I been born in New York City, I probably would have made a good Communist. But being born in where I was, it made me a very good Klansman." In this one short statement, Pierce encompasses several key points made in this book. People in the South until at least the last third or so of the twentieth century received their most basic grounding in the region's history and in their personal connection to that history not from mass media, not from public education, but from stories related by members of their immediate communities, starting with the extended family. The place of Reconstruction in these cycles of stories is key to understanding how people, white and black, saw the society around them. For Pierce, growing up as the civil rights movement was getting under way, the stories of the Ku Klux Klan during Reconstruction encouraged him to join the Ku Klux Klan to work against the change he saw happening around him, a reaction more extreme than some, but by no means uncommon. With the perspective of age, Pierce acknowledges the power that stories of Reconstruction held for the South when he grew up. Memory of Reconstruction shaped the South in the twentieth century. Perhaps understanding how that happened can help shape the South in the twenty-first century.[10]

NOTES

ABBREVIATIONS USED IN NOTES

AAA	Agricultural Adjustment Administration
ASNLH	Association for the Study of Negro Life and History
CGW/ASNLH	Papers of Carter G. Woodson and the Association for the Study of Negro Life and History, 1915–1950
CGW/LOC	The Carter G. Woodson Collection of Negro Papers and Related Documents
CIC	Commission on Interracial Cooperation Papers, 1919–1944
CIO	Congress of Industrial Organizations
CU	Special Collections, Strom Thurmond Institute, Clemson University, Clemson, S.C.
DU	Rare Book, Manuscript, and Special Collections Library, Duke University, Durham, N.C.
DUA	Duke University Archives, Durham, N.C.
FWP	Federal Writers' Project
GAR	Grand Army of the Republic
KKK	Ku Klux Klan
LSR	Laura Spelman Rockefeller Memorial Collection
NAACP	National Association for the Advancement of Colored People
NYA	National Youth Administration
PDC	Pendleton District Commission, Pendleton, S.C.
PDP	South Carolina Progressive Democratic Party
SCDAH	South Carolina Department of Archives and History, Columbia, S.C.
SCHS	South Carolina Historical Society, Charleston, S.C.
SCL	South Caroliniana Library, University of South Carolina, Columbia, S.C.
SHA	Southern Historical Association

SHC   Southern Historical Collection, Manuscript Department, Wilson Library, University of North Carolina at Chapel Hill
SISS   Senate Internal Security Subcommittee
SNYC   Southern Negro Youth Congress
TWOC   Textile Workers Organizing Committee
UDC   United Daughters of the Confederacy
UDC-WHC   United Daughters of the Confederacy, Wade Hampton Chapter
UNCA   University Archives, Manuscript Department, Wilson Library, University of North Carolina at Chapel Hill
WPA   Works Progress Administration

INTRODUCTION

1. Ciardi, *How Does a Poem Mean?*

2. Marx, *Eighteenth Brumaire*, 15.

3. Olick and Robbins, "Social Memory Studies," 108 (second quotation), 112 (first and fourth quotations); Nora, "Reasons for the Current Upsurge," (third quotation).

4. Brundage, *Southern Past;* C. R. Wilson, *Baptized in Blood;* Foster, *Ghosts of the Confederacy;* Blight, *Race and Reunion;* Hale, *Making Whiteness,* 75–84.

5. Kantrowitz, *Ben Tillman,* 3; Poole, *Never Surrender;* Holden, *In the Great Maelstrom,* 5.

6. Hobsbawm, "Mass-Producing Traditions," 263; Kammen, *Mystic Chords of Memory,* 93–100 (quotation, 94). Blight, *Race and Reunion,* 120–22, points out the importance that actors during Reconstruction placed on shaping future interpretations of the period.

7. Nora, "Between Memory and History," 7. On historical memory in the South, see the essays in Brundage, *Where These Memories Grow,* especially Brundage's introductory essay, "No Deed But Memory," and also his *Southern Past.*

8. Vansina, *Oral Tradition as History;* Glassie, "Practice and Purpose of History," 963 (quotation); Glassie, *Passing the Time in Ballymenone;* Montell, *Killings;* Paredes, *"With His Pistol in His Hand";* Fentress and Wickham, *Social Memory.*

9. Fentress and Wickham, *Social Memory,* 47.

10. Nora, "Between Memory and History"; Vansina, *Oral Tradition as History,* 120–21; Glassie, *Passing the Time in Ballymenone,* 118–19, 147, 152–53, 195–97, 199, 375–76; Ives, *Bonny Earl of Murray,* 111–13; Patterson, *Tree Accurst,* 65–67, 71, 79–80, 100–11; Baker, "Under the Rope," 322.

11. Lord, *Singer of Tales;* Fentress and Wickham, *Social Memory,* 49–51.

12. Scott, *Domination and the Arts of Resistance,* xii; Fraser, "Rethinking the Public Sphere," 67; Bodnar, *Remaking America,* 13–17.

13. Zerubavel, *Recovered Roots,* 10; Foucault, *Power/Knowledge,* 38.

ONE. CREATING MEANING
DURING RECONSTRUCTION

1. Zuczek, *State of Rebellion*, 103–7, argues convincingly that local opposition had moderated Ku Klux Klan outrages before federal intervention. Williams, *Great South Carolina Ku Klux Klan Trials*, demonstrates the half-hearted nature of the federal prosecutions of Ku Klux Klan members.

2. Foner, *Free Soil, Free Labor*, 11–13; Richardson, *Death of Reconstruction*, 6–40.

3. Durden, *James Shepherd Pike*, 3–5, 14–35, 187–88, 201–204 (first quotation, 31; second quotation, 187–88); "A State in Ruins," *New York Tribune*, 5 March 1872 (third quotation).

4. Richardson, *Death of Reconstruction*, 107.

5. Pike, *Prostrate State*, 12 (first quotation), 83 (second and third quotations); Richardson, *Death of Reconstruction*, 106 (fourth quotation); Durden, *James Shepherd Pike*, 215. For more on the Taxpayers' Conventions, see Williamson, *After Slavery*, 157; Martin, *Southern Hero*, 189; Richardson, *Death of Reconstruction*, 93–94, 111–13; Kantrowitz, *Ben Tillman*, 60.

6. Godkin, "Socialism in South Carolina," 247–48 (quotation 247); Zuczek, *State of Rebellion*, 139, 141.

7. Zuczek, *State of Rebellion*, 151.

8. Foner, *Reconstruction*, 423–24, 444, 550–51, 558–63; Rable, *But There Was No Peace*, 122–62. As Steven Hahn points out in *A Nation under Our Feet*, 295–313, politics in the South throughout most of the nineteenth century was more a matter of paramilitary power than electoral democracy.

9. Zuczek, *State of Rebellion*, 151–52, 161–65 (quotation 161); Williamson, *After Slavery*, 330–31; Kantrowitz, *Ben Tillman*, 64–71; Martin, *Southern Hero*, 207–11.

10. Zuczek, *State of Rebellion*, 166, 168–69, 172–78; Simkins and Woody, *South Carolina during Reconstruction*, 564–69; Kantrowitz, *Ben Tillman*, 74; Poole, "Never Surrender," 213 (quotation). For a day-by-day account of the campaign, see A. B. Williams, *Hampton and His Red Shirts*.

11. Woodward, *Reunion and Reaction*.

TWO. WADE HAMPTON'S LEGEND
IN BEN TILLMAN'S WORLD

1. Kantrowitz, *Ben Tillman*, 2.

2. U.S. Congress, Joint Congressional Committee on Inaugural Ceremonies, *Inaugural Addresses*, 184; Hirshon, *Farewell to the Bloody Shirt*, 168–214.

3. Herbert, *Why the Solid South?* Hammett, *Hilary Abner Herbert*, 1, 14, 24–42, 43–51, 52 (first quotation), 62, 142; Herbert, "How We Redeemed Alabama"; Herbert, "Reminiscences," 370, Hilary A. Herbert Papers, SHC (second quotation); Herbert to Zebulon B. Vance et al., 8 April 1889, P.C. 15.14, Zebulon Baird Vance Papers, North Carolina Department of Archives and History, Raleigh, N.C. (third quotation). The twelve addressees of the 1889 letter were William L. Wilson (West Virginia), J. Randolph Tucker (Washington, D.C.), Zebulon B. Vance

(North Carolina), Wade Hampton (South Carolina), Henry G. Turner (Georgia), Samuel D. Pasco (Florida), James Q. George (Mississippi), William B. Bate (Tennessee), S. M. Robertson (Louisiana), Charles D. Stewart (Texas), John H. Rogers (Arkansas), and George G. Vest (Washington, D.C.).

4. Garlington, *Men of the Time,* 197–98. An overview of political corruption during this period may be found in M. W. Summer, *Era of Good Stealings.* See also Richardson, *Death of Reconstruction,* 57–60, 93. Hemphill, "Reconstruction in South Carolina," 110 (quotation).

5. By the time of this speech, the new Tillmanite Senate in South Carolina had voted to replace Hampton. Simkins, *Pitchfork Ben Tillman,* 186–87; Hirshon, *Farewell to the Bloody Shirt,* 215–35; *Congressional Record,* vol. 22, pt. 2, 51st Cong., 2nd sess., Senate, 16 Jan. 1891, 1421 (first quotation), 1419 (second and third quotations).

6. Tindall, "South Carolina Constitutional Convention," 20.

7. Kousser, *Shaping of Southern Politics;* Tindall, "South Carolina Constitutional Convention," 1 (first quotation), 20 (second quotation), 26, 135–41; Ball, *State that Forgot,* 138; *Columbia State,* 15 May 1895 (third quotation).

8. Woodward, *Strange Career of Jim Crow,* commemorative ed., 85–86; Feldman, *Disfranchisement Myth,* 36–37 (first quotation), 98 (second quotation).

9. Kantrowitz, *Ben Tillman,* 256–58; Wilk, "Phoenix Riot," 48 (first quotation), 49 (second quotation).

10. "Camp Moultrie, Sons of C. V., Charleston," *Confederate Veteran* 2 (November 1894): 327; "Patriotic Sons of Veterans," *Confederate Veteran* 4 (July 1895): 215–17; *Confederate Veteran* 4 (December 1896): 409; *Echoes from "Hampton Day,"* 4 (quotation). For another consideration of Hampton Day and South Carolina's remembrance of Hampton, see Holden, "'Is Our Love for Wade Hampton Foolishness?'"

11. McArthur and Burton, "Gentleman and an Officer," 82–91; Field, *Hampton Legion;* Wells, *Hampton and Reconstruction,* 140.

12. *Charleston Daily Courier,* 22 March 1865.

13. *Confederate Veteran* 3, no. 6 (June 1895): 175; *Charleston News and Courier,* 15 May 1895; *Charleston News and Courier,* 16 May 1895.

14. *Charleston News and Courier,* 14 May 1895.

15. *Columbia State,* 15 May 1895. The speech is also reprinted in *Echoes from "Hampton Day."*

16. Many of these publications were first-person accounts of Wells's service in the Civil War and therefore concerned Wade Hampton. See the following articles, all by Edward L. Wells: "Experiences of a Northern Man"; "Who Burnt Columbia?"; "Morning Call on General Kilpatrick"; "Hampton at Fayetteville"; "Comment on 'The Crisis of the Confederacy'"; "Review of John S. Wise"; "Review of B. K. Benson"; "Review of Mrs. St. Julien Ravenel"; "Review of Mrs. George Bryan Conrad." Edward L. Wells to "Dear General" [Wade Hampton], 12 February 1896, Edward L. Wells to James Grant Wilson, 25 June 1898, and Edward L. Wells to B. F. Johnson, 13 June 1899, all in Edward L. Wells Papers; Wells, *Hampton and His Cavalry.*

17. Wells, *Hampton and Reconstruction,* iv.

18. Wells, *Hampton and Reconstruction*, 86, 87, 91–97 (quotation 86).

19. *American Historical Review* 13, no. 2 (January 1908): 426; "Review of Edward L. Wells, *Hampton and Reconstruction*," *Independent*, 53 (17 October 1907), 946; *Columbia State*, 12 May 1907.

20. Novick, *That Noble Dream*, 21, 53 (quotation); *American Historical Review* 1, no. 1 (October 1895).

21. For another phase of this process, see Brundage, *Southern Past*, 117–20.

22. "Vita," Hollis, *Early Period of Reconstruction*, 130; Dunning, *Essays on the Civil War and Reconstruction*; Dunning, *Reconstruction, Political and Economic*; Novick, *That Noble Dream*, 230–34; Foner, *Reconstruction*, xix–xxii.

23. Hollis, *Early Period of Reconstruction*, 45–46.

24. Ibid., 76 n. 36, 83 (second quotation), 125 (first quotation); Fermer, *James Gordon Bennett*, 141–54, 297–309. On fears of insurrection in South Carolina during this period, see Saville, *Work of Reconstruction*, 148–49; Carter, "Anatomy of Fear," 347–48; and Hahn, "Nation under Our Feet," 146–59.

25. Jones, *Stormy Petrel*, 138 (first quotation); G. A. Wauchope, "Review of Reynolds, *Reconstruction in South Carolina*" from *Baltimore Sun*, reprinted in *Columbia State*, 10 June 1906 (second quotation); Reynolds, *Reconstruction in South Carolina*, 2 (third quotation).

26. Wauchope, "Review of Reynolds"; F. W. Moore, "Review of Reynolds," 180–81; Conkin, "History of Vanderbilt's History Department"; Dodd, "South Carolina Reconstruction"; "Reconstruction in South Carolina," *Outlook* 83 (4 August 1906), 816 (fourth quotation); "The Civil War and After," *Independent* 61 (13 September 1906), 639 (fifth quotation); Macaulay, "South Carolina Reconstruction Historiography," 24 (seventh quotation).

27. Lyotard, *Postmodern Condition*, 18–23.

28. *Columbia State*, 12 May 1907 (first quotation); Novick, *That Noble Dream*, 37; *Columbia State*, 6 May 1906 (third quotation). For other Dunning School state histories, see, for instance, Fleming, *Civil War and Reconstruction*; Garner, *Reconstruction in Mississippi*; and Woolley, *Reconstruction of Georgia*. The chronology of 1865 to 1877 for Reconstruction is itself the product of certain historical assumptions and beliefs. It would be challenged by W. E. B. Du Bois in *Black Reconstruction* and later by Eric Foner in *Reconstruction* by changing the center of the narrative to the freed slaves.

29. News of Hampton's death occupied most of the 12 and 13 April 1902 editions of South Carolina's daily newspapers. The details of my account come from the *Charleston News and Courier*, the *Columbia State*, and the *Greenville Daily News*. Guthke, *Last Words*, 54. Hampton was one of the dying Confederates represented in Pendleton, *Last Words of Confederate Heroes*, 7–8.

30. Rogers, "South Mourns a Leader"; Massey, *Upcountry Reflections*, 163.

31. Leach, *Land of Desire*, 63; *Columbia State*, 12 April 1902; *Columbia State*, 13 April 1902 (quotation); *Greenville Daily News*, 13 April 1902.

32. *Laurens Advertiser*, 16 April 1902; *Charleston News and Courier*, 14 April 1902; *Newberry Herald and News*, 15 April 1902; *Greenville Daily News*, 13 and 20 April 1902; *Georgetown Times*, 16 April 1902; *Columbia State*, 12 April 1902.

33. *Columbia State,* 16 April 1902. The most detailed coverage of the funeral is in the *Columbia State,* 14 April 1902, but all papers in the state and many others throughout the country carried accounts on that date.

34. *Columbia State,* 12 April 1902 (first quotation) and 16 May 1902; *Greenville News,* 16 and 22 April 1902; Savage, *Standing Soldiers, Kneeling Slaves,* 6 (second quotation).

35. *Greenville News,* 23, 27, and 30 April and 2 May 1902; *Final Report of the Commission to Provide for a Monument,* 5, 8–9; "Monument of Wade Hampton," *Confederate Veteran* 15 (March 1907): 134; *Columbia State,* 14 May and 22, 23, 25 October 1903.

36. Ruckstull, *Great Works of Art,* 517–42, and "Ruckstull Dies at 89," *Art Digest* 18; Bogart, "In Search of a United Front," 162 (quotation); "Baltimore Monument—Ruckstuhl," *Confederate Veteran* 11, no. 3 (March 1903): 133; "Unveiling of Maryland Monument," *Confederate Veteran* 11, no. 6 (June 1903): 268–69.

37. "Monument of Wade Hampton," *Confederate Veteran* 15 (March 1907): 134 (first quotation); Wellman, *Giant in Gray,* illustrations and captions following page 176 (second quotation); Claude E. Sawyer to W. P. Houseal, 17 November 1926, Statements Concerning the Election of 1876, Historical Commission, Department of Archives and History, SCDAH (third quotation); *Greenville News,* 21 November 1906 (fourth quotation); *New York Daily Tribune,* 19 November 1906, 3; Savage, *Standing Soldiers, Kneeling Slaves,* 133.

THREE. CELEBRATING THE RED SHIRTS

1. Horace Williams to Carlee McClendon, 5 May 1970, Tricentennial Commission (S219007), Director, County Correspondence, 1968–71, Anderson folder, SCDAH; Samuel W. Kluttz to J. W. Daniel, 13 December 1930, Folder 20, James W. Daniel Papers, SCL; J. Tompkins, *Sensational Designs,* xiii, xi; E. L. Ayers, *Promise of the New South,* 339–72 (quotation 372). Although Ayers does not explain it in these terms, the transition he describes corresponds to the transition in whites' attitudes toward blacks that Joel Williamson charted from a "Liberal" phase in the years immediately after Reconstruction to a "Radical" phase around the beginning of the twentieth century. Williamson, *Crucible of Race,* 109–39.

2. Two good summaries of the reconciliationist literature of the 1880s and 1890s are Silber, *Romance of Reunion,* 105–22, and Blight, *Race and Reunion,* 216–17, 221.

3. P. Brooks, *Melodramatic Imagination,* 20 (first quotation), 200 (second quotation), 12–13 (third quotation), 199; Fox-Genovese and Genovese, "Divine Sanction of the Social Order."

4. Blight, *Race and Reunion,* 222–27; Page, "Red Rock," *Scribner's Magazine* 23, no. 1: 34–52; 23, no. 2: 161–78; 23, no. 3: 292–310; 23, no. 498): 481–96; 23, no. 5: 613–32; 23, no. 6: 689–708; 24, no. 1: 113–22; 24, no. 2: 237–51; 24, no. 3: 350–70; 24, no. 4: 470–88; 24, no. 5: 578–96; *New York Times,* 12 May 1900, BR9. I am passing over George Washington Cable's 1894 novel *John March, Southerner.* Cable wrote the novel in the late 1880s, after he had already been chased out of the South for

his liberal views on race, and the novel made little impression on the public. E. L. Ayers, *Promise of the New South,* 347–48.

5. Dixon, *Clansman.* For a good discussion of Dixon's views on race as expressed in his writings, see Williamson, *Crucible of Race,* 140–79.

6. J. W. Daniel, *Maid of the Foot-Hills;* Watson, *Builders,* 91. J. W. Daniel, *Girl in Checks; Out from under Caesar's Frown; Ramble among Surnames;* and *Cateechee of Keeowee.* James Walter Daniel Papers, SCL.

7. Daniel likely heard of Jolly as a child in the next county, and he would have heard stories about the outlaw while pastoring Methodist churches in Anderson County in 1881 and from 1884 to 1886: Watson, *Builders,* 91. Vandiver, *Traditions and History,* 228, 249; "Cabin Home of Manse Jolly, One-Man Army, Still Stands," newspaper clipping dated 5 October 1940, p. 6, Watson Scrapbooks, SCL; McCully, "Letter from a Reconstruction Renegade"; Manse Jolly Papers (bound typescript), South Carolina Room, Anderson County Library, Anderson, S.C.; De Forest, *Union Officer in the Reconstruction,* 14–16; "'Manse' Jolly," photocopy of undated clipping (internal references in the article place its date shortly after 1916), from *Anderson Daily Tribune,* Manse Jolly File, PDC (quotation); typescript of letter from James George Harper, April 1926, Jolly File; Rufus M. Newton, "Manse Jolly, Anderson Guerilla, Kept Federal Garrison in Terror," *Columbia State,* 7 August 1932; Rufus M. Newton, "Manse Jolly, Anderson Guerilla, Became More and More Revengeful," *Columbia State,* 14 August 1932; "Jolly Took Off 92 Years Ago," *Anderson Independent,* 29 January 1958. See also the extensive clipping collection in Jolly File.

8. Daniel, *Maid of the Foot-Hills,* 89, 122–23, 139–46. Daniel may have had in mind an incident supposed to have occurred in Anderson during Reconstruction when Prince Rivers, a black officer garrisoned there with the federal army, sat down in the middle of the Baptist Church during a morning service one Sunday. Vandiver, *Traditions and History,* 250–51.

9. De Forest, "Report of Outrages"; Leland, *Voice from South Carolina,* 65–74.

10. Trelease, *White Terror,* 362–80; Daniel, *Maid of the Foot-Hills,* 158–62; U.S. Congress, Joint Select Committee, *Testimony,* 3:212, 5:1364–65, 1472, 1757–69, 1795–99. David W. Blight discusses how this report was positioned by its Republican and Democratic authors as a potent record of two opposing views of Reconstruction. He states, "The minority [Democrat] report from the Klan hearings could have served as an initial script for Dixon's and Griffith's *Birth of a Nation,*" as indeed it did serve as an important source for Daniel's and Page's novels. Blight, *Race and Reunion,* 114–22 (quotation, 122).

11. Daniel, *Maid of the Foot-Hills,* 76–79 (quotation, 79), 103–6; "Cabin Home of Manse Jolly," clipping; "Manse Jolly, Confederate Guerilla, with $25,000 Reward upon His Head, Rides into Federal Camp and 'Calls' Yankee Bluff," clipping dated 9 June 1928, p. 2, Watson Scrapbooks. On Furman's death, see "Letter of S. K. Dendy, Sr., to Southern Daughters," in South Carolina Division, UDC, *Recollections and Reminiscences,* 4:481; S. T. King, *Reminiscences of My Life in Camp,* 43–44; Trowbridge, "Six Months in the Freedmen's Bureau," 203–4; and Higginson, *Army Life in a Black Regiment,* 210. On Myers, see W. J. Elliott, "Random

Recollections of Fairfield County," clipping on p. 18 of "Fairfield Addenda 1946" Scrapbook, Fairfield County Museum, Genealogy Room, Winnsboro, S.C. On Hardin, see Metz, *John Wesley Hardin*, 8–23.

12. Daniel, *Maid of the Foot-Hills*, 56–64, 71–72, 118–21, 148 (quotation), 152, 171–83, 198–225, 242–48. According to Thomas B. Keys, *Army and Crawford Keys* (in manuscript collections), 99, "Many Anderson District natives considered Manse S. Jolly a southern Robin Hood."

13. Daniel, *Maid of the Foot-Hills*, 7 (quotation), 38–46, 118–20, 152–55, 171, 192–97, 242–48.

14. Ibid., 7; P. Brooks, *Melodramatic Imagination*, 44; McConachie, *Melodramatic Formations*, 124.

15. P. Brooks, *Melodramatic Imagination*, 27 (first quotation); Hobson, *But Now I See*, 1–17, esp. 13; Daniel, *Maid of the Foot-Hills*, 118–27, 171–83, 214 (third quotation), 215–24.

16. Simkins and Woody, *South Carolina during Reconstruction*, 501.

17. Neville, *Kinship and Pilgrimage*, 23–24, 51–57, 87–94; Weiss, "Tourism in America," 304–6; Foster, *Ghosts of the Confederacy*, 128–44; Dearing, *Veterans in Politics*.

18. *Anderson Daily Mail*, 28 May 1897; enlistment certificate in Jesse C. Stribling Papers, CU; *Anderson Intelligencer*, 19 May 1897; *Pickens Sentinel*, 18 October 1883, 6 March 1890, 19 February 1891, 5 November 1891.

19. The Pendleton Farmers' Society was founded in 1815 in order to improve farming methods and agricultural production. Stribling was elected president in 1908, and planning began for the ninety-fourth annual meeting of the Pendleton Farmers Society, set for the late summer. Pendleton Farmers' Society, *Pendleton Farmers' Society*, 20–22; *Anderson Daily Mail*, 28 May 1927; Reynolds, *Reconstruction in South Carolina*; Daniel, *Maid of the Foot-Hills*; Wells, *Hampton and Reconstruction*.

20. *Columbia State*, 23 August 1908.

21. Ibid.; photographs in Red Shirt File, PDC.

22. Anderson was in the process of reorganizing its Chamber of Commerce to overcome the lingering effects of the Panic of 1907. *Anderson Daily Mail*, 28 June 1909.

23. Carlton, *Mill and Town*, 59–71, esp. 62–65; U.S. Department of Commerce, Bureau of the Census, *Thirteenth Census*, 3:650; Anderson population in 1909 from Norryce, *General Sketch of Anderson*; Kohn, *Cotton Mills of South Carolina*, 86–89, 108, 110, 214–17; *Anderson Daily Mail*, 30 July 1909; Vandiver, *Traditions and History*, 313.

24. McLaurin, *Paternalism and Protest*, 51. The first historian of the southern textile industry, Broadus Mitchell, pointed out the importance of Reconstruction to the growth of the industry as well. See Mitchell, *Rise of Cotton Mills*, 56–57, 62, 98–99. On Smyth, see Jacobs, *Pioneer*, 24, 31; D. A. Tompkins, *Cotton Mill, Commercial Features*, v; *Spartanburg Herald*, 21 August 1910 (third quotation).

25. On the labor shortage and recruiting workers from the mountains, see J. D. Hall et al., *Like a Family*, 107–11; Mitchell, *Rise of Cotton Mills*, 189–91; Link, *Para-*

dox of Southern Progressivism, 169–71. On the Panic of 1907, see Kolko, *Triumph of Conservatism,* 153–56. Carlton, *Mill and Town,* 249 (quotation); J. H. Moore, *Columbia and Richland County,* 311–12; McLaurin, "Early Labor Union Organizational Efforts," 58–59; Davidson, *Child Labor Legislation,* 139–42, 178–84.

26. McLaurin, *Paternalism and Protest,* 52; Link, *Paradox of Southern Progressivism,* 180–81.

27. *Anderson Daily Mail,* 3 July 1909 and 25 August 1909. One of the 1876 bands left detailed records: Pendleton Cornet Band Records, CU. On Orr Mills, see, for instance, Kohn, *Cotton Mills of South Carolina,* 166. Also, Orr Mills was featured in nearly all the photographs of mills in the promotional booklet by Norryce, *General Sketch of Anderson.* Carlton, citing N. G. Gonzales in the *Columbia State* newspaper, calls Orr Mills a "show mill" in *Mill and Town,* 192.

28. *Anderson Daily Mail,* 24 August 1909 (first quotation); Norryce, *General Sketch of Anderson; Anderson Daily Mail,* 26 August 1909 (second quotation).

29. Tillman's speech was printed in the *Anderson Daily Mail,* 4 September 1909. Later, a version that included descriptions of three other race riots was published as Tillman, *Struggles of 1876.*

30. Tillman, *Struggles of 1876,* 13 (first quotation), 27 (second quotation), 28 (third quotation). *Anderson Daily Mail,* 4 September 1909. For several years previous, Tillman had been working as an apostle of violent southern racism to the rest of the nation through speeches in the Senate and on the chautauqua circuit. He also may have wanted to depict himself as young and strong to counter the publicity of his poor health following a stroke in 1908. Kantrowitz, *Ben Tillman,* 287–89; Simkins, *Pitchfork Ben Tillman,* 462–63.

31. Downey, "Planting a Capitalist South," 23–27; Trent, *William Gilmore Simms,* 154; Hagood, *Meet Your Grandfather,* 113–14; 1860 Federal Census of Population, Free Inhabitants, South Carolina, Barnwell District, Dunbarton P.O., dwelling #558, p. 442; 1860 Federal Census of Population, Slave Inhabitants, South Carolina, Barnwell District, p. 240; *Columbia State,* 24 September 1911; Hennessy, *Return to Bull Run,* 400, 563; Barrett, *Sherman's March,* 52; Williamson, *After Slavery,* 267; 1870 Federal Manuscript Census of Population, Barnwell Post Office, Barnwell Township, Barnwell Co., S.C., p. 91.

32. Zuczek, *State of Rebellion,* 175–77; Kantrowitz, *Ben Tillman,* 74; 1870 Federal Manuscript Census of Population, Barnwell Post Office, Barnwell Township, Barnwell Co., S.C., 90.

33. Quoted in Drago, *Hurrah For Hampton!* 103.

34. *Columbia State,* 24 September 1911 (quotation) and 28 September 1911.

35. *Columbia State,* 28 and 29 September 1911. On Blease, see Simon, *Fabric of Defeat,* 11–35, and Williamson, *Crucible of Race,* 428–29.

36. *Anderson Daily Mail,* 29 September 1911; *Columbia State,* 27 September 1911.

37. F. W. P. Butler, "M'Kie Meriwether," *Columbia State,* 23 January 1914. The man directing the assault on the armory when Meriwether died was General Matthew C. Butler, the father of F. W. P. Butler. Garlington, *Men of the Time,* 66. Francis Wilkinson Pickens Butler was named for the Civil War governor of South

Carolina, his maternal grandfather. Martin, *Southern Hero*, 9. The career of the bill may be followed in South Carolina, *Journal of the House of Representatives Beginning Tuesday, January 13, 1914*, 290, 351, 1084, 1094, 1340, 1343, and South Carolina, *Journal of the Senate Beginning Tuesday, January 13, 1914*, 888, 905, 1005, 1067.

38. D. D. Wallace, *South Carolina*, 659; marginalia in Duke University's copy of McCravy, *Memories*, 16, bearing the inscription "A. S. Salley, Columbia, S.C., May 15, 1941" on the flyleaf; South Carolina, *Journal of the House of Representatives Beginning Tuesday, January 10, 1911*, 407 (first quotation), 920 (second quotation); U. R. Brooks, *Butler and His Cavalry*; "Pleads for a Monument to Confederate Chiefs," *Columbia State*, 1 February 1914; *Spartanburg Herald*, 18 August 1910.

39. Butler, "M'Kie Meriwether"; Simkins and Woody, *South Carolina during Reconstruction*, 567 (quotation); Carlton, *Mill and Town*, 246–49; Kantrowitz, *Ben Tillman*, 296–99. Meriwether could also serve better than Gary as a symbol of the goal of unity embodied in the project of white supremacy. Meriwether died in 1876 at age twenty-four, long before he had the opportunity to become embroiled in the factionalism that slowly ate away at the Democratic Party after 1876. Gary, on the other hand, had an open and nasty break with Hampton soon after he took off his red shirt. He died in 1881, but his legacy of political contrariness was carried forward by his protégé, Ben Tillman. Kantrowitz, *Ben Tillman*, 91–98; Cooper, *Conservative Regime*, 53–64.

40. *Columbia State*, 6 and 7 March 1914; South Carolina, *Acts and Joint Resolutions Regular Session of 1914*, 946 (first quotation); South Carolina, *Acts and Joint Resolutions Regular Session of 1915*, 427; *Columbia State*, 17 February 1916 (second quotation).

41. Henderson, "White Man's Revolution," 179, 181.

42. Ibid., 172, 174; J. W. Daniel, "By-Ways of State History," clipping from *Southern Christian Advocate* in Folder 1, Box 2, James Walter Daniel Papers, SCL.

43. Rogin, "'Sword Became a Flashing Vision,'" 151.

FOUR. MEMORIES AND COUNTERMEMORY

1. Fentress and Wickham, *Social Memory*, 41–86; Vansina, *Oral Tradition as History*, 98–100; Baker, "Under the Rope," 320–21, 335–38.

2. Blight, *Race and Reunion*.

3. Hahn, *Nation under Our Feet*, 135–46, 234–35, 249–51, 259–64; Richardson, *Death of Reconstruction*, 41–121; Kelly, "Not All Black and White"; Painter, *Exodusters*, 15; Trouillot, *Silencing the Past*, 73.

4. The most thorough and insightful account of how children were brought up with these historical memories is Katharine Du Pre Lumpkin's account of her childhood in Columbia, *Making of a Southerner*, 111–47. For a similar account from Charleston two decades later, see Rubin, "General Longstreet and Me." An evocative account of storytelling at veterans' reunions is provided by Katharine Du Pre Lumpkin's sister Grace Lumpkin in her novel *To Make My Bread*, 190–93.

For a general introduction to political speeches in the South during this period, see Braden, "The Rhetoric of Exploitation: Southern Demagogues in Action," in Braden, *Oral Tradition in the South,* 83–106.

5. Bonham, "A Boy's Memories," 1, Milledge Lipscomb Bonham Papers, SCL; Morgan, *Recollections of a Rebel Reefer.*

6. L. R. Ayers, "Red Shirt Election." The earlier typescript of this piece is in Loula Rockwell Ayers Recollections, SHC. Bonham, "A Boy's Memories," 2; Frances Reeves Jeffcoat, Introduction to South Carolina Division, UDC, *Recollections and Reminiscences,* 1:iii–v; Minute Book of the United Daughters of the Confederacy—Wade Hampton Chapter, June 1910–November 1913, 28, Confederate Relic Room, Columbia, S.C.

7. "Tells of Schools in Old Building," *Columbia State,* 29 September 1927; Caroline S. Coleman, "Girl Was 'Red Shirt' in 1876," *Charleston News and Courier,* 15 March 1942 (quotation); Nelle C. Wells, "Manning Woman Recalls Reconstruction Period," *Charleston News and Courier,* 15 April 1956; Victor B. Stanley Jr., "Table Preserved as Relic of 1876," *Charleston News and Courier,* 14 November 1937.

8. Sarah Ball Copeland, "Glimpses of Laurens County History," clipping dated 20 January 1927, p. 3, in Harry Legare Watson Scrapbooks (microfilm), SCL; Bonham, "Boy's Memories," 37.

9. Toole, *Ninety Years in Aiken County,* 17 (first quotation); Dr. Julius A. Mood, "Doctor Mood Writes Recollections Grave and Gay of His Rich Life; Went through Burning of Columbia," *Columbia State,* 17 December 1933 (second quotation).

10. Morgan, *Recollections of a Rebel Reefer,* 1–13, 320–22, 326–28 (quotation 327); Du Bois, *Black Reconstruction,* 409, 423; Bushman, *Refinement of America,* 390–98.

11. Schrager, "What Is Social in Oral History?" 22–33.

12. Bonham, "Boy's Memories," 39 (first and second quotations), 40 (second quotation); Utsey, *Who's Who in South Carolina,* 51; Camak, "Fairfield County, Thomas C. Camak" (third quotation). It is not insignificant that Camak described his participation in Redemption in terms drawn directly from the New Testament (1 Corinthians 13:11).

13. W. W. Ball, "How the Red-Shirts Rode with Hampton," *Charleston News and Courier,* 21 November 1906; Tillman, *Struggles of 1876,* 34; W. A. Strother, "Reminiscences of the Red Shirts of 1876," in South Carolina Division, UDC, *Recollections and Reminiscences,* 4:471; L. R. Ayers, "Red Shirt Election," 60–61. Fiction writers also found the scene of women sewing red shirts appealing: see Daniel, *Maid of the Foot-Hills,* 212.

14. South Carolina Division, UDC, *Recollections and Reminiscences,* 1:507. "Memoir of Sally Elmore Taylor," 166–69, Series 3, Folder 6, Franklin Harper Elmore Papers, SHC, 165–69 (quotation, 166).

15. Brundage, "No Deed but Memory," 3–4; Alexander C. Shaffer, "Service in the South," p. 100 1/2, Edward Terry Hendrie Shaffer Papers, SCL; Zuczek, *State of Rebellion,* 76, 197; *Columbia State,* 31 December 1902.

16. Brundage, "Whispering Consolation to Generations Unborn," 342–43; Brundage, *Southern Past*, 55–104; Clark, *Defining Moments*.

17. *Columbia State*, 2 January 1902 (quotation). On Emancipation Day celebrations in South Carolina, see Wiggins, "African American Celebrations," 17–18; Tindall, *South Carolina Negroes*, 288–89; and Clark, "Celebrating Freedom." Folklorist William H. Wiggins Jr. provides a broad study of Emancipation Day and related celebrations in *O Freedom!* though it does not convey a good sense of how the celebrations developed over time.

18. *Columbia State*, 1 January 1892; *Columbia State*, 2 January 1901; *Jacksonville Times-Union*, 2 January 1901. Standard accounts of parades in U.S. history (such as Davis, *Parades and Power*, and Ryan, "American Parade") have tended to think of them as pluralistic representations of a unified civic culture, but Emancipation Day parades existed in opposition to a determinedly nonpluralistic society. Such parades were, to borrow Raymond Williams's taxonomy, emergent, trying to bring something new—social equality or at least respect for African Americans—into being, in opposition to the dominant culture of white supremacy. Williams laid out his indispensable taxonomy of cultural change in *Marxism and Literature*, 121–27.

19. Blight, *Race and Reunion*, 64–84; Davies, "Problem of Race Segregation"; *Savannah Tribune*, 6 June 1914; *Columbia State*, 3 June 1899; *Charleston News and Courier*, 31 May 1890.

20. Edgar, *South Carolina*, 360. On the Florence Stockade, see Harrold, *Libby, Andersonville, Florence*, 55–56; Grigsby, *Smoked Yank*, 177–98; G. W. King, "Death Camp at Florence." Accounts of Decoration Day are found in *Columbia State*, 1 June 1901; *Savannah Tribune*, 30 May 1914; *Columbia State*, 1 June 1901; *Columbia State*, 1 June 1902; *Columbia State*, 30 and 31 May 1897; *Charleston News and Courier*, 30 May 1893; *Columbia State*, 29 May 1893; *Columbia State*, 1 June 1898; *Columbia State*, 31 May 1902; *Darlington News*, 4 June 1896.

21. *Darlington News*, 20 May 1890; *Charleston News and Courier*, 31 May 1890; Brayton, *Address Delivered on Decoration Day*, 8 (first quotation), 10 (second quotation).

22. Hirsch, *Portrait of America*.

23. Heywood, "Aunt Mariah Heywood"; Sherman, "Slave Interview."

24. Rawick, *American Slave*, supplement, series 1, 5:482–83, 489. See also Rawick, *American Slave*, 2, pt. 3:313.

25. Hampton, "Slave Narrative"; Haynes, "Aunt Dolly Haynes."

26. Glassberg, *American Historical Pageantry*. Thanks to songwriter Bill Morrissey for the phrasing of the last sentence.

27. *Columbia State*, 3 January 1905, 2 January 1896.

28. *Columbia State*, 3 January 1899; Tindall, *South Carolina Negroes*, 81, 87.

29. *Columbia State*, 2 January 1904; Clark, "Celebrating Freedom," 111–12, 116–17; Blight, *Race and Reunion*, 91.

30. *Darlington News*, 30 May 1889; *Charleston News and Courier*, 31 May 1893; *Darlington News*, 4 June 1896; *Columbia State*, 3 June 1899 (quotation); *Charleston News and Courier*, 31 May 1890; *Columbia State*, 3 June 1899. For subsequent

celebrations of Decoration Day in Florence, see the *Columbia State* on the following dates: 1 June 1902, 31 May 1904, 2 June 1912, 2 June 1913, 1 June 1914, 31 May 1920, 1 June 1920, 31 May 1922, 31 May 1923, 31 May 1928. A few years earlier, African Americans had been forced out of Decoration Day celebrations at Mobile. See *Charleston News and Courier*, 31 May 1892; *Charleston News and Courier*, 31 May 1895.

31. *Beaufort Gazette*, 6 June 1913, 4 June 1915; Champie, *Brief History of the Marine Corps*, 2–5; *Beaufort Gazette*, 1 June 1917 (quotation).

32. *Beaufort Gazette*, 4 June 1920, 3 June 1921, 1 June 1923, 4 June 1925; *Columbia Palmetto Leader*, 20 June 1925; *Beaufort Gazette*, 27 May 1926, 2 June 1927, 31 May 1928, 7 June 1928, 13 June 1929, 5 June 1930, 4 June 1931; *New York Tribune*, 2 June 1929; interview with Eva Chaplin by Sally S. Graham, St. Helena Island, S.C., 5 August 1994, Tray 11B, Behind the Veil Collection, DU; interview with Kathleen Daise by Sally S. Graham, St. Helena Island, S.C., 1 August 1994, Tray 11B, Behind the Veil Collection; *Beaufort Gazette*, 26 May and 2 June 1938. For more on Christensen and his family, see Tetzlaff, *Cultivating a New South*.

33. Brundage, "Whispering Consolation to Generations Unborn," 350–52.

34. W. K. Hughes, "Veteran Negro Janitor."

35. McCreight, "Ku Klux Stories"; "The Ellenton Riot," K-1–2, item #10, Federal Writers' Project Collection, SCL; Coleman, "Mrs. Jennie Isabel Coleman"; "The K.K.K. at Mt. Pleasant," B-1–16, item #3, Federal Writers' Project Collection; Rawick, *American Slave*, supplement, series 1, 5:488–89 (first quotation); G. L. Summer, *Folklore of South Carolina*, 49–55; Rawick, *American Slave*, 2, pt. 2:120–21 (second quotation). The ex-slave narratives are full of accounts of violence during Reconstruction. For more on this, see Mercer, "Tapping the Slave Narrative Collection," 367–70.

36. "Joshua Rivers, Son of the Negro Leader, Tells the Story of the Hamburg Riot of 1876," B-4–18, item #12, Federal Writers' Project Collection; "B. F. Randolph," H-2–18, item #1, Federal Writers' Project Collection.

37. McCreight, "Ku Klux Stories"; Rawick, *American Slave*, 14, pt. 2:247–51; "The K.K.K. at Mt. Pleasant," B-1–16, item #3, Federal Writers' Project Collection.

38. William W. Lumpkin, "Where and Why I Was a Kuklux," Civil War Collections, Box 76, Folder 66, North Carolina State Archives, Raleigh, N.C.; J. D. Hall, "'You Must Remember This,'" 443–53; K. D. Lumpkin, *Making of a Southerner*, 121–27.

FIVE. RECONSTRUCTION AND POLITICS IN THE ROOSEVELT ERA

1. *Charleston Evening Post*, 28 September 1932; Toole, *Ninety Years in Aiken County*, 66; *Florence Morning News*, 28 October 1932 (quotation); Lewinson, *Race, Class, and Party*, 170–76; Key, *Southern Politics in State and Nation*, 288–89; Tindall, *South Carolina Negroes*, 67.

2. Ball had read Bowers's book enthusiastically when it came out, and he had

it in mind as he wrote his own book later. W. W. Ball to W. E. Gonzales, 28 August 1929, Box 18, Ball Papers; W. W. Ball to D. L. Chambers, 29 January 1931 and 20 February 1931, Box 19, Ball Papers (first quotation); W. W. Ball to D. L. Chambers, 26 March 1932, Box 20, Ball Papers (second quotation); Thomas F. McDow to W. W. Ball, 8 December 1931, Box 19, Ball Papers (third quotation); E. H. Shanklin to W. W. Ball, 28 March 1932, Box 20, Ball Papers; Bowers, *Tragic Era*; Ball, *State that Forgot*, 142, 154–61; Holden, *In the Great Maelstrom*, 89, 101.

3. Ball, *State that Forgot*, 15; W. W. Ball, "How the Red-Shirts Rode with Hampton," *Charleston News and Courier*, 21 November 1906; Ball, *Boy's Recollections*.

4. Ernest L. Ewbank Sr. to W. W. Ball, 26 October 1932 (quotation), Ellison A. Smyth to W. W. Ball, 28 October 1932, and Robert D. Bass to W. W. Ball, 25 November 1932, Box 21, Ball Papers; *Greenwood Index-Journal*, 14 October 1932. For responses to the book, see letters from 12 October 1932 to 31 October 1932, Box 21, Ball Papers.

5. Folder 82, Alexander S. Salley Jr. Papers, SCL (first quotation); circular from Owen Daly, 5 August 1908, Folder 166, Salley Papers; Folder 1, Salley Papers; William E. Dodd, "South Carolina Reconstruction," *New York Times Saturday Review of Books*, 18 August 1906, 506 (second quotation).

6. *Columbia State*, 22 July 1932 (first quotation); *Camden Chronicle*, 4 November 1932 (second quotation); *Florence Morning News*, 27 October 1932 (third quotation); Hayes, *South Carolina and the New Deal*, 16. W. J. Cash noted a similar equation of Herbert Hoover with the Radical Republicans of Reconstruction in 1932. See Cash, *Mind of the South*, 374.

7. Tindall, *Emergence of the New South*, 111–42; Kirby, "Southern Exodus," 594.

8. Sullivan, *Days of Hope*, 43; Rable, "South and the Politics of Antilynching," 212; Sitkoff, *New Deal for Blacks*, 48–49; P. Daniel, *Breaking the Land*, 63–151.

9. Hayes, *South Carolina and the New Deal*, 162–65; Sullivan, *Days of Hope*, 43.

10. Sullivan, *Days of Hope*, 43–48 (quotation, 48); Hayes, *South Carolina and the New Deal*, 167–68; P. Daniel, *Breaking the Land*, 193–94; Hoffman, "Genesis of the Modern Movement"; Lewinson, *Race, Class, and Party*, 153–54.

11. Simon, *Fabric of Defeat*, 112; Waldrep, *Southern Workers*, 89, 95–105; Irons, *Testing the New Deal*; Salmond, *General Textile Strike of 1934*.

12. On historical pageants, see Glassberg, *American Historical Pageantry*. Examples from South Carolina include Walmsley, *Making of South Carolina*, and South Carolina, *Historical Pageant of South Carolina*. *Charleston News and Courier*, 28 July 1935 (quotation) and 17 March 1935; *Greenville Piedmont*, 16 October 1935.

13. Sullivan, *Days of Hope*, 59; Robertson, *Sly and Able*, 64–65, 121–22, 144–56, 189, 191, 196; Hayes, *South Carolina and the New Deal*, 137–38, 141–42; Tindall, *Emergence of the New South*, 607–8.

14. *New York Times*, 25 June 1936; Robertson, *Sly and Able*, 190–93.

15. A. F. Lever to James F. Byrnes, 28 June 1936, Box 12, Senatorial, Misc., 1936, L, James F. Byrnes Papers, CU (first quotation); A. F. Lever to James F. Byrnes, 30 June and 9 July 1936, and A. F. Lever to Cassie Connor, 31 July 1936, Box 12, Senatorial, Misc., 1936, L, Byrnes Papers; *Columbia State*, 8 July 1936 (second quotation); *Columbia State*, 7, 9, 15, and 31 July 1936; typescript attached to letter from James F. Byrnes to A. F. Lever, 3 August 1936, Box 12, Senatorial, Misc., 1936, L, Byrnes Papers (third quotation) (another version of this letter was published as an editorial in the *Columbia State*, 31 July 1936); *Columbia State*, 10 July 1936 (fourth quotation); Robertson, *Sly and Able*, 199.

16. Leuchtenburg, *Roosevelt and the New Deal*, 190–96, 231–51; Sullivan, *Days of Hope*, 61.

17. Simon, *Fabric of Defeat*, 197–203.

18. *Columbia State*, 30 July 1938.

19. *Congressional Record*, vol. 79, pt. 6, 74th Cong., 1st sess., 29 April 1935, 6520 (first quotation), 30 April 1935, 6616 (second quotation); *Congressional Record*, vol. 83, pt. 1, 75th Cong., 3rd sess., 8 January 1938, 228 (third and fourth quotations), 229 (fifth quotation).

20. *Columbia State*, 30 July 1938 (first quotation), 1 and 2 August 1938, and 3 August 1938 (second quotation). A listing of the campaign stops during August is found in the *Columbia State*, 2 August 1938.

21. Ziegler, "Senator Walter George's 1938 Campaign," 346 (quotation); Robertson, *Sly and Able*, 268, 271–75; Egerton, *Speak Now against the Day*, 119.

22. *Columbia State*, 3 August 1938 (first quotation), 1 August 1938 (second quotation). Haiti had particular salience in South Carolina since a number of white Haitian planters had fled to the state following the country's 1791 slave uprising and revolution. See Geggus, "Caradeux and Colonial Memory."

23. *New York Times*, 30 August 1938, 1 (first quotation); *Charleston News and Courier*, 1 September 1938 (second quotation); *Charlotte Observer*, 31 August 1938 (third quotation); *Orangeburg Times and Democrat*, 31 August 1938 (fourth quotation); *Charleston News and Courier*, 31 August 1938.

24. Sullivan, *Days of Hope*, 97–101 (quotation, 101); Egerton, *Speak Now against the Day*, 152–53, 185–97; Simon, "Race Reactions," 239–42.

25. Lau, "Freedom Road Territory," 141–53. African Americans also got involved in the mayoral election in Winston-Salem in 1939. See R. R. Korstad, *Civil Rights Unionism*, 139.

26. 1870 Census of Population, South Carolina, Greenville County, Greenville, p. 647; *Greenville Enterprise and Mountaineer*, 8 November 1876; *Augusta Chronicle*, 5 July 1887; Baker, "'Hoover Scare' in South Carolina," 268, 282; *Greenville Enterprise and Mountaineer*, 3 July 1889; Wilhelmina Jackson, "Greenville Notes," 7 February 1940, Box 36, File 3, Ralph J. Bunche Papers, Schomburg Center for Research in Black Culture, New York (quotation). My thanks to Peter F. Lau for providing me with a copy of this document.

27. H. Lewis, *Blackways of Kent*, 172 (quotation); Logan, *Negro in American Life and Thought*; Payne, *I've Got the Light of Freedom*, 178.

28. The best contemporary overview of these events, and the source of the quotation, is James D. Parham, "The Klan Rides Again!" undated newspaper clipping, reel 53, 7:194, frame 2103, *Commission on Interracial Cooperation Papers, 1919–1944* ([Sanford, N.C.]: Microfilming Corporation of America, 1983) (hereafter CIC); Lau, "Freedom Road Territory," 158–60; Hale, *Making Whiteness,* 182–86; Coggeshall, *Carolina Piedmont Country,* 131–32.

29. In this, the Ku Klux Klan of the 1930s showed a subtle appreciation of the power of public opinion not unlike they had done during the 1860s and 1870s when they often forced victims who had been beaten to publish notices in the local newspapers renouncing membership in the Republican Party and political activity generally. See Trelease, *White Terror,* 360, and Nelson, *Iron Confederacies,* 131–32.

30. "K K K Rescinds Ban on Rides," newspaper clipping datelined 2 October [1939], reel 53, 7:194, frame 2093, CIC.

31. "No Excuse for 'Night-Riding' in Today's South Carolina," newspaper clipping labeled [Columbia] *State,* 6 October 1939, reel 53, 7:194, frame 2086, CIC; "'Saving' White 'Supremacy' by Mask and Night Shirt," undated newspaper clipping reprinted from *Charleston News and Courier,* reel 53, 7:194, frame 2087, CIC; "There's No Need in South Carolina for Hooded and Robed Gangs," undated newspaper clipping from *Orangeburg Times and Democrat,* reel 53, 7:194, frame 2088, CIC.

32. "Sidney Park Pastor Invites Klan to Church," undated newspaper clipping, reel 53, 7:194, frame 2082, CIC. Further biographical information on Colclough may be found in Lakey, *History of the CME Church,* 507–10. Folklorist Gladys-Marie Frye noted that African Americans across the South from the 1860s to the 1960s conflated the antebellum slave patrols and the postbellum Ku Klux Klan. Frye, *Night Riders in Black Folk History,* 112–13, 121–22, 155–57.

33. Lau, "Freedom Road Territory," 158–59; author's interview with A. J. Whittenberg, Greenville, S.C., 22 August 1998, notes and tape in author's possession.

34. Lau, "Freedom Road Territory," 184–90, 212; Sullivan, *Days of Hope,* 147–49.

35. *Charleston News and Courier,* 4 April 1944 (first quotation), 10 April 1944 (second quotation), and 14 April 1944 (third quotation); Tindall, *South Carolina Negroes,* 19–29.

36. *Charleston News and Courier,* 15 April 1944 (quotation); Lau, "Freedom Road Territory," 207–17.

37. Lau, "Freedom Road Territory," 216–17; Robert Behre, "Linconville's Past Rich, Hidden," *Charleston Post and Courier,* 6 February 1994, 1A; Powers, *Black Charlestonians,* 223–24; Bleser, *Promised Land,* 19–21; Williamson, *After Slavery,* 207; South Carolina, *Journal of the House of Representatives Being the Regular Session, Beginning Tuesday, January 10, 1933,* 27, 40, 76, 89, 102, 174, 1021; South Carolina, *Journal of the Senate Being the Regular Session, Beginning Tuesday, January 10, 1933,* 53; *Charleston News and Courier,* 16, 18, and 19 January 1933; South Carolina, *Acts and Joint Resolutions, Regular Session of 1936,* 2052 (no. 1049).

38. O. E. McKaine, "Keynote Speech," Box 8, A. J. Clement Papers, SCL.

SIX. RADICALS' RECONSTRUCTION

1. Ringer, "Intellectual Field," 269.

2. J. D. Hall, "Women Writers," 7 (quotation); R. R. Korstad, *Civil Rights Unionism;* Richards, "Southern Negro Youth Congress"; Egerton, *Speak Now against the Day;* Gilmore, *Defying Dixie.* For a discussion of "racialized capitalism" and a view of Jim Crow that incorporates class as an element coequal with race, see R. R. Korstad, *Civil Rights Unionism,* 55; J. D. Hall, "Long Civil Rights Movement," 1243; Kelly, "Sentinels for New South Industry," 339; and, in a broader historical context, Robinson, *Black Marxism,* xiii, 26.

3. On the black radical tradition, see Robinson, *Black Marxism;* Edwards, "'Autonomy' of Black Radicalism"; Singh, "Retracing the Black-Red Thread"; Holcomb, "New Negroes." On African Americans, Communists, and the South, see Solomon, *Cry Was Unity;* Kelley, *Hammer and Hoe.*

4. Richardson, *Death of Reconstruction,* 41–155; Hahn, *Nation under Our Feet,* 216–64; W. Wilson, "Reconstruction of the Southern States," 1. The debate on just how radical Radical Reconstruction was or was not is summarized in Foner, "Reconstruction Revisited," and Weisberger, "Dark and Bloody Ground."

5. Meier and Rudwick, *Black History,* 1–19. The concept of a counterpublic comes from Fraser, "Rethinking the Public Sphere," 67. To my understanding, Fraser's concept of "subaltern counterpublics"—"parallel discursive arenas where members of subordinated social groups invent and circulate counterdiscourses to formulate oppositional interpretations of their identities, interests, and needs" (p. 67)—is similar to the concept of "free space," which historian Sara M. Evans and political scientist Harry C. Boyte describe as "public places in the community . . . the environments in which people are able to learn a new self-respect, a deeper and more assertive group identity, public skills, and values of cooperation and civic virtue . . . settings between private lives and large-scale institutions where ordinary citizens can act with dignity, independence, and vision. . . . Free spaces foster the discovery of new democratic potential among people and new political facts about the world, the construction of networks and contacts with other groups, expanded identities, and control of a space that is relatively independent of elite control." See Evans and Boyte, *Free Spaces,* 166.

6. Carter G. Woodson to W. S. Richardson, 9 September 1921 and 25 April 1922 (first quotation), Series 3 (Appropriations, 1917–45), Subseries 8 (Interracial Relations), Folder 966 (Association for the Study of Negro Life and History, 1921–26), *Laura Spelman Rockefeller Memorial Collection* (Wilmington, Del.: Scholarly Resources, 1998), microfilm (hereafter LSR); *Laura Spelman Rockefeller Memorial Final Report,* 20 (second quotation); Memorandum by W. S. Richardson, 14 September 1921, Series 3 (Appropriations, 1917–45), Subseries 8 (Interracial Relations), Folder 966 (Association for the Study of Negro Life and History, 1921–26), LSR (third quotation); "Notes," *Journal of Negro History* 8, no. 2 (Apr. 1923): 244–45 (fourth quotation).

7. Work et al., "Some Negro Members of Reconstruction Conventions," 63 (quotation); Thompson, "John G. Thompson," 120–25; Lynch, "Some Historical

Errors"; Lynch, "More about the Historical Errors." For reader contributions see, for example, "Letters on Reconstruction Records," *Journal of Negro History,* 467–75; "Correspondence," *Journal of Negro History,* 241–47; H. A. Wallace, "Communications," 296–98; Park, "Extracts from Newspapers," 299–311; Hayne, Work, and Chamberlain, "Materials from the Scrapbook of William A. Hayne," *Journal of Negro History,* 311–40; Hart, Wallace, Dickerman, and Monroe, "Communications," 419–26.

8. "Proceedings of the Annual Meeting of the Association for the Study of Negro Life and History," *Journal of Negro History,* 120; Carter G. Woodson to A. A. Taylor, 5 July 1922, Series 4, *Papers of Carter G. Woodson and the Association for the Study of Negro Life and History* (microfilm; hereafter CGW/ASNLH); S. G. Hall, "Research As Opportunity," 40–44; "Notes," *Journal of Negro History* 7, no. 1 (January 1922): 120; Taylor, "Negro Congressmen a Generation After"; Taylor, "Negro in South Carolina," pts. 1 and 2; Taylor, *Negro in South Carolina.*

9. Taylor, *Negro in South Carolina,* 2. John Hope Franklin noted that Taylor's histories of Reconstruction in South Carolina and Virginia "were the first extensive attempts to challenge the writings of the Dunning school of Reconstruction historiography." Franklin, "Alrutheus Ambush Taylor," 240.

10. Taylor, *Negro in South Carolina,* 32–33 (first quotation), 70 (second and third quotations), 82–124, 125, 153–85, 247, 261–89.

11. White, "Remnants of Dark Ages"; Fish, "Review of A. A. Taylor," 653; Yates Snowden to W. T. Couch, 3 October 1930, University of North Carolina Press Records, Sub-Group 4, "Simkins, F. B. & R. H. Woody, *South Carolina during Reconstruction,*" University of North Carolina Archives, Wilson Library, University of North Carolina (hereafter UNCA).

12. *Francis Butler Simkins, 1897–1966,* 19; Robert H. Woody to Nick Renda, 27 January 1969, Box 2, "Simkins, Francis B." folder, Box 2, Robert H. Woody Papers, Duke University Archives (hereafter DUA); Robert H. Woody, "Recollections, 1985," p. 18, Box 1, Woody Papers; Woody, "South Carolina Reform Movements"; Woody, "Studies in the Economic and Political Reconstruction"; W. T. Couch to J. Milton Ariail, 1 October 1930, J. M. Ariail to W. T. Couch, 5 October 1930 (first quotation), and Yates Snowden to W. T. Couch, 3 October 1930, University of North Carolina Press Records, Sub-Group 4, "Simkins, F. B. & R. H. Woody, *South Carolina during Reconstruction*"; "New Book on Reconstruction by Simkins and Woody," clipping from *Edgefield Advertiser,* 30 March 1932, unfoldered items, Box 3, Woody Papers; "Minneapolis Meeting of the American Historical Association," 445.

13. Simkins and Woody, *South Carolina during Reconstruction,* viii (first quotation), 48–52, 355–58, 381–95, 425–43, 561 (second quotation), 556 (third quotation).

14. Robert H. Woody to Nick Renda, 27 January 1969, Box 2, "Simkins, Francis B." folder, Box 2, Woody Papers; Simkins and Woody, *South Carolina during Reconstruction,* 570–90.

15. Simkins and Woody, *South Carolina during Reconstruction,* 564 (first quotation), 566 (second quotation).

16. G. G. Johnson, "South during the 'Fiery Epoch,'" 304; Commager, "Reconstruction Reconsidered," 295 (second quotation); Beale, "Review of Simkins and Woody," 346–47.

17. "New Book on Reconstruction by Simkins and Woody," clipping from *Edgefield Advertiser,* 30 March 1932, unfoldered items, Box 3, Woody Papers (quotation). For Woodson's authorship of this unattributed article, see Francis B. Simkins to W. T. Couch, 25 February 1932, University of North Carolina Press Records, Sub-Group 4, "Simkins, F. B. & R. H. Woody, *South Carolina during Reconstruction.*" Representative reviews from southern newspapers include G. O. M., "Reconstruction Period Dealt With in New Work," clipping from *Raleigh Times,* 3 September 1932, and James Elliott Walmsley, "Prize-Winning History Praised," clipping from *Richmond Times Dispatch,* 24 October 1932, both in unfoldered items, Box 3, Woody Papers.

18. Quoted from a speech Simkins gave in Edgefield ca. 1956 in *Francis Butler Simkins, 1897–1966,* 49–50 (first quotation); Robert H. Woody to Nick Renda, 27 January 1969, Box 2, "Simkins, Francis B." folder, Box 2, Woody Papers (second quotation).

19. V. J. Williams, *Rethinking Race,* 4–36. Boas supported the publication of the *Journal of Negro History,* 30; Tannenbaum, *Darker Phases of the South;* Yates Snowden to W. T. Couch, 3 October 1930, University of North Carolina Press Records, Sub-Group 4, "Simkins, F. B. & R. H. Woody, *South Carolina during Reconstruction*" (quotation); Simkins, "Negro in South Carolina Law," "Race Legislation in South Carolina," pts. 1 and 2, "Election of 1876 in South Carolina," pts. 1 and 2, "Latin-American Opinion of Pan-Americanism," "Guzman Blanco."

20. *Francis Butler Simkins, 1897–1966,* 19, 34; Freyre, "Social Life in Brazil"; Freyre, *Tempo morto e outros tempos,* 139 (first and third quotations); *Francis Butler Simkins, 1897–1966,* 19; Simkins, *Tillman Movement in South Carolina,* dedication (second quotation). On Freyre, see also Freyre, *Casa-grande e senzala;* Maybury-Lewis, Introduction to *Masters and the Slaves;* Needell, "Identity, Race, Gender, and Modernity"; Skidmore, "Raízes de Gilberto Freyre"; and Skidmore, *Black into White,* 190–92.

21. *Columbia State,* 20 April 1924; Francis Butler Simkins to Carter G. Woodson, 12 May 1923, Series 2, CGW/ASNLH (Simkins misdated this letter; it was written in May 1924 rather than May 1923, as the date of the book review that "appeared a week ago in the Columbia (S.C.) *State*" demonstrates); Francis B. Simkins to Carter G. Woodson, 10 June 1924, Series 2, CGW/ASNLH.

22. D. L. Lewis, *W. E. B. Du Bois,* 304, 350, 360 (quotation), 363–64.

23. Blight, "W. E. B. Du Bois," 46 (second quotation), 57 (first quotation); D. L. Lewis, *W. E. B. Du Bois,* 305–7, 310; Robinson, *Black Marxism,* 185–240.

24. Du Bois, *Black Reconstruction,* xix (quotation), 36–41, 55–83.

25. Ibid., 130–31, 373, 381–525.

26. D. L. Lewis, *W. E. B. Du Bois,* 361 (first quotation), 376–77, 378 (second quotation); D. L. Lewis, Introduction to *Black Reconstruction* by DuBois, xvi; Du Bois, "Freedmen's Bureau"; Du Bois, "Reconstruction and Its Benefits"; Novick, *That Noble Dream,* 230–34.

27. Du Bois, *Black Reconstruction,* 717 (second quotation), 721, 725 (first quotation).

28. Ibid., 722 (first quotation), 726 (second quotation), 728 (third quotation).

29. Degras, *Communist International, 1919–1943,* 2:552–57; Solomon, *Cry Was Unity,* 68–111; Salmond, *Gastonia, 1929;* Allen, *Organizing in the Depression South,* 17–18.

30. Kelley, *Hammer and Hoe,* 1–10; Kelly, *Race, Class, and Power;* Letwin, *Challenge of Interracial Unionism;* Allen, *Organizing in the Depression South,* 21–28, 33–46.

31. Kelley, *Hammer and Hoe,* 78–91.

32. Jim Allen, "Workers Hail Paris Commune," *Southern Worker,* 21 March 1931; "100 Years Ago—Nat Turner," *Southern Worker,* 5 September 1931; O. Hall, "Denmark Vesey," 9–10.

33. Harris Gilbert, "Movie Whips Up Lynch Spirit," *Southern Worker,* 28 March 1931.

34. Al Murphy to Nell Irvin Painter, March 1978, Folder B-83/iv, Southern Oral History Program Collection, SHC (first quotation); Kelley, *Hammer and Hoe,* 39 (second quotation), 99 (third quotation); Haywood, *Black Bolshevik,* 7.

35. Al Murphy to Nell Irvin Painter, March 1978, Folder B-83/iv, Southern Oral History Program Collection; Kelley, *Hammer and Hoe,* 48, 178; Olive Matthews Stone, "Curriculum Vitae," Folder 1, Olive Matthews Stone Papers, SHC; Interview with Olive Matthews Stone by Sherna Gluck, 27 June 1975, G-59-3, in the Southern Oral History Program Collection, SHC (quotation); Cole, "Personality and Cultural Research," 524; O. M. Stone, "Agrarian Conflict in Alabama"; Allen, *Organizing in the Depression South,* 30.

36. Charney, *Long Journey,* 60–61 (first quotation); front matter in Allen, *Reconstruction* (second quotation); Denning, *Cultural Front,* 131 (third quotation); Hardy, *First American Revolution.* The basic document describing this shift can be found in Degras, *Communist International, 1919–1943,* 3:355–70. On the Popular Front and African Americans, see Solomon, *Cry Was Unity,* 269–70.

37. Allen, *Reconstruction,* 8 (first quotation), 44 (second quotation), 51, 72, 114.

38. Ibid., 91 (first quotation), 114 (second quotation), 130–35 (third quotation 131).

39. Richard Enmale, "Editor's Foreword," in Allen, *Reconstruction,* 7 (first quotation), 14 (third quotation); Allen, *Reconstruction,* 215 (second quotation).

40. Lawson, *Thaddeus Stevens,* 12. For more on Lawson, see Buhle, Buhle, and Georgakas, *Encyclopedia of the American Left,* 789, 903. For more of Lawson's contributions to African American history during this period, see Lawson, *Study Outline History of the American Negro People;* Lawson, *Struggle against White Chauvinism.* Lawson would also continue to put her scholarship on Reconstruction in the service of social change, publishing the first biography of Mississippi's Reconstruction senator, Hiram Revels, in 1960. See Lawson, *Gentleman from Mississippi.*

41. Cobb, "World War II"; Egerton, *Speak Now against the Day,* 201–341; Sullivan, *Days of Hope,* 133–68; R. R. Korstad, *Civil Rights Unionism;* Cash, *Mind of the South.*

42. Fast, *Being Red,* 3–6, 17–29, 32, 51–53, 62, 71, 75–76; Fast, *Two Valleys;* Fast, *Conceived in Liberty;* Fast, *Citizen Tom Paine;* Meisler, "Forgotten Dreams of Howard Fast"; Fast, "History in Fiction," 9 (quotation); Fast, *Freedom Road.*

43. Magdol, *Right to the Land,* 174–99; Campbell, *Providence;* K'Meyer, *Interracialism and Christian Community.*

44. Fast, *Freedom Road,* 12, 17 (first quotation), 74–76 (second quotation 76).

45. Ibid., 77 (first quotation), 262 (second quotation).

46. Ibid., 262–63; Fast, "Negro Finds His History," 17.

47. Fast, *Being Red,* 80, 83–85; "News of the Screen," *New York Times,* 17 December 1946, 44; Mayberry, "Two Down," 196 (first quotation); Weeks, "Black Hatred," 127; *New Yorker* 20 (19 August 1944), 58 (second quotation); Trilling, "Fiction in Review," 219 (third quotation).

48. Tarleton Collier, "Emergence from Slavery," *Louisville Courier-Journal,* 20 August 1944; John Selby, "New Yorker 'Experts' on Race Situation in South Carolina," *Columbia State,* 20 August 1944; Marjorie Hunter, "Negro during Reconstruction," *Raleigh News and Observer,* 20 August 1944.

49. Cheney, "Uncle Sam's Other Province," 147 (first quotation), 149 (second quotation), 150 (third quotation); Wright, "Myth-Makers and the South's Dilemma," 548; Tyson, *Radio Free Dixie,* 31–38, 40–42, 48–50, 53, 60; Egerton, *Speak Now against the Day,* 363–65. During World War II, white southerners harbored continual fears of African American violence. See Odum, *Race and Rumors of Race.*

50. R. R. Korstad, *Civil Rights Unionism;* Griffith, *Crisis of American Labor;* Minchin, *What Do We Need a Union For?* Sullivan, *Days of Hope,* 193–220; Egerton, *Speak Now against the Day,* 393–97; K. Korstad, "Black and White Together," 72 (quotation). Helpful background for this period in South Carolina is found in Simon, "Race Reactions."

51. C. A. Hughes, "We Demand Our Rights," 38, 43–45; Cohen, *When the Old Left Was Young;* Richards, "Southern Negro Youth Congress," 42–43; Kelley, *Hammer and Hoe,* 195–219.

52. Gellman, "Radical Past for a Progressive Future"; Program for "First Annual Lecture Series on Negro Life and Culture" sponsored by Arts Committee, Richmond Youth Federation, Folder 30 (Southern Negro Youth Council), Stone Papers; "Program for Fourth All-Southern Negro Youth Conference, April 18–21, 1940, New Orleans, La.," Folder 9, Series I, Junius I. Scales Papers, SHC; Report of 4/12/45, BH File 100–147, Katharine Du Pre Lumpkin FBI file (cross references), in possession of Jacquelyn Dowd Hall, Chapel Hill, N.C.; Richards, "Southern Negro Youth Congress," 124; Scales and Nickson, *Cause at Heart,* 162–68; *Columbia State,* 19–22 October 1946; Fast, "They're Marching Up Freedom Road," 21; *Columbia State,* 19 October 1946 (first quotation); "Pre-Conference News-Bulletin, Southern Youth Legislature, Columbia, S.C.," Folder 9, Series I, Scales

Papers (second quotation); "The Southern Negro Youth Conference presents Paul Robeson," Folder 9, Series I, Scales Papers; O'Dell, "'I Wasn't Interested in Living'" (third quotation).

53. Du Bois, "Behold the Land," 117 (first quotation), 118 (second and third quotations).

54. Culver and Hyde, *American Dreamer*, 415, 436–37, 451; R. R. Korstad, *Civil Rights Unionism*, 267–68.

55. Culver and Hyde, *American Dreamer*, 433–59.

56. Borstelmann, *Cold War and the Color Line*, 45–84; Wexler, *Fire in a Canebrake*; Frederickson, *Dixiecrat Revolt*, 58–63; Egerton, *Speak Now against the Day*, 359–75, 413–16; Frederickson, "'Slowest State.'"

57. Frederickson, *Dixiecrat Revolt*, 70, 3, 104–5, 148.

58. Sullivan, *Days of Hope*, 259–70.

59. Walker, "New Objective," 16–17; "Oakley Park," 16; Walker, "South Carolina Governor Thurmond"; Carson, "Great Triumvirate," 7–8 (first quotation); *Greenville News*, 29 October 1948; *Greenville News*, 3 November 1948 (second quotation).

60. Katharine Du Pre Lumpkin, "Eli Hill" typescript, Folders 53–54, Series 2, Katharine Du Pre Lumpkin Papers, SHC.

61. K. D. Lumpkin, *Making of a Southerner*; J. D. Hall, "'You Must Remember This.'"

62. Katharine Du Pre Lumpkin to Alfred A. Knopf, 8 May 1949, Folder 14, Series 1, Lumpkin Papers.

63. William Faulkner, "Upon Receiving the Nobel Prize," 119 (first quotation); Lumpkin, "Eli Hill" typescript, 137–55; Katharine Du Pre Lumpkin, "Application for Literary Fellowship," [1949], Folder 14, Series 1, Lumpkin Papers (second quotation).

64. Katharine Du Pre Lumpkin to Alfred A. Knopf, 8 May 1949, Folder 14, Series 1, Lumpkin Papers; Craig Wylie to Katharine Du Pre Lumpkin, 15 June 1951, Folder 15, Series 1, Lumpkin Papers.

65. Katharine Du Pre Lumpkin to Craig Wylie, 10 June 1951, Folder 15, Series 1, Lumpkin Papers (first quotation); Katharine Du Pre Lumpkin, "Notes on there being no truly 'moderate position' in the post–Civil War period," Folder 15, Series 1, Lumpkin Papers (second quotation).

SEVEN. THE STRANGE CAREER OF
THE SECOND RECONSTRUCTION

1. On the transition to the cold war phase of the civil rights movement, see Korstad and Lichtenstein, "Opportunities Found and Lost," 811; J. D. Hall, "Long Civil Rights Movement," 1245–50; Dudziak, *Cold War Civil Rights*, 11–14; Marable, *Race, Reform, and Rebellion*, 12–41.

2. Nora, "Between Memory and History." Two articles heralded the shift in Reconstruction historiography: Simkins, "New Viewpoints on Southern Recon-

struction," and Beale, "On Rewriting Reconstruction History." On the broader changes in southern history during this period, see B. L. Johnson, "Regionalism, Race, and the Meaning," 324–93.

3. A. B. Williams, *Hampton and His Red Shirts*. The columns appeared in the *Columbia State* on Sundays between 8 August 1926 and 13 March 1927. The effort to get Williams's book published is detailed in a number of letters between 1927 and 1935, mostly in Box 18, W. W. Ball Papers, Rare Book, Manuscript, and Special Collections Library, Duke University, Durham, N.C. Readers' responses can be found throughout this period. Coulter, "Review of Williams," 455.

4. Beale, "On Rewriting Reconstruction History," 808 (first and second quotations); Coulter, *South during Reconstruction*, xi (third quotation), ix (fourth quotation); Bailey, "E. Merton Coulter," 32–48; Hamilton, "Review of Coulter"; B. L. Johnson, "Regionalism, Race, and the Meaning," 366–68. On J. W. Daniel's novel, see the discussion in chapter 3.

5. Franklin, "Whither Reconstruction Historiography?" 454, 461; Collins, *Whither Solid South?*

6. Simkins, "Review of Williams," 281–82; Wellman, *Giant in Gray;* Jarrell, *Wade Hampton and the Negro;* Simkins, "Review of Wellman, *Giant in Gray*," 146; Simkins, "New Viewpoints of Southern Reconstruction," 51. Sometime in the late 1940s, Simkins took a puzzling conservative turn in his views on southern history; see Humphreys, "South Carolina Rustic."

7. Kluger, *Simple Justice*, 3–26, 287–366; P. Daniel, *Lost Revolutions*, 26; Quint, *Profile in Black and White*, 16 (second quotation); A. H. Stone, "Mississippian's View," 191 (third and fourth quotations), 192 (fifth quotation).

8. Woodward, *Thinking Back*, 85–86; Roper, *C. Vann Woodward*, 6, 28–55.

9. Woodward, *Thinking Back*, 86 (first quotation); Roper, *C. Vann Woodward*, 55–59 (second quotation 59).

10. Woodward, *Thinking Back*, 13–20; Roper, *C. Vann Woodward*, 63–96 (quotation 63); Salmond, *General Textile Strike of 1934*, 223–25; Egerton, *Speak Now against the Day*, 130–34; Singal, *War Within*, 261–338.

11. Woodward, *Tom Watson;* Woodward, *Thinking Back*, 27 (first quotation), 44 (second quotation).

12. Roper, *C. Vann Woodward*, 149–51; Woodward, *Thinking Back*, 56 (quotation); Woodward, *Reunion and Reaction;* Woodward, *Origins of the New South;* Cobb, "'On the Pinnacle in Yankeeland.'"

13. Woodward, *Thinking Back*, 55–56; Novick, *That Noble Dream*, 335 (second quotation); Fitzpatrick, *History's Memory*, 189 (third quotation).

14. Roper, *C. Vann Woodward*, 161–62; Schrecker, *No Ivory Tower*, 165–66 (quotation, 166). For the lingering effects of McCarthyism in academia on contemporary scholarship, see J. D. Hall, "'Archive Fever.'"

15. Woodward, "Irony of Southern History." On the rise and fall of regionalism in the United States, see Dorman, *Revolt of the Provinces*. On Woodward's role as a public intellectual dealing with segregation, see also the account by Polsgrove, *Divided Minds*, 28–37, which is similar to my analysis, but with a different

emphasis and a rather more negative view of Woodward's development of the idea of a "New Reconstruction." On the SHA in this period, see B. L. Johnson, "Regionalism, Race, and the Meaning," 394–432.

16. Woodward, "Irony of Southern History," 5, 17, 19.

17. Kluger, *Simple Justice*, 617–56 (quotation, 638).

18. Egerton, *Speak Now against the Day*, 615–18; Bartley, *Rise of Massive Resistance*, 74; Quint, *Profile in Black and White*, 25 (second quotation).

19. Woodward, *Strange Career of Jim Crow* (1955), viii (first quotation), 5 (second quotation), 9 (third quotation).

20. Simkins, "Review of Jarrell, *Wade Hampton and the Negro*," 737.

21. Woodward, "'New Reconstruction' in the South," 501, 502, 508; Woodward, "Irony of Southern History," 17. For a history of *Commentary* magazine during this period, see Abrams, *Commentary Magazine, 1945–1959*.

22. Woodward, *Strange Career of Jim Crow*, new and rev. ed.; Carleton, "Second Reconstruction"; Fairclough, *To Redeem the Soul*, 11–35; McMillen, *Citizens' Council*.

23. *Congressional Record*, vol. 103, 85th Cong., 1st sess., 10774 (first quotation), 10775 (second quotation) (2 July 1957), 11232 (third quotation) (10 July 1957).

24. Quoted in Kallen, "Meaning of Tragedy," 773; McMillen, *Citizens' Council*, 358. On Little Rock, see Kirk, "'Massive Resistance and Minimum Compliance.'" On the backlash against *Brown*, see Klarman, "How *Brown* Changed Race Relations," and Badger, "*Brown* and Backlash."

25. Dudziak, *Cold War Civil Rights*, 115–51.

26. *Greenville News*, 24 December (first quotation) and 29 December (second quotation) 1957.

27. *Charleston News and Courier*, 14 May 1895.

28. Quint, *Profile in Black and White*, 37 (first quotation); "Should Leave the Red Shirts to History," *Greenville News*, 28 December 1957. For another example of the power that violence still had to stifle dissent in South Carolina in 1957, see Tyson, "Dynamite and 'The Silent South,'" about an unprosecuted Ku Klux Klan bombing in Gaffney.

CONCLUSION

1. M. L. King, "Honoring Dr. Du Bois, No. 2, 1968," 34 (first quotation), 35 (second quotation); M. L. King, "Our God Is Marching On." On this final phase of King's career, see Fairclough, *To Redeem the Soul*, 353–83; Harding, *Martin Luther King*; McKnight, *Last Crusade*.

2. In the absence of secondary literature on the South Carolina Tricentennial, see the voluminous records of the Tricentennial Commission, SCDAH. *Anderson Independent*, 3 September 1970 (quotation); Liverance, *Anderson County*, 22.

3. Edgar, *South Carolina*, 543 (quotation); Edelman, "Southern School Desegregation," 39–40; Mary Dodgen Few, "Wade Hampton" in Liverance, *Anderson County*, 14.

4. P. Bradley Morrah Jr. to Governor James B. Edwards, 29 April 1975, South

Carolina American Revolution Bicentennial Commission (hereafter SCARBC), Central Correspondence, Box 3, "Black Involvement" folder (277.0), SCDAH; John E. Hills to Stanley E. DeVeaux, 25 November 1974, SCARBC, Central Correspondence, Box 1, "Achievement '76, 1974 correspondence" folder (50.0), SCDAH. For details of local events, see SCARBC, Central Correspondence, Box 3, folder 238.0. On the bicentennial, see Bodnar, *Remaking America,* 226–44; Spillman, "When Do Collective Memories Last?"; Litwack, "Trouble in Mind."

5. South Carolina League of the South, "Position Papers" (first quotation); Red Shirts, "Jion the Red Shirt's" (*sic*) (second quotation).

6. *Columbia State,* 1 December 1985 (first quotation); *Columbia State,* 30 May 2003, A13 (second and third quotations); Oliphant, *Simms' History of South Carolina;* Jones, *South Carolina.* On Oliphant, see Baker, "Mary C. Simms Oliphant." To get a sense of the durability of Oliphant's textbook, it is worth noting that several generations of southern historians from South Carolina all learned from this book, including George B. Tindall, Joel Williamson, Gaines M. Foster, Dan T. Carter, and myself.

7. *Columbia State,* 29 November 1997; *Greenville News,* 1 August 2001; *Columbia State,* 31 January 2000; Foner, *Freedom's Lawmakers,* 152; Woody, "Jonathan Jasper Wright." For more on the controversy over Wright, see *Columbia State,* 20 February 1997, 15 March 1997, 19 January 1998.

8. Linda Brown, "Marker Honors Stephen A. Swails," *Kingstree News,* 10 June 1998, accessed online http://www.kingstreenews.com/19980610/Marker.HTM (27 July 2005).

9. *Congressional Record,* vol. 149, 108th Cong., 1st sess., 8 January 2003, H137, and 16 June 2003, S7936; *Hilton Head Island Packet,* 26 May 2003; "Hopes Dim for Reconstruction History Park" (quotation); *Columbia State,* 28 February 2005.

10. Pierce, "Statement to Greensboro Truth and Reconciliation Commission." For background on the events in Greensboro in 1979, see Wheaton, *Codename GREENKILL.* The best source of information on the Greensboro Truth and Reconciliation Commission is their Web site: http://www.greensborotrc.org.

BIBLIOGRAPHY

MANUSCRIPT COLLECTIONS

South Caroliniana Library, University of South Carolina, Columbia

Milledge Lipscomb Bonham Papers
A. J. Clement Papers
James Walter Daniel Papers
Edward Terry Hendrie Shaffer Papers
Alexander S. Salley Jr. Papers
Harry Legare Watson Scrapbooks
Works Projects Administration—Federal Writers Project Collection

South Carolina Department of Archives and History, Columbia

Department of Archives and History, Historical Commission, Statements concerning the 1876 Election, S108157
South Carolina American Revolution Bicentennial Commission, RG 107000
Tricentennial Commission, RG 219000

Confederate Relic Room, Columbia

Minute Book of the United Daughters of the Confederacy—Wade Hampton Chapter, June 1910–November 1913

Special Collections, Strom Thurmond Institute, Clemson University

James F. Byrnes Papers
Pendleton Cornet Band Records
Jesse C. Stribling Papers

BIBLIOGRAPHY

South Carolina Room, Anderson County Public Library, Anderson, S.C.

Manse Jolly Papers
Thomas B. Keys, *The Army and Crawford Keys: Aftermath of the Brown's Ferry Outrage*

Pendleton District Commission, Pendleton, S.C.

Manse Jolly File
Red Shirt File

Genealogy Room, Fairfield County Museum, Winnsboro, S.C.

"Fairfield Addenda 1946" Scrapbook

South Carolina Historical Society, Charleston

Edward L. Wells Papers (microfiche edition)
Edward L. Wells Papers

Southern Historical Collection, University of North Carolina at Chapel Hill

Loula Rockwell Ayers Recollections
Franklin Harper Elmore Papers
Hilary A. Herbert Papers
Katharine Du Pre Lumpkin Papers
Junius I. Scales Papers
Southern Oral History Program Collection
Olive Matthews Stone Papers

University Archives, University of North Carolina at Chapel Hill

University of North Carolina Press Records

Rare Books, Manuscripts, and Special Collections Library, Duke University

W. W. Ball Papers
Behind the Veil Collection

University Archives, Duke University

Robert H. Woody Papers

North Carolina Department of Archives and History, Raleigh, N.C.

Civil War Collections
Zebulon Baird Vance Papers

BIBLIOGRAPHY

Jacquelyn Dowd Hall, Chapel Hill, N.C.

BH File 100–147, Katharine Du Pre Lumpkin FBI file (cross references)

Schomburg Center for Research in Black Culture, New York

Ralph J. Bunche Papers

COLLECTIONS ON MICROFILM

Laura Spelman Rockefeller Memorial Collection. Wilmington, Del.: Scholarly Resources, 1998.

Commission on Interracial Cooperation Papers, 1919–1944. [Sanford, N.C.]: Microfilming Corporation of America, 1983.

Papers of the International Labor Defense. Frederick, Md.: University Publications of America, 1987.

Papers of Carter G. Woodson and the Association for the Study of Negro Life and History, 1915–1950. Bethesda, Md.: University Publications of America, 1998.

United States. Census Office. 8th census. 1860. Free Population Schedule, Barnwell District, South Carolina. Washington, D.C.: National Archives and Records Administration.

———. Census Office. 8th census. 1860. Slave Population Schedule, Barnwell District, South Carolina. Washington, D.C.: National Archives and Records Administration.

———. Census Office. 9th census. 1870. Population Schedule, Barnwell County, South Carolina. Washington, D.C.: National Archives and Records Administration.

———. Census Office. 9th census. 1870. Population Schedule, Greenville County, South Carolina. Washington, D.C.: National Archives and Records Administration.

NEWSPAPERS AND PERIODICALS

Anderson Independent
Anderson Intelligencer
Anderson Daily Mail
Augusta Chronicle
Beaufort Gazette
Camden Chronicle
Charleston Daily Courier
Charleston Evening Post
Charleston News and Courier
Charleston Post and Courier
Charlotte Observer
Columbia Palmetto Leader

Columbia State
Congressional Record
Confederate Veteran (Nashville, Tenn.)
Darlington News
Florence Morning News
Georgetown Times
Greenville Enterprise and Mountaineer
Greenville News
Greenville Piedmont
Greenwood Index-Journal
Hilton Head Island Packet
The Independent (New York)
Jacksonville Times-Union
Kingstree News
Louisville Courier-Journal
Laurens Advertiser
New York Times
New York Tribune
Newberry Herald and News
Orangeburg Times and Democrat
Outlook (New York)
Pickens Sentinel
Raleigh News and Observer
Savannah Tribune
Scribner's Magazine (New York)
Southern Worker (Birmingham, Ala.)
Spartanburg Herald

OTHER SOURCES

Abrams, Nathan. *Commentary Magazine, 1945–1959: A Journal of Significant Thought and Opinion.* London: Vallentine Mitchell, 2006.

Allen, James S. *Organizing in the Depression South: A Communist's Memoir.* Minneapolis: MEP, 2001.

———. *Reconstruction: The Battle for Democracy.* New York: International, 1937.

Ayers, Edward L. *The Promise of the New South: Life after Reconstruction.* New York: Oxford University Press, 1992.

Ayers, Loula Rockwell. "The Red Shirt Election." *Atlantic Monthly* 194, no. 5 (November 1954): 60–61.

Badger, Tony. "*Brown* and Backlash." In *Massive Resistance: Southern Opposition to the Second Reconstruction,* ed. Clive Webb, 76–98. New York: Oxford University Press, 2005.

Bailey, Fred Arthur. "E. Merton Coulter and the Political Culture of Southern Historiography." In *Reading Southern History: Essays on Interpreters and In-*

terpretations, ed. Glenn Feldman, 32–48. Tuscaloosa: University of Alabama Press, 2001.

Baker, Bruce E. "The 'Hoover Scare' in South Carolina, 1887: An Attempt to Organize Black Farm Labor." *Labor History* 40, no. 3 (August 1999): 261–82.

———. "Mary C. Simms Oliphant." In *South Carolina Encyclopedia,* ed. Walter Edgar. Columbia: University of South Carolina, 2006.

———. "Under the Rope: Lynching and Memory in Laurens County, South Carolina." In *Where These Memories Grow: History, Memory, and Southern Identity,* ed. W. Fitzhugh Brundage. Chapel Hill: University of North Carolina Press, 2000.

Ball, W. W. "A Boy's Recollections of the Red Shirt Campaign of 1876 in South Carolina." Columbia, S.C.: The Club, 1911.

———. *The State that Forgot: South Carolina's Surrender to Democracy.* Indianapolis: Bobbs-Merrill, 1932.

Barrett, John G. *Sherman's March through the Carolinas.* Chapel Hill: University of North Carolina Press, 1956.

Bartley, Numan V. *The Rise of Massive Resistance: Race and Politics in the South during the 1950's.* Baton Rouge: Louisiana State University Press, 1969.

Beale, Howard K. "On Rewriting Reconstruction History." *American Historical Review* 45, no. 4 (July 1940): 807–27.

———. "Review of Simkins and Woody, *South Carolina during Reconstruction.*" *American Historical Review* 38, no. 2 (January 1933): 345–47.

Bleser, Carol K. Rothrock. *The Promised Land: The History of the South Carolina Land Commission, 1869–1890.* Columbia: University of South Carolina Press, 1969.

Blight, David W. *Race and Reunion: The Civil War in American Memory.* Cambridge, Mass.: Harvard University Press, 2001.

———. "W. E. B. Du Bois and the Struggle for American Historical Memory." In *History and Memory in African-American Culture,* ed. Geneviève Fabre and Robert O'Meally. New York: Oxford University Press, 1994.

Bodnar, John. *Remaking America: Public Memory, Commemoration, and Patriotism in the Twentieth Century.* Princeton, N.J.: Princeton University Press, 1992.

Bogart, Michele H. "In Search of a United Front: American Architectural Sculpture at the Turn of the Century." *Winterthur Portfolio* 19 (Summer/Autumn 1984): 151–76.

Borstelmann, Thomas. *The Cold War and the Color Line: American Race Relations in the Global Arena.* Cambridge, Mass.: Harvard University Press, 2001.

Bowers, Claude G. *The Tragic Era: The Revolution after Lincoln.* New York: Houghton Mifflin, 1929.

Braden, Waldo W. *The Oral Tradition in the South.* Baton Rouge: Louisiana State University Press, 1983.

Brayton, Ellery M. *An Address Delivered on Decoration Day, May 30, 1890, at the National Cemetery, Beaufort, S.C.* Columbia, S.C.: Bryan Printing, 1890.

Brooks, Peter. *The Melodramatic Imagination: Balzac, Henry James, Melodrama, and the Mode of Excess.* New Haven: Yale University Press, 1976.

Brooks, U. R. *Butler and His Cavalry in the War of Secession, 1861–1865.* Columbia, S.C.: State Co., 1909.

Brundage, W. Fitzhugh. "No Deed But Memory." In *Where These Memories Grow: History, Memory, and Southern Identity,* ed. W. Fitzhugh Brundage. Chapel Hill: University of North Carolina Press, 2000.

———. *The Southern Past: A Clash of Race and Memory.* Cambridge, Mass.: Harvard University Press, 2005.

———, ed. *Where These Memories Grow: History, Memory, and Southern Identity.* Chapel Hill: University of North Carolina Press, 2000.

———. "Whispering Consolation to Generations Unborn: Black Memory in the Era of Jim Crow." In *Warm Ashes: Issues in Southern History at the Dawn of the Twenty-First Century,* ed. Winfred B. Moore Jr., Kyle S. Sinisi, and David H. White Jr. Columbia: University of South Carolina Press, 2003.

Buhle, Mari Jo, Paul Buhle, and Dan Georgakas. *Encyclopedia of the American Left.* 2nd ed. New York: Oxford University Press, 1998.

Bushman, Richard L. *The Refinement of America: Persons, Houses, Cities.* New York: Knopf, 1992.

Cable, George Washington. *John March, Southerner.* New York: Charles Scribner's Sons, 1894.

Camak, Thomas C. "Fairfield County, Thomas C. Camak, 83 Years Old." American Life Histories: Manuscripts from the Federal Writers' Project, 1936–1940. 1938. http://lcweb2.loc.gov/ammem/wpaintro/wpahome.html (18 November 2006).

Campbell, Will D. *Providence.* Waco, Texas: Baylor University Press, 2002.

Carleton, William G. "The Second Reconstruction: An Analysis from the Deep South." *Antioch Review* 18, no. 2 (Summer 1958): 171–82.

Carlton, David L. *Mill and Town in South Carolina, 1880–1920.* Baton Rouge: Louisiana State University Press, 1982.

Carson, Mrs. J. R. "The Great Triumvirate of the Reconstruction Period in South Carolina." *United Daughters of the Confederacy Magazine* 11, no. 9 (September 1948): 7–8.

Carter, Dan T. "The Anatomy of Fear: The Christmas Day Insurrection Scare of 1865." *Journal of Southern History* 42 (August 1976): 345–64.

Cash, W. J. *The Mind of the South.* New York: Alfred A. Knopf, 1941.

Champie, Elmore A. *A Brief History of the Marine Corps Recruit Depot, Parris Island, South Carolina, 1891–1962.* Washington, D.C.: Historical Branch, G-3 Division Headquarters, U.S. Marine Corps, 1962.

Charney, George. *A Long Journey.* Chicago: Quadrangle Books, 1968.

Cheney, Brainard. "Uncle Sam's Other Province: Propaganda Novels about the South." *Sewanee Review* 53 (1945): 147–52.

Ciardi, John. *How Does a Poem Mean?* Boston: Houghton Mifflin, 1959.

Clark, Kathleen Ann. "Celebrating Freedom: Emancipation Day Celebrations and African American Memory in the Early Reconstruction South." In *Where These Memories Grow: History, Memory, and Southern Identity,* ed. W. Fitzhugh Brundage. Chapel Hill: University of North Carolina Press, 2000.

———. *Defining Moments: African American Commemoration and Political Culture in the South, 1863–1913.* Chapel Hill: University of North Carolina Press, 2005.

Cobb, James C. "'On the Pinnacle in Yankeeland': C. Vann as a [Southern] Renaissance Man." *Journal of Southern History* 67, no. 4 (November 2001): 715–40.

———. "World War II and the Mind of the Modern South." In *Redefining Southern Culture: Mind and Identity in the Modern South,* ed. Cobb, 25–43. Athens: University of Georgia Press, 1999.

Coggeshall, John M. *Carolina Piedmont Country.* Jackson: University Press of Mississippi, 1996.

Cohen, Robby. *When the Old Left Was Young: Student Radicals and America's First Mass Student Movement, 1929–1941.* New York: Oxford University Press, 1993.

Cole, William E. "Personality and Cultural Research in the Tennessee Valley." *Social Forces* 13, no. 4 (May 1935): 521–27.

Coleman, Jennie Isabel. "Mrs. Jennie Isabel Coleman." American Life Histories: Manuscripts from the Federal Writers' Project, 1936–1940. [1936]. http://lcweb2.loc.gov/ammem/wpaintro/wpahome.html (18 November 2006).

Collins, Charles Wallace. *Whither Solid South? A Study in Politics and Race Relations.* New Orleans: Pelican, 1947.

Commager, Henry Steele. "Reconstruction Reconsidered." *New Republic* 71 (27 July 1932): 295.

Conkin, Paul K. "The History of Vanderbilt's History Department." Vanderbilt Department of History. http://sitemason.vanderbilt.edu/history/history (7 November 2003).

Cooper, William J. *The Conservative Regime: South Carolina, 1877–1890.* Baltimore: Johns Hopkins Press, 1968.

"Correspondence." *Journal of Negro History* 6, no. 2 (April 1921): 241–47.

Coulter, E. Merton. "Review of Williams, *Hampton and His Red Shirts.*" *Mississippi Valley Historical Review* 22, no. 3 (December 1935): 454–55.

———. *The South during Reconstruction, 1865–1877.* Baton Rouge: Louisiana State University Press, 1947.

Culver, John C., and John Hyde. *American Dreamer: A Life of Henry A. Wallace.* New York: W. W. Norton, 2000.

Daniel, J. W. *Cateechee of Keeowee, a Descriptive Poem.* Nashville: Publishing house of the Methodist Episcopal Church, South, 1898.

———. *The Girl in Checks; or, The Mystery of the Mountain Cabin.* Nashville: Printed for the author, 1890.

———. *A Maid of the Foot-Hills; or, Missing Links in the Story of Reconstruction.* New York: Neale, 1905.

———. *Out from under Caesar's Frown; or, The Belle of the Dismal.* Nashville: Printed for the author, 1891.

———. *A Ramble among Surnames.* Nashville: Publishing house of the M. E. Church, South, 1893.

Daniel, Pete. *Breaking the Land: The Transformation of Cotton, Tobacco, and Rice Cultures since 1880.* Urbana: University of Illinois Press, 1985.

———. *Lost Revolutions: The South in the 1950s.* Chapel Hill: University of North Carolina Press, 2000.

Davidson, Elizabeth H. *Child Labor Legislation in the Southern Textile States.* Chapel Hill: University of North Carolina Press, 1939.

Davies, Wallace E. "The Problem of Race Segregation in the Grand Army of the Republic." *Journal of Southern History* 13, no. 3 (August 1947): 354–72.

Davis, Susan G. *Parades and Power: Street Theatre in Nineteenth-Century Philadelphia.* Philadelphia: Temple University Press, 1986.

De Forest, J. W. "A Report of Outrages." *Harper's New Monthly Magazine* 38 (December 1868): 75–84.

De Forest, John William. *A Union Officer in the Reconstruction,* ed. James H. Croushore and David Morris Potter. 1948; reprint, Baton Rouge: Louisiana State University Press, 1997.

Dearing, Mary R. *Veterans in Politics: The Story of the G. A. R.* Baton Rouge: Louisiana State University Press, 1952.

Degras, Jane, ed. *The Communist International, 1919–1943: Documents.* Vols. 2 and 3. New York: Oxford University Press, 1960, 1965.

Denning, Michael. *The Cultural Front: The Laboring of American Culture in the Twentieth Century.* New York: Verso, 1997.

Dixon, Thomas, Jr. *The Clansman: An Historical Romance of the Ku Klux Klan.* New York: Doubleday, Page, 1905.

Dodd, William E. "South Carolina Reconstruction." *New York Times Saturday Review of Books,* 18 August 1906, 506.

Dorman, Robert L. *Revolt of the Provinces: The Regionalist Movement in America, 1920–1945.* Chapel Hill: University of North Carolina Press, 1993.

Downey, Thomas More. "Planting a Capitalist South: The Transformation of Western South Carolina, 1790–1860." Ph.D. diss., University of South Carolina, 2000.

Drago, Edmund L. *Hurrah for Hampton! Black Red Shirts in South Carolina during Reconstruction.* Fayetteville: University of Arkansas Press, 1998.

Du Bois, W. E. B. "Behold the Land." *Southern Exposure* 9, no. 1 (Spring 1981): 117–18.

———. *Black Reconstruction in America, 1860–1880.* 1935; reprint, with an introduction by David L. Lewis, New York: Free Press, 1992.

———. "The Freedmen's Bureau." *Atlantic Monthly* 87 (March 1901): 354–65.

———. "Reconstruction and Its Benefits." *American Historical Review* 15, no. 4 (July 1910): 781–99.

Dudziak, Mary L. *Cold War Civil Rights: Race and the Image of American Democracy.* Princeton: Princeton University Press, 2000.

Dunning, William Archibald. *Essays on the Civil War and Reconstruction and Related Topics.* New York: Macmillan, 1898.

———. *Reconstruction, Political and Economic, 1865–1877.* New York: Harper and Brothers, 1907.

Durden, Robert Franklin. *James Shepherd Pike: Republicanism and the American Negro, 1850–1882.* Durham, N.C.: Duke University Press, 1957.

Echoes from "Hampton Day," May 14th, 1895. Compiled and arranged for the Camp. Charleston, S.C.: Walker, Evans & Cogswell, 1895.

Edelman, Marian Wright. "Southern School Desegregation, 1954–1973: A Judicial-Political Overview." *Annals of the American Academy of Political and Social Science* 407 (May 1973): 32–42.

Edgar, Walter. *South Carolina: A History.* Columbia: University of South Carolina Press, 1998.

Edwards, Brent Hayes. "The 'Autonomy' of Black Radicalism." *Social Text* 19, no. 2 (Summer 2001): 1–13.

Egerton, John. *Speak Now against the Day: The Generation Before the Civil Rights Movement in the South.* New York: Knopf, 1994.

Evans, Sara M., and Harry C. Boyte. *Free Spaces: The Sources of Democratic Change in America.* New York: Harper and Row, 1986.

Fairclough, Adam. *To Redeem the Soul of America: The Southern Christian Leadership Conference and Martin Luther King, Jr.* Athens: University of Georgia Press, 1987.

Fast, Howard. *Being Red.* Boston: Houghton Mifflin, 1990.

———. *Citizen Tom Paine.* New York: Duell, Sloane, and Pearce, 1943.

———. *Conceived in Liberty: A Novel of Valley Forge.* New York: Simon and Schuster, 1939.

———. *Freedom Road.* New York: Duell, Sloane, and Pearce, 1944.

———. "History in Fiction." *New Masses* 50 (18 January 1944): 8–9.

———. "Negro Finds His History." *New Masses* 55 (15 May 1945): 17.

———. "They're Marching up Freedom Road." *New Masses* 61 (5 November 1946): 20–21.

———. *Two Valleys.* New York: Dial Press, 1933.

Faulkner, William. "Upon Receiving the Nobel Prize for Literature." *Essays, Speeches, and Public Letters.* New York: Random House, 1965.

Feldman, Glenn. *The Disfranchisement Myth: Poor Whites and Suffrage Restriction in Alabama.* Athens: University of Georgia Press, 2004.

Fentress, James, and Chris Wickham. *Social Memory.* Oxford: Basil Blackwell, 1992.

Fermer, Douglas. *James Gordon Bennett and the New York Herald: A Study of Editorial Opinion in the Civil War Era, 1854–1867.* New York: St. Martin's Press, 1986.

Field, Ron. *The Hampton Legion.* Part 1: *Regimental History.* Lower Swell, Gloucestershire, England: Design Folio, 1994.

Final Report of the Commission to Provide for a Monument to the Memory of Wade Hampton. Columbia, S.C.: Gonzales and Bryan, 1906.

Fish, Carl Russell. "Review of A. A. Taylor, *The Negro in South Carolina during Reconstruction.*" *American Historical Review* 30, no. 3 (April 1925): 653.

Fitzpatrick, Ellen. *History's Memory: Writing America's History, 1880–1980*. Cambridge, Mass.: Harvard University Press, 2002.

Fleming, Walter L. *Civil War and Reconstruction in Alabama*. New York: Macmillan, 1905.

Foner, Eric. *Freedom's Lawmakers: A Directory of Black Officeholders during Reconstruction*. Rev. ed. Baton Rouge: Louisiana State University Press, 1996.

———. *Free Soil, Free Labor, Free Men: The Ideology of the Republican Party Before the Civil War*. 1970; reprint, New York: Oxford University Press, 1995.

———. *Reconstruction: America's Unfinished Revolution, 1863–1877*. New York: Harper & Row, 1988.

———. "Reconstruction Revisited." *Reviews in American History* 10, no. 4 (December 1982): 82–100.

Foster, Gaines M. *Ghosts of the Confederacy: Defeat, the Lost Cause, and the Emergence of the New South, 1865 to 1913*. New York: Oxford University Press, 1987.

Foucault, Michel. *Power/Knowledge: Selected Interviews and Other Writings, 1972–1977*. Ed. and trans. Colin Gordon. New York: Pantheon, 1980.

Fox-Genovese, Elizabeth, and Eugene D. Genovese, "The Divine Sanction of the Social Order: Religious Foundations of the Southern Slaveholders' World View." *Journal of the American Academy of Religion* 55, no. 2 (1987): 211–33.

Francis Butler Simkins, 1897–1966: Historian of the South. Columbia, S.C.: State Printing, [1967?].

Franklin, John Hope. "Alrutheus Ambush Taylor." *Journal of Negro History* 39, no. 3 (July 1954): 240–42.

———. "Whither Reconstruction Historiography?" *Journal of Negro Education* 17, no. 4 (Autumn 1948): 446–61.

Fraser, Nancy. "Rethinking the Public Sphere: A Contribution to the Critique of Actually Existing Democracy." *Social Text* 25/26 (1990): 56–80.

Frederickson, Kari. *The Dixiecrat Revolt and the End of the Solid South, 1932–1968*. Chapel Hill: University of North Carolina Press, 2001.

———. "'The Slowest State' and 'Most Backward Community': Racial Violence in South Carolina and Federal Civil-Rights Legislation, 1946–1948." *South Carolina Historical Magazine* 98, no. 2 (April 1997): 177–202.

Freyre, Gilberto. *Casa-grande e senzala: Formação da família brasileira sob o regime de economía patriarcal*. Rio de Janeiro: Maia & Schmidt, 1933.

———. "Social Life in Brazil in the Middle of the Nineteenth Century." *Hispanic American Historical Review* 5, no. 4 (November 1922): 597–630.

———. *Tempo morto e outros tempos: Trechos de um diário de adolescência e primeira mocidade, 1915–1930*. Rio de Janeiro: Livravia José Olympio, 1975.

Frye, Gladys-Marie. *Night Riders in Black Folk History*. Knoxville: University of Tennessee Press, 1975.

Garlington, J. C. *Men of the Time; Sketches of Living Notables; A Biographical Encyclopedia of Contemporaneous South Carolina Leaders*. Spartanburg, S.C.: Garlington, 1892.

Garner, James W. *Reconstruction in Mississippi*. New York: Macmillan, 1901.

Geggus, David P. "The Caradeux and Colonial Memory." In *The Impact of the*

Haitian Revolution in the Atlantic World, ed. David P. Geggus. Columbia: University of South Carolina Press, 2001.

Gellman, Erik S. "A Radical Past for a Progressive Future: Black Culture and the National Negro Congress." Paper presented at the Annual Meeting of the American Historical Association, Washington, D.C., 11 January 2004. Paper in possession of author.

Gilmore, Glenda. *Defying Dixie: Southerners at War with White Supremacy, 1919–1948*. New York: Norton, forthcoming.

Glassberg, David. *American Historical Pageantry: The Uses of Tradition in the Early Twentieth Century*. Chapel Hill: University of North Carolina Press, 1990.

Glassie, Henry. *Passing the Time in Ballymenone: Culture and History of an Ulster Community*. Philadelphia: University of Pennsylvania Press, 1982.

———. "The Practice and Purpose of History." *Journal of American History* 81, no. 3 (December 1994): 961–68.

Godkin, E. L. "Socialism in South Carolina." *Nation* 18, no. 459 (16 April 1874): 247–48.

Griffith, Barbara S. *The Crisis of American Labor: Operation Dixie and the Defeat of the CIO*. Philadelphia: Temple University Press, 1988.

Grigsby, Melvin. *The Smoked Yank*. Rev. ed. Sioux Falls, S.D.: Dakota Bell, 1888.

Guthke, Karl S. *Last Words: Variations on a Theme in Cultural History*. Princeton, N.J.: Princeton University Press, 1992.

Hagood, Johnson. *Meet Your Grandfather: A Sketch-Book of the Hagood-Tobin Family*. [Charleston?]: privately published, 1946.

Hahn, Steven. *A Nation under Our Feet: Black Political Struggles in the Rural South from Slavery to the Great Migration*. Cambridge, Mass.: Harvard University Press, 2003.

Halbwachs, Maurice. *The Collective Memory*. Trans. Francis J. Ditter Jr. and Vida Yazdi Ditter. New York: Harper & Row, 1980.

Hale, Grace Elizabeth. *Making Whiteness: The Culture of Segregation in the South, 1890–1940*. New York: Pantheon, 1998.

Hall, Jacquelyn Dowd. "'Archive Fever' or Lost in the Records of the FBI." Paper presented at the "Homeland Insecurity: Civil Liberties, Repression, and Citizenship in the 1950s" conference, Smith College, Northampton, Mass., 24 January 2003. Paper in possession of author.

———. "The Long Civil Rights Movement and the Political Uses of the Past." *Journal of American History* 91, no. 4 (March 2005): 1233–63.

———. "Women Writers, the 'Southern Front,' and the Dialectical Imagination." *Journal of Southern History* 69, no. 1 (February 2003): 3–36.

———. "'You Must Remember This': Autobiography as Social Critique." *Journal of American History* 89 (September 1998): 439–65.

Hall, Jacquelyn Dowd, James Leloudis, Robert Korstad, Mary Murphy, LuAnn Jones, and Christopher B. Daly. *Like a Family: The Making of a Southern Cotton Mill World*. Chapel Hill: University of North Carolina Press, 1987.

Hall, Otto. "Denmark Vesey—A Lesson in Self-Defense." *Labor Defender* 10, no. 2

(February 1934): 9–10. Available in microfilm on reel 1, *Papers of the International Labor Defense* (Frederick, Md.: University Publications of America, 1987).

Hall, Stephen Gilroy. "Research as Opportunity: Alrutheus Ambush Taylor, Black Intellectualism, and the Remaking of Reconstruction Historiography, 1893–1954." *UCLA Historical Journal* 16 (1996): 39–60.

Hamilton, J. G. de Roulhac. "Review of Coulter, *The South during Reconstruction, 1865–1877.*" *Journal of Southern History* 14, no. 1 (February 1948): 134–36.

Hammett, Hugh B. *Hilary Abner Herbert: A Southerner Returns to the Union.* Philadelphia: American Philosophical Society, 1976.

Hampton, Lawrence. "Slave Narrative." Born in Slavery: Slave Narratives from the Federal Writers' Project, 1936–1938. [1936]. http://memory.loc.gov/ammem/ snhtml/snhome.html (18 November 2006).

Harding, Vincent. *Martin Luther King: The Inconvenient Hero.* New York: Orbis Books, 1996.

Hardy, Jack. *The First American Revolution.* New York: International, 1937.

Harris, Trudier. "Porch-Sitting as a Creative Southern Tradition." *Southern Cultures* 2, nos. 3/4 (1996): 441–458.

Harrold, John. *Libby, Andersonville, Florence: The Capture, Imprisonment, Escape and Rescue of John Harrold, A Union Soldier in the War of the Rebellion.* Atlantic City, N.J.: Daily Union Book and Job Printing Office, 1892.

Hart, Albert Bushnell, Henry A. Wallace, G. S. Dickerman, and Frederic S. Monroe. "Communications." *Journal of Negro History* 7, no. 4 (October 1922): 419–26.

Hayes, Jack Irby, Jr. *South Carolina and the New Deal.* Columbia: University of South Carolina Press, 2001.

Hayne, William A., Monroe N. Work, and D. H. Chamberlain. "Materials from the Scrapbook of William A. Hayne." *Journal of Negro History* 7, no. 3 (July 1922): 311–40.

Haynes, Dolly. "Aunt Dolly Haynes." Born in Slavery: Slave Narratives from the Federal Writers' Project, 1936–1938. [1936]. http://memory.loc.gov/ammem/ snhtml/snhome.html (18 November 2006).

Haywood, Harry. *Black Bolshevik: Autobiography of an Afro-American Communist.* Chicago: Liberator Press, 1978.

Hemphill, John J. "Reconstruction in South Carolina." In *Why the Solid South? or, Reconstruction and Its Results,* ed. Hilary A. Herbert. 1890; reprint, New York: Negro Universities Press, 1969.

Henderson, Daniel S. "The White Man's Revolution in South Carolina." In *Life and Addresses of D. S. Henderson,* ed. P. F. Henderson, D. S. Henderson Jr., and T. R. Henderson. Columbia, S.C.: R. L. Bryan, 1922.

Hennessy, John J. *Return to Bull Run: The Campaign and Battle of Second Manassas.* New York: Simon & Schuster, 1993.

Herbert, Hilary Abner. "How We Redeemed Alabama." *Century Magazine* 85 (April 1913): 854–62.

Herbert, Hilary A., ed. *Why the Solid South? or, Reconstruction and Its Results.* 1890; reprint, New York: Negro Universities Press, 1969.

Heywood, Mariah. "Aunt Mariah Heywood." Born in Slavery: Slave Narratives from the Federal Writers' Project, 1936–1938. 1937. http://memory.loc.gov/ammem/snhtml/snhome.html (18 November 2006).

Higginson, Thomas Wentworth. *Army Life in a Black Regiment.* East Lansing: Michigan State University Press, 1960.

Hirsch, Jerrold. *Portrait of America: A Cultural History of the Federal Writers' Project.* Chapel Hill: University of North Carolina Press, 2003.

Hirshon, Stanley P. *Farewell to the Bloody Shirt: Northern Republicans and the Southern Negro, 1877–1893.* Bloomington: Indiana University Press, 1962.

Hobsbawm, Eric. "Mass-Producing Traditions: Europe, 1870–1914." In *The Invention of Tradition,* ed. Eric Hobsbawm and Terence Ranger. New York: Cambridge University Press, 1983.

Hobson, Fred C. *But Now I See: The White Southern Racial Conversion Narrative.* Baton Rouge: Louisiana State University Press, 1999.

Hoffman, Edwin D. "The Genesis of the Modern Movement for Equal Rights in South Carolina, 1930–1939." *Journal of Negro History* 45, no. 4 (October 1959): 346–69.

Holcomb, Gary E. "New Negroes, Black Communists, and the New Pluralism." *American Quarterly* 53, no. 2 (June 2001): 367–76.

Holden, Charles J. *In the Great Maelstrom: Conservatives in Post–Civil War South Carolina.* Columbia: University of South Carolina Press, 2002.

———. "'Is Our Love for Wade Hampton Foolishness?' South Carolina and the Lost Cause." In *The Myth of the Lost Cause and Civil War History,* ed. Gary W. Gallagher and Alan T. Nolan. Bloomington: Indiana University Press, 2000.

Hollis, John Porter. *The Early Period of Reconstruction in South Carolina.* Johns Hopkins University Studies in Historical and Political Science, series 23, nos. 1–2. Baltimore: Johns Hopkins Press, 1905.

"Hopes Dim for Reconstruction History Park," 1 March 2005, AikenOnline. com. http://aiken.augusta.com/stories/030105/new_N1029.1.shtml (9 August 2005).

Hughes, C. Alvin. "We Demand Our Rights: The Southern Negro Youth Congress, 1937–1949." *Phylon* 48, no. 1 (1987): 38–50.

Hughes, Walter K. "A Veteran Negro Janitor." American Life Histories: Manuscripts from the Federal Writers' Project, 1936–1940. 1938. http://lcweb2.loc .gov/ammem/wpaintro/wpahome.html (18 November 2006).

Humphreys, James S. "South Carolina Rustic: Historian Francis Butler Simkins, a Life." Ph.D. diss., University of Southern Mississippi, 2005.

Hutcheson, Allen Carrington. "Maryville, South Carolina: An All-Black Town and Its White Neighbors." B.A. honors thesis, Harvard College, 1995.

Irons, Janet. *Testing the New Deal: The General Textile Strike in the American South.* Urbana: University of Illinois Press, 2000.

Ives, Edward D. *The Bonny Earl of Murray: The Man, the Murder, the Ballad.* Urbana: University of Illinois Press, 1997.

Jackson, Walter A. "White Liberal Intellectuals, Civil Rights and Gradualism, 1954–1960." In *The Making of Martin Luther King and the Civil Rights Movement,* ed. Brian Ward and Tony Badger, 96–114. London: Macmillan, 1996.

Jacobs, William Plumer. *The Pioneer.* Clinton, S.C.: Jacobs and Co. Press, 1935.

Jarrell, Hampton. *Wade Hampton and the Negro: The Road Not Taken.* Columbia: University of South Carolina Press, 1950.

Johnson, Bethany Leigh. "Regionalism, Race, and the Meaning of the Southern Past: Professional History in the American South, 1896–1961." Ph.D. diss., Rice University, 2001.

Johnson, Guion Griffis. "The South during the 'Fiery Epoch.'" *Social Forces* 12, no. 2 (December 1933): 303–4.

Jones, Lewis P. *South Carolina: One of the Fifty States.* Orangeburg, S.C.: Sandlapper, 1985.

———. *Stormy Petrel: N. G. Gonzales and His State.* Columbia: University of South Carolina Press, 1973.

Kallen, Horace M. "The Meaning of Tragedy in the Freedom of Man." *Journal of Philosophy* 55, no. 18 (August 1958): 772–80.

Kammen, Michael. *The Mystic Chords of Memory: The Transformation of Tradition in American Culture.* New York: Knopf, 1991.

Kantrowitz, Stephen. *Ben Tillman and the Reconstruction of White Supremacy.* Chapel Hill: University of North Carolina Press, 2000.

Kelley, Robin D. G. *Hammer and Hoe: Alabama Communists during the Great Depression.* Chapel Hill: University of North Carolina Press, 1990.

Kelly, Brian. "Not All Black and White: Labour Militancy, Republican Factionalism and the Crisis of Reconstruction in South Carolina." Paper presented to American History Research Seminar, Rothermere American Institute, Oxford University, 28 October 2004. Paper in possession of author.

———. *Race, Class, and Power in the Alabama Coalfields, 1908–1921.* Urbana: University of Illinois Press, 2001.

———. "Sentinels for New South Industry: Booker T. Washington, Industrial Accommodation, and Black Workers in the Jim Crow South." *Labor History* 44, no. 3 (August 2003): 337–57.

Kennedy, Gwen Neville. *Kinship and Pilgrimage: Rituals of Reunion in American Protestant Culture.* New York: Oxford University Press, 1987.

Key, V. O. *Southern Politics in State and Nation.* New York: Vintage, 1949.

King, G. Wayne. "Death Camp at Florence." *Civil War Times Illustrated* 12, no. 9 (January 1974): 34–42.

King, Martin Luther, Jr. "Honoring Dr. Du Bois, No. 2, 1968." In *Freedomways Reader: Prophets in Their Own Country,* ed. Esther Cooper Jackson. Boulder, Colo.: Westview Press, 2000.

———. "Our God Is Marching On." A Call to Conscience: The Landmark Speeches of Martin Luther King Jr. Martin Luther King Papers Project, 25 March 1965. http://www.stanford.edu/group/King/publications/speeches/Our_God_is_marching_on.html (11 August 2005).

King, Susie Taylor. *Reminiscences of My Life in Camp with the 33rd United States Colored Troops, Late 1st S. C. Volunteers.* Boston: published by author, 1902.

Kirby, Jack Temple. "The Southern Exodus, 1910–1960: A Primer for Historians." *Journal of Southern History* 49, no. 4 (November 1983): 585–600.

Kirk, John A. "'Massive Resistance and Minimum Compliance': The Origins of the 1957 Little Rock School Crisis and the Failure of School Desegregation in the South." In *Massive Resistance: Southern Opposition to the Second Reconstruction,* ed. Clive Webb. New York: Oxford University Press, 2005, 76–98.

Klarman, Michael J. "How Brown Changed Race Relations: The Backlash Thesis." *Journal of American History* 81, no. 1 (June 1994): 81–118.

Kluger, Richard. *Simple Justice: The History of Brown v. Board of Education and Black America's Struggle for Equality.* New York: Knopf, 1975.

K'Meyer, Tracy Elaine. *Interracialism and Christian Community in the Postwar South: The Story of Koinonia Farm.* Charlottesville: University of Virginia Press, 1997.

Kohn, August. *The Cotton Mills of South Carolina.* Columbia, S.C.: Department of Agriculture, Commerce, and Immigration, 1907.

Kolko, Gabriel. *The Triumph of Conservatism: A Reinterpretation of American History, 1900–1916.* New York: Free Press of Glencoe, 1963.

Korstad, Karl. "Black and White Together: Organizing in the South with the Food, Tobacco, Agricultural and Allied Workers Union (FTA-CIO), 1946–1952." In *The CIO's Left-Led Unions,* ed. Steve Rosswurm. New Brunswick, N.J.: Rutgers University Press, 1992.

Korstad, Robert Rodgers. *Civil Rights Unionism: Tobacco Workers and the Struggle for Democracy in the Mid-Twentieth-Century South.* Chapel Hill: University of North Carolina Press, 2003.

Korstad, Robert, and Nelson Lichtenstein. "Opportunities Found and Lost: Labor, Radicals, and the Early Civil Rights Movement." *Journal of American History* 75, no. 3 (December 1988): 786–811.

Kousser, J. Morgan. *The Shaping of Southern Politics: Suffrage Restriction and the Establishment of the One-Party South, 1880–1910.* New Haven: Yale University Press, 1974.

Lakey, Othal Hawthorne. *The History of the CME Church.* Memphis: CME Publishing House, 1985.

Lau, Peter F. "Freedom Road Territory: The Politics of Civil Rights Struggle in South Carolina during the Jim Crow Era." Ph.D. diss., Rutgers University, 2002.

The Laura Spelman Rockefeller Memorial Final Report. New York: n.p., 1933.

Lawson, Elizabeth. *The Gentleman from Mississippi: Our First Negro Senator.* New York: Elizabeth Lawson, 1960.

———. *The Struggle against White Chauvinism.* New York: New York State Education Dept., Communist Party, 1949.

———. *Study Outline History of the American Negro People, 1619–1918.* New York: Workers Book Shop, 1939.

———. *Thaddeus Stevens: Militant Democrat and Fighter for Negro Rights.* New York: International, 1942.

Leach, William. *Land of Desire: Merchants, Power, and the Rise of a New American Culture.* New York: Pantheon, 1993.

Leland, John A. *A Voice from South Carolina: Twelve Chapters Before Hampton,*

Two Chapters after Hampton, with a Journal of a Reputed Ku-Klux, and an Appendix. Charleston: Walker, Evans, and Cogswell, 1879.

"Letters on Reconstruction Records." *Journal of Negro History* 5, no. 4 (October 1920): 467–75.

Letwin, Daniel. *The Challenge of Interracial Unionism: Alabama Coal Miners, 1878–1921.* Chapel Hill: University of North Carolina Press, 1998.

Leuchtenburg, William E. *Franklin D. Roosevelt and the New Deal, 1932–1940.* New York: Harper & Row, 1963.

Lewinson, Paul. *Race, Class, and Party: A History of Negro Suffrage and White Politics in the South.* New York: Oxford University Press, 1932.

Lewis, David L. Introduction to *Black Reconstruction in America, 1860–1880,* by W. E. B. Du Bois. New York: Free Press, 1992.

———. *W. E. B. Du Bois: The Fight for Equality and the American Century, 1919–1963.* New York: Holt, 2000.

Lewis, Hylan. *Blackways of Kent.* Chapel Hill: University of North Carolina Press, 1955.

Link, William A. *The Paradox of Southern Progressivism, 1880–1930.* Chapel Hill: University of North Carolina Press, 1992.

Litwack, Leon F. "Trouble in Mind: The Bicentennial and the Afro-American Experience." *Journal of American History* 74, no. 2 (September 1987): 315–37.

Liverance, Sara Vandiver, ed. *Anderson County South Carolina Tricentennial Celebration, August 30–September 5, 1970, Souvenir Program.* [Anderson, S.C.?]: Anderson County Tricentennial Committee, 1970.

Logan, Rayford. *The Negro in American Life and Thought: The Nadir, 1877–1901.* New York: Dial Press, 1954.

Lord, Albert Bates. *The Singer of Tales.* Cambridge, Mass.: Harvard University Press, 1960.

Lumpkin, Grace. *To Make My Bread.* New York: Macaulay, 1932.

Lumpkin, Katharine Du Pre. *The Making of a Southerner.* New York: Knopf, 1946.

Lynch, John R. "More about the Historical Errors of James Ford Rhodes." *Journal of Negro History* 3, no. 2 (April 1918): 139–57.

———. "Some Historical Errors of James Ford Rhodes." *Journal of Negro History* 2, no. 4 (October 1917): 345–68.

Lyotard, Jean-François. *The Postmodern Condition: A Report on Knowledge.* Trans. Geoff Bennington and Brian Massumi. Minneapolis: University of Minnesota Press, 1984.

Macaulay, Neill W., Jr. "South Carolina Reconstruction Historiography." *South Carolina Historical Magazine* 65 (1964): 24.

Magdol, Edward. *A Right to the Land: Essays on the Freedmen's Community.* Westport, Conn.: Greenwood, 1977.

Marable, Manning. *Race, Reform, and Rebellion: The Second Reconstruction in Black America, 1945–1982.* New York: Macmillan, 1984.

Martin, Samuel J. *Southern Hero: Matthew Calbraith Butler, Confederate General, Hampton Red Shirt, and U.S. Senator.* Mechanicsburg, Pa.: Stackpole, 2001.

Marx, Karl. *The Eighteenth Brumaire of Louis Bonaparte.* New York: International, 1963.

Massey, Jane Duncan. *Upcountry Reflections, 1900–1903 and 1906: Some Personal Diaries Belonging to Jane Duncan Todd Massey, and Other Bits of History from Oconee County, South Carolina.* Comp. and ed. Sara Hunter Kellar. Titusville, Fla.: Sarah H. Kellar, 1993.

Mayberry, George. "Two Down." *New Republic* 111 (14 August 1944): 196.

Maybury-Lewis, David H. P. Introduction to *The Masters and the Slaves: A Study in the Development of Brazilian Civilization,* by Gilberto Freyre. Berkeley: University of California Press, 1986.

McArthur, Judith N., and Orville Vernon Burton. *"A Gentleman and an Officer": A Military and Social History of James B. Griffin's Civil War.* New York: Oxford University Press, 1996.

McConachie, Bruce A. *Melodramatic Formations: American Theatre and Society, 1820–1870.* Iowa City: University of Iowa Press, 1992.

McCravy, Edwin Parker. *Memories.* Easley, S.C.: Observer Printing, 1941.

McCreight, David A. "Ku Klux Stories." American Life Histories: Manuscripts from the Federal Writers' Project, 1936–1940. 1937. http://lcweb2.loc.gov/ammem/wpaintro/wpahome.html (18 November 2006).

McCully, Robert S. "Letter from a Reconstruction Renegade." *South Carolina Historical Magazine* 77, no. 1 (January 1976): 34–40.

McKnight, Gerald D. *The Last Crusade: Martin Luther King, Jr., the FBI, and the Poor People's Campaign.* Boulder, Colo.: Westview Press, 1998.

McLaurin, Melton A. "Early Labor Union Organizational Efforts in South Carolina Cotton Mills, 1880–1905." *South Carolina Historical Magazine* 72 (January 1971): 44–59.

———. *Paternalism and Protest: Southern Cotton Mill Workers and Organized Labor, 1875–1905.* Westport, Conn.: Greenwood, 1971.

McMillen, Neil R. *The Citizens' Council: Organized Resistance to the Second Reconstruction.* Urbana: University of Illinois Press, 1971.

Meier, August, and Elliott Rudwick. *Black History and the Historical Profession, 1915–1980.* Urbana: University of Illinois Press, 1986.

Meisler, Stanley. "The Forgotten Dreams of Howard Fast." *Nation,* 30 May 1959, 498–500.

Mercer, P. M. "Tapping the Slave Narrative Collection for the Response of Black South Carolinians to Emancipation and Reconstruction." *Australian Journal of Politics and History* 25, no. 3 (1979): 358–73.

Metz, Leon. *John Wesley Hardin: Dark Angel of Texas.* El Paso: Mangan Books, 1996.

Minchin, Timothy J. *What Do We Need a Union For? The TWUA in the South, 1945–1955.* Chapel Hill: University of North Carolina Press, 1997.

"Minneapolis Meeting of the American Historical Association." *American Historical Review* 37, no. 3 (April 1932): 429–50.

Mitchell, Broadus. *The Rise of Cotton Mills in the South.* 1921, reprint, Columbia: University of South Carolina Press, 2001.

Montell, William Lynwood. *Killings: Folk Justice in the Upper South.* Lexington: University Press of Kentucky, 1986.

Moore, Frederick W. "Review of Reynolds, *Reconstruction in South Carolina, 1865–1877." American Historical Review* 12, no. 1 (October 1906): 180–81.

Moore, John Hammond. *Columbia and Richland County: A South Carolina Community, 1740–1990.* Columbia: University of South Carolina Press, 1993.

Morgan, James Morris. *Recollections of a Rebel Reefer.* Boston: Houghton Mifflin, 1917.

Needell, Jeffrey D. "Identity, Race, Gender, and Modernity in the Origins of Gilberto Freyre's Oeuvre." *American Historical Review* 100, no. 1 (February 1995): 51–77.

Nelson, Scott Reynolds. *Iron Confederacies: Southern Railways, Klan Violence, and Reconstruction.* Chapel Hill: University of North Carolina Press, 1999.

Neville, Gwen Kennedy. *Kinship and Pilgrimage: Rituals of Reunion in American Protestant Culture.* New York: Oxford University Press, 1987.

Nora, Pierre. "Between Memory and History: Les Lieux de Mémoire." *Representations* 26 (Spring 1989): 7–25.

———. 2002. "Reasons for the Current Upsurge in Memory." Eurozine. http://www.eurozine.com/pdf/2002-04-19-nora-en.pdf (1 August 2005).

Norryce, C. W., ed. *A General Sketch of the City of Anderson.* Anderson, S.C.: Roper Printing, 1909.

Novick, Peter. *That Noble Dream: The "Objectivity Question" and the American Historical Profession.* New York: Cambridge University Press, 1988.

"Oakley Park." *United Daughters of the Confederacy Magazine* 11, no. 5 (May 1948): 16.

O'Dell, Jack. "'I Wasn't Interested in Living in the United States If I Wasn't Going to Be in the Movement': Jack O'Dell on Civil Rights Organizing." History Matters. http://historymatters.gmu.edu/d/6926/ (14 July 2003).

Odum, Howard W. *Race and Rumors of Race: Challenge to American Crisis.* Chapel Hill: University of North Carolina Press, 1943.

Olick, Jeffrey K. and Joyce Robbins. "Social Memory Studies: From 'Collective Memory' to the Historical Sociology of Mnemonic Practices." *Annual Review of Sociology* 24 (1998): 105–40.

Oliphant, Mary C. Simms, ed. *Simms' History of South Carolina, Revised by Mrs. Mary C. Simms Oliphant.* Columbia, S.C.: State Co., 1917.

Page, Thomas Nelson. "Red Rock: A Chronicle of Reconstruction." *Scribner's Magazine* 23, no. 1 (January 1898): 34–52, no. 2 (February 1898): 161–78, no. 3 (March 1898): 292–310, no. 4 (April 1898): 481–96, no. 5 (May 1898): 613–32, no. 6 (June 1898): 689–708, and 24, no. 1 (July 1898): 113–22, no. 2 (August 1898): 237–51, no. 3 (September 1898): 350–70, no. 4 (October 1898): 470–88, no. 5 (November 1898): 578–96.

———. *Red Rock: A Chronicle of Reconstruction.* New York: Charles Scribner's Sons, 1898.

Painter, Nell Irvin. *Exodusters: Black Migration to Kansas after Reconstruction.* New York: Knopf, 1976.

Paredes, Américo. *"With His Pistol in His Hand": A Border Ballad and Its Hero.* Austin: University of Texas Press, 1958.

Park, R. E. "Extracts from Newspapers Showing the Disorders of Reconstruction." *Journal of Negro History* 7, no. 3 (July 1922): 299–311.

Patterson, Daniel W. *A Tree Accurst: Bobby McMillon and Stories of Frankie Silver.* Chapel Hill: University of North Carolina Press, 2000.

Payne, Charles M. *I've Got the Light of Freedom: The Organizing Tradition and the Mississippi Freedom Struggle.* Berkeley: University of California Press, 1985.

Pendleton Farmers' Society, Committee on History. *Pendleton Farmers' Society.* Atlanta: Foote & Davies, 1908.

Pendleton, V. L. *Last Words of Confederate Heroes.* Raleigh: Mutual, 1913.

Pierce, Joseph Gorrell. "Statement to Greensboro Truth and Reconciliation Commission," 16 July 2005, Greensboro, N.C. Transcript available at http://www .greensborotrc.org/pierce.doc (24 January 2007).

Pike, James S. *The Prostrate State: South Carolina under Negro Government.* New York: D. Appleton, 1874.

Polsgrove, Carol. *Divided Minds: Intellectuals and the Civil Rights Movement.* New York: W. W. Norton, 2001.

Poole, W. Scott. *Never Surrender: Confederate Memory and Conservatism in the South Carolina Upcountry.* Athens: University of Georgia Press, 2004.

———. "Never Surrender: The Lost Cause and the Making of Southern Conservatism in the South Carolina Upcountry, 1850–1903." Ph.D. diss., University of Mississippi, 2001.

Powers, Bernard E., Jr. *Black Charlestonians: A Social History, 1822–1885.* Fayetteville: University of Arkansas Press, 1994.

"The Proceedings of the Annual Meeting of the Association for the Study of Negro Life and History." *Journal of Negro History* 8, no. 1 (January 1923): 116–22.

Quint, Howard H. *Profile in Black and White: A Frank Portrait of South Carolina.* Washington, D.C.: Public Affairs Press, 1958.

Rable, George C. *But There Was No Peace: The Role of Violence in the Politics of Reconstruction.* Athens: University of Georgia Press, 1984.

———. "The South and the Politics of Antilynching Legislation, 1920–1940." *Journal of Southern History* 51, no. 2 (May 1985): 201–20.

Rawick, George P., ed. *The American Slave: A Composite Autobiography.* Westport, Conn.: Greenwood, 1972.

———. *The American Slave: A Composite Autobiography.* Supplement, series 1. Westport, Conn.: Greenwood, 1978.

"Reconstruction in South Carolina." *Outlook* 83 (4 August 1906): 816.

The Red Shirts. "Jion the Red Shirt's [sic]." July 2005. http://www.redshirts.org/ join.htm (26 July 2005).

"Review of Edward L. Wells, *Hampton and Reconstruction.*" *Independent* 53 (17 October 1907): 946.

Reynolds, John S. *Reconstruction in South Carolina, 1865–1877.* Columbia, S.C.: State Co., 1905.

Richards, Johnetta Gladys. "The Southern Negro Youth Congress: A History." Ph.D. diss., University of Cincinnati, 1987.

Richardson, Heather Cox. *The Death of Reconstruction: Race, Labor, and Politics in the Post-Civil War North, 1865–1901*. Cambridge, Mass.: Harvard University Press, 2001.

Ringer, Fritz. "The Intellectual Field, Intellectual History, and the Sociology of Knowledge." *Theory and Society* 19, no. 3 (June 1990): 269–94.

Robertson, David. *Sly and Able: A Political Biography of James F. Byrnes*. New York: W. W. Norton, 1994.

Robinson, Cedric J. *Black Marxism: The Making of a Black Radical Tradition*. Chapel Hill: University of North Carolina Press, 2000.

Rogers, William Warren. "The South Mourns a Leader: The Death of John C. Calhoun." *Alabama Historical Quarterly* 36, no. 2 (Summer 1974): 167–71.

Rogin, Michael. "'The Sword Became a Flashing Vision': D. W. Griffith's *The Birth of a Nation*." *Representations* 9 (Winter 1985): 150–95.

Roper, John Herbert. *C. Vann Woodward, Southerner*. Athens: University of Georgia Press, 1987.

Rubin, Louis D., Jr. "General Longstreet and Me: Refighting the Civil War." *Southern Cultures* 8, no. 1 (Spring 2002): 21–46.

"Ruckstull Dies at 89." *Art Digest* 16 (June 1942).

Ruckstull, F. W. *Great Works of Art and What Makes Them Great*. Garden City, N.J.: Garden City Publishing, 1925.

Ryan, Mary. "The American Parade: Representations of the Nineteenth-Century Social Order." In *The New Cultural History*, ed. Lynn Hunt. Berkeley: University of California Press, 1989.

Salmond, John A. *Gastonia, 1929: The Story of the Loray Mill Strike*. Chapel Hill: University of North Carolina Press, 1995.

———. *The General Textile Strike of 1934: From Maine to Alabama*. Columbia: University of Missouri Press, 2002.

Savage, Kirk. *Standing Soldiers, Kneeling Slaves: Race, War, and Monument in Nineteenth-Century America*. Princeton, N.J.: Princeton University Press, 1997.

Saville, Julie. *The Work of Reconstruction: From Slave to Wage Laborer in South Carolina, 1860–1870*. New York: Cambridge University Press, 1994.

Scales, Junius Irving, and Richard Nickson. *Cause at Heart: A Former Communist Remembers*. Athens: University of Georgia Press, 1987.

Schrager, Samuel. "What Is Social in Oral History?" *International Journal of Oral History* 4, no. 2 (June 1983): 76–98.

Schrecker, Ellen W. *No Ivory Tower: McCarthyism and the Universities*. New York: Oxford University Press, 1986.

Scott, James C. *Domination and the Arts of Resistance: Hidden Transcripts*. New Haven: Yale University Press, 1990.

Sherman, William. "Slave Interview." Born in Slavery: Slave Narratives from the Federal Writers' Project, 1936–1938. 1936. http://memory.loc.gov/ammem/snhtml/snhome.html (23 August 2005).

Silber, Nina. *The Romance of Reunion: Northerners and the South, 1865–1900.* Chapel Hill: University of North Carolina Press, 1993.

Simkins, Francis Butler. "The Election of 1876 in South Carolina," parts 1 and 2. *South Atlantic Quarterly* 21, no. 3 (July 1922): 225–40, and 21, no. 4 (October 1922): 335–51.

———. "Guzman Blanco: An Appreciation." *South Atlantic Quarterly* 23, no. 4 (October 1924): 310–18.

———. "Latin-American Opinion of Pan-Americanism." *South Atlantic Quarterly* 22, no. 3 (July 1923): 216–27.

———. "The Negro in South Carolina Law." M.A. thesis, Columbia University, 1920.

———. "New Viewpoints of Southern Reconstruction." *Journal of Southern History* 5 (1938): 16–34.

———. *Pitchfork Ben Tillman, South Carolinian.* Baton Rouge: Louisiana State University Press, 1944.

———. "Race Legislation in South Carolina since 1865," parts 1 and 2. *South Atlantic Quarterly* 20, no. 1 (January 1921): 61–71, and 20, no. 2 (April 1921): 165–77.

———. "Review of Jarrell, *Wade Hampton and the Negro.*" *Mississippi Valley Historical Review* 37, no. 4 (March 1951): 736–38.

———. "Review of Williams, *Hampton and His Red Shirts.*" *Journal of Southern History* 2, no. 2 (May 1936): 281–83.

———. "Review of Wellman, *Giant in Gray.*" *Mississippi Valley Historical Review* 37, no. 1 (June 1950): 145–46.

———. *The Tillman Movement in South Carolina.* Durham, N.C.: Duke University Press, 1926.

Simkins, Francis Butler, and Robert Hilliard Woody. *South Carolina during Reconstruction.* Chapel Hill: University of North Carolina Press, 1932.

Simon, Bryant. *A Fabric of Defeat: The Politics of South Carolina Millhands, 1910–1948.* Chapel Hill: University of North Carolina Press, 1998.

———. "Race Reactions: African American Organizing, Liberalism, and White Working-Class Politics in Postwar South Carolina." In *Jumpin' Jim Crow: Southern Politics from Civil War to Civil Rights,* ed. Jane Dailey, Glenda Elizabeth Gilmore, and Bryant Simon. Princeton, N.J.: Princeton University Press, 2000.

Singal, Daniel Joseph. *The War Within: From Victorian to Modernist Thought in the South, 1919–1945.* Chapel Hill: University of North Carolina Press, 1982.

Singh, Nikhil Pal. "Retracing the Black-Red Thread." *American Literary History* 15, no. 4 (Winter 2003): 830–40.

Sitkoff, Harvard. *A New Deal for Blacks: The Emergence of Civil Rights as a National Issue.* Vol. 1: *The Depression Decade.* New York: Oxford University Press, 1978.

Skidmore, Thomas E. *Black into White: Race and Nationality in Brazilian Thought.* 1974; reprint, Durham, N.C.: Duke University Press, 1993.

———. "Raízes de Gilberto Freyre." *Journal of Latin American Studies* 54, no. 1 (February 2002): 1–20.

Solomon, Mark. *The Cry Was Unity: Communists and African Americans, 1917–1936.* Jackson: University Press of Mississippi, 1998.

South Carolina. *Acts and Joint Resolutions of the General Assembly of the State of South Carolina Passed at the Regular Session of 1914.* Columbia, S.C.: Gonzales and Bryan, State Printers, 1914.

———. *Acts and Joint Resolutions of the General Assembly of the State of South Carolina Passed at the Regular Session of 1915.* Columbia, S.C.: Gonzales and Bryan, State Printers, 1915.

———. *Acts and Joint Resolutions of the General Assembly of the State of South Carolina, Regular Session of 1936.* [Columbia]: Joint Committee on Printing, General Assembly of South Carolina, [1936].

———. *An Historical Pageant of South Carolina.* Columbia, S.C.: State Co., [1925].

———. *Journal of the House of Representatives of the First Session of the 80th General Assembly of the State of South Carolina, Being the Regular Session, Beginning Tuesday, January 10, 1933.* [Columbia]: Joint Committee on Printing, General Assembly of South Carolina, [1933].

———. *Journal of the House of Representatives of the General Assembly of the State of South Carolina Being the Regular Session, Beginning Tuesday, January 10, 1911.* Columbia, S.C.: Gonzales and Bryan, State Printers, 1911.

———. *Journal of the House of Representatives of the General Assembly of the State of South Carolina Being the Regular Session, Beginning Tuesday, January 13, 1914.* Columbia, S.C.: Gonzales and Bryan, State Printers, 1914.

———. *Journal of the Senate of the First Session of the 80th General Assembly of the State of South Carolina, Being the Regular Session, Beginning Tuesday, January 10, 1933.* [Columbia]: Joint Committee on Printing, General Assembly of South Carolina, [1933].

———. *Journal of the Senate of the General Assembly of the State of South Carolina Being the Regular Session, Beginning Tuesday, January 13, 1914.* Columbia, S.C.: Gonzales and Bryan, State Printers, 1914.

South Carolina Division, United Daughters of the Confederacy. *Recollections and Reminiscences, 1861–1865 through World War I.* 12 vols. [S.C.]: South Carolina Division, United Daughters of the Confederacy, 1990–.

South Carolina League of the South. Position Papers, July 2005. http://sclos.org/LPP-01.htm (18 November 2006).

Spillman, Lyn. "When Do Collective Memories Last? Founding Moments in the United States and Australia." *Social Science History* 22, no. 4 (Winter 1998): 445–77.

Stone, Alfred H. "A Mississippian's View of Civil Rights, States Rights, and the Reconstruction Background." *Journal of Mississippi History* 10, no. 3 (July 1948): 181–239.

Stone, Olive Matthews. "Agrarian Conflict in Alabama: Sections, Races, and Classes in a Rural State from 1800 to 1938." Ph.D. diss., University of North Carolina at Chapel Hill, 1939.

Sullivan, Patricia. *Days of Hope: Race and Democracy in the New Deal Era.* Chapel Hill: University of North Carolina Press, 1996.

Summer, G. Leland. *Folklore of South Carolina, including Central and Dutch Fork sections of the state and much data on the early Quaker and Covenanter customs, etc.* N.p., 1950.

Summer, Mark Wahlgren. *The Era of Good Stealings.* New York: Oxford University Press, 1993.

Tannenbaum, Frank. *Darker Phases of the South.* New York: G. P. Putnam's Sons, 1924.

Taylor, Alrutheus Ambush. "Negro Congressmen a Generation After," parts 1 and 2. *Journal of Negro History* 7, no. 2 (April 1922): 121–71.

———. "The Negro in South Carolina during Reconstruction," parts 1 and 2. *Journal of Negro History* 9, no. 3 (July 1924), and no. 4 (October 1924).

———. *The Negro in South Carolina during the Reconstruction.* Washington, D.C.: Association for the Study of Negro Life and History, 1924.

Tetzlaff, Monica Maria. *Cultivating a New South: Abbie Holmes Christensen and the Politics of Race and Gender, 1852–1938.* Columbia: University of South Carolina Press, 2002.

Thompson, John G. "John G. Thompson, the Original Carpet-bagger." *Journal of Negro History* 5, no. 1 (January 1920): 120–25.

Tillman, Benjamin R. *The Struggles of 1876: How South Carolina Was Delivered from Carpet-bag and Negro Rule.* Speech at the Red-Shirt reunion at Anderson, S.C. Personal reminiscences and incidents by Senator B. R. Tillman. N.p., 1909.

Tindall, George Brown. *The Emergence of the New South, 1913–1945.* Baton Rouge: Louisiana State University Press, 1967.

———. "The South Carolina Constitutional Convention of 1895." M.A. thesis, University of North Carolina, 1948.

———. *South Carolina Negroes, 1877–1900.* Columbia: University of South Carolina Press, 1952.

Tompkins, D. A. *Cotton Mill, Commercial Features: A Textbook.* Charlotte, N.C.: Published by the author, 1899.

Tompkins, Jane. *Sensational Designs: The Cultural Work of American Fiction, 1790–1860.* New York: Oxford University Press, 1985.

Toole, Gasper Loren, II. *Ninety Years in Aiken County: Memoirs of Aiken County and Its People.* N.p.: [1957?].

Trelease, Allen W. *White Terror: The Ku Klux Klan Conspiracy and Southern Reconstruction.* New York: Harper and Row, 1971.

Trent, William P. *William Gilmore Simms.* Boston: Houghton, Mifflin, 1892.

Trilling, Diana. "Fiction in Review." *Nation* 159 (19 August 1944), 219.

Trouillot, Michel-Rolph. *Silencing the Past: Power and the Production of History.* Boston: Beacon Press, 1995.

Trowbridge, Charles Tyler. "Six Months in the Freedmen's Bureau with a Colored Regiment." In *Glimpses of the Nation's Struggle, Sixth Series, Papers Read before the Minnesota Commandery of the Military Order of the Loyal Legion of the United States, January, 1903–1908.* Minneapolis: Aug. Davis, 1909.

Tyson, Timothy B. "Dynamite and 'The Silent South': A Story from the Second

Reconstruction." In *Jumpin' Jim Crow: Southern Politics from Civil War to Civil Rights,* ed. Jane Dailey, Glenda Elizabeth Gilmore, and Bryant Simon, 275–97. Princeton, N.J.: Princeton University Press, 2000.

———. *Radio Free Dixie: Robert F. Williams and the Roots of Black Power.* Chapel Hill: University of North Carolina Press, 1999.

U.S. Congress, Joint Congressional Committee on Inaugural Ceremonies. *Inaugural addresses of the presidents of the United States: from George Washington, 1789, to George Bush, 1989.* Bicentennial ed. 101st Cong., 1st sess., 1989. Washington, D.C.: GPO, 1989.

———, Joint Select Committee to Inquire into the Conditions of Affairs in the Late Insurrectionary States. *Testimony Taken by the Joint Select Committee to Inquire into the Conditions of Affairs in the Late Insurrectionary States.* Washington: Government Printing Office, 1872. (KKK Hearings)

U.S. Department of Commerce, Bureau of the Census. *Thirteenth Census of the United States, Taken in the Year 1910.* Vol. 3: *Population, 1910, Reports by States, with Statistics for Counties, Cities and Other Civil Divisions, Nebraska–Wyoming, Alaska, Hawaii, and Puerto Rico.* Washington, D.C.: GPO, 1913.

Utsey, Walker Scott, ed. *Who's Who in South Carolina, 1934–1935.* Columbia, S.C.: Current Historical Association, 1935.

Vandiver, Louise Ayer. *Traditions and History of Anderson County.* Atlanta: Ruralist Press, 1928.

Vansina, Jan. *Oral Tradition as History.* Madison: University of Wisconsin Press, 1985.

Waldrep, G. C., III. *Southern Workers and the Search for Community: Spartanburg County, South Carolina.* Urbana: University of Illinois Press, 2000.

Walker, Mrs. J. Frost. "A New Objective—'Red Shirt Shrine.'" *United Daughters of the Confederacy Magazine* 11, no. 5 (May 1948): 16–17.

———. "South Carolina Governor Thurmond and Bride at Oakley Park." *United Daughters of the Confederacy Magazine* 11, no. 3 (March 1948): 11–12.

Wallace, David Duncan. *South Carolina: A Short History.* Chapel Hill: University of North Carolina Press, 1951.

Wallace, Henry A. "Communications." *Journal of Negro History* 7, no. 3 (July 1922): 296–98.

Walmsley, James Elliott. *The Making of South Carolina: A Historical Pageant.* Rock Hill, S.C.: Record Printing, 1921.

Watson, E. O. *Builders: Sketches Methodist Preachers in South Carolina with Historical Data.* [Columbia, S.C.]: Southern Christian Advocate, 1932.

Weeks, Edmund. "Black Hatred." *Atlantic Monthly* 174 (9 September 1944): 127.

Weisberger, Bernard A. "The Dark and Bloody Ground of Reconstruction Historiography." *Journal of Southern History* 25, no. 4 (November 1959): 427–47.

Weiss, Thomas. "Tourism in America before World War II." *Journal of Economic History* 64, no. 2 (June 2004): 289–327.

Wellman, Manly Wade. *Giant in Gray: A Biography of Wade Hampton of South Carolina.* New York: Charles Scribner's Sons, 1949.

Wells, Edward L. "Comment on 'The Crisis of the Confederacy.'" *Southern Historical Society Papers* 33 (1905): 79–82.

———. "Experiences of a Northern Man in the Confederate Army: Running the Blockade." *Southern Historical Society Papers* 9 (1881): 369–78.

———. *Hampton and His Cavalry in '64.* Richmond: B. F. Johnson, 1899.

———. *Hampton and Reconstruction.* Columbia, S.C.: State Co., 1907.

———. "Hampton at Fayetteville." *Southern Historical Society Papers* 13 (1885): 144–48.

———. "A Morning Call on General Kilpatrick." *Southern Historical Society Papers* 12 (1884): 123–30.

———. "Review of B. K. Benson, Who Goes There." *Publications of the Southern History Association* 5, no. 1 (January 1901): 62–63.

———. "Review of John S. Wise, The End of an Era." *Publications of the Southern History Association* 4, no. 4 (July 1900): 272–75.

———. "Review of Mrs. George Bryan Conrad, Reminiscences of a Southern Woman." *Publications of the Southern History Association* 5, no. 6 (November 1901): 519–21.

———. "Review of Mrs. St. Julien Ravenel, Life and Times of William Lowndes of South Carolina." *Publications of the Southern History Association* 5, no. 5 (September 1901): 415–17.

———. "Who Burnt Columbia? Testimony of a Confederate Cavalryman." *Southern Historical Society Papers* 10 (1882): 109–19.

Wexler, Laura. *Fire in a Canebrake: The Last Mass Lynching in America.* New York: Scribner, 2003.

Wheaton, Elizabeth. *Codename GREENKILL: The 1979 Greensboro Killings.* Athens: University of Georgia Press, 1987.

White, Walter F. "Remnants of Dark Ages." *New York Herald Tribune Books,* 27 September 1925, V:11.

Whittenberg, A. J. Personal interview, Greenville, S.C., 22 August 1998. Notes and tapes in possession of author.

Wiggins, William H., Jr. "African American Celebrations: An Historical and Cultural Overview (1865–1969)." In *Jubilation! African American Celebrations in the Southeast,* ed. William H. Wiggins Jr. and Douglas DeNatale. Columbia: McKissick Museum, University of South Carolina, 1993.

———. *O Freedom! Afro-American Emancipation Celebrations.* Knoxville: University of Tennessee Press, 1987.

Wilk, Daniel L. "The Phoenix Riot and the Memories of Greenwood County." *Southern Cultures* 8, no. 4 (Winter 2002): 29–55.

Williams, Alfred B. *Hampton and His Red Shirts: South Carolina's Deliverance in 1876.* Charleston: Walker, Evans, and Cogswell, 1935.

Williams, Lou Falkner. *The Great South Carolina Ku Klux Klan Trials, 1871–1872.* Athens: University of Georgia Press, 1996.

Williams, Raymond. *Marxism and Literature.* Oxford: Oxford University Press, 1977.

Williams, Vernon J., Jr. *Rethinking Race: Franz Boas and His Contemporaries.* Lexington: University Press of Kentucky, 1996.

Williamson, Joel. *After Slavery: The Negro in South Carolina During Reconstruction, 1861–1877.* Chapel Hill: University of North Carolina Press, 1965.

———. *The Crucible of Race: Black-White Relations in the South since Emancipation.* New York: Oxford University Press, 1984.

Wilson, Charles Reagan. *Baptized in Blood: The Religion of the Lost Cause, 1865–1920.* Athens: University of Georgia Press, 1980.

Wilson, Woodrow. "The Reconstruction of the Southern States." *Atlantic Monthly* 87 (January 1901): 1–15.

Woodward, C. Vann. "The Irony of Southern History." *Journal of Southern History* 19, no. 1 (February 1953): 3–19.

———. "The 'New Reconstruction' in the South: Desegregation in Historical Perspective." *Commentary* 21, no. 6 (June 1956): 501–8.

———. *The Origins of the New South, 1877–1913.* Baton Rouge: Louisiana State University Press, 1951.

———. *Reunion and Reaction: The Compromise of 1877 and the End of Reconstruction.* 2nd ed. New York: Doubleday Anchor Books, 1956.

———. *The Strange Career of Jim Crow.* 1955; new and rev. ed., New York: Oxford University Press, 1957; commemorative ed., New York: Oxford University Press, 2002.

———. *Thinking Back: The Perils of Writing History.* Baton Rouge: Louisiana State University Press, 1986.

———. *Tom Watson, Agrarian Rebel.* New York: Macmillan, 1938.

Woody, R. H. "Jonathan Jasper Wright, Associate Justice of the Supreme Court of South Carolina, 1870–1877." *Journal of Negro History* 18, no. 2 (April 1933): 114–31.

Woody, Robert H. "The South Carolina Reform Movements of 1870 and 1872." Duke University, A.M. thesis, 1928.

———. "Studies in the Economic and Political Reconstruction of South Carolina." Duke University, Ph.D. diss., 1930.

Woolley, Edwin C. *The Reconstruction of Georgia.* New York: Columbia University Press, 1901.

Work, Monroe N., et al. "Some Negro Members of Reconstruction Conventions and Legislatures and of Congress." *Journal of Negro History* 5, no. 1 (January 1920): 63–119.

Wright, Louis B. "Myth-Makers and the South's Dilemma." *Sewanee Review* 53 (1945): 544–58.

Zerubavel, Yael. *Recovered Roots: Collective Memory and the Making of Israeli National Tradition.* Chicago: University of Chicago Press, 1995.

Ziegler, Luther Harmon, Jr. "Senator Walter George's 1938 Campaign." *Georgia Historical Quarterly* 43, no. 4 (December 1959): 333–52.

Zuczek, Richard. *State of Rebellion: South Carolina during Reconstruction.* Columbia: University of South Carolina Press, 1996.

INDEX

Italicized page numbers refer to illustrations.

THE AMERICAN SOUTH SERIES

Anne Goodwyn Jones and Susan V. Donaldson, editors
Haunted Bodies: Gender and Southern Texts

M. M. Manring
Slave in a Box: The Strange Career of Aunt Jemima

Stephen Cushman
Bloody Promenade: Reflections on a Civil War Battle

John C. Willis
Forgotten Time: The Yazoo-Mississippi Delta after the Civil War

Charlene M. Boyer Lewis
*Ladies and Gentlemen on Display: Planter Society at the Virginia Springs,
1790–1860*

Christopher Metress, editor
The Lynching of Emmett Till: A Documentary Narrative

Dianne Swann-Wright
A Way out of No Way: Claiming Family and Freedom in the New South

James David Miller
South by Southwest: Planter Emigration and Identity in the Slave South

Richard F. Hamm
*Murder, Honor, and Law: Four Virginia Homicides from Reconstruction
to the Great Depression*

Andrew H. Myers
*Black, White, and Olive Drab: Racial Integration at Fort Jackson,
South Carolina, and the Civil Rights Movement*

Bruce E. Baker
*What Reconstruction Meant: Historical Memory
in the American South*